Indian Foreign and Security Policy in South Asia

This book examines Indian foreign policy and security relations in its Eastern regional neighbourhood.

Indian Foreign and Security Policy in South Asia conducts an in-depth analysis into India's foreign policy towards the three main countries in India's Eastern neighbourhood – Sri Lanka, Nepal, and Bangladesh. In particular, it deals with India's role in the final years of the civil war in Sri Lanka, its approach to the peace and democratisation process in Nepal, and Indian foreign policy towards Bangladesh on a range of issues including Islamist militancy, migration, border security, and insurgency.

Set within an analytical framework centred on the notions of 'empire', 'hegemony', and 'leadership', the study reveals that India pursued predominantly hegemonic strategies and was not able to generate genuine followership among its smaller neighbours. The South Asian case therefore shows the discrepancy that may exist between the possession of power capabilities and the ability to exercise actual influence: a conclusion which lifts the study from geographical specifics, and extends its relevance to other cases and cross-regional comparisons.

This book will be of much interest to students of Indian foreign policy, Asian security, foreign policy analysis, strategic studies and IR in general.

Sandra Destradi is a research fellow at GIGA Institute of Asian Studies, and was awarded a PhD in Political Science at Hamburg University.

Asian Security Studies

Series Editors: Sumit Ganguly, Indiana University, Bloomington and Andrew Scobell

US Army War College

Few regions of the world are as fraught with security questions as Asia. Within this region, it is possible to study great power rivalries, irredentist conflicts, nuclear and ballistic missile proliferation, secessionist movements, ethnoreligious conflicts and inter-state wars. This book series publishes the best possible scholarship on the security issues affecting the region, including detailed empirical studies, theoretically-oriented case studies and policy-relevant analyses, as well as more general works.

China and International Institutions
Alternate paths to global power
Marc Lanteigne

China's Rising Sea Power
The PLA Navy's Submarine Challenge
Peter Howarth

If China Attacks Taiwan
Military strategy, politics and economics
Edited by Steve Tsang

Chinese Civil-Military Relations
The transformation of the People's Liberation Army
Edited by Nan Li

The Chinese Army Today
Tradition and transformation for the 21st Century
Dennis J. Blasko

Taiwan's Security
History and prospects
Bernard D. Cole

Religion and Conflict in South and Southeast Asia
Disrupting violence
Edited by Linell E. Cady and Sheldon W. Simon

Political Islam and Violence in Indonesia
Zachary Abuza

US-Indian Strategic Cooperation into the 21st Century
More than words
Edited by Sumit Ganguly, Brian Shoup and Andrew Scobell

India, Pakistan and the Secret Jihad
The covert war in Kashmir, 1947–2004
Praveen Swami

China's Strategic Culture and Foreign Policy Decision-Making
Confucianism, leadership and war
Huiyun Feng

Indian Foreign and Security Policy in South Asia

Regional power strategies

Sandra Destradi

Routledge
Taylor & Francis Group

LONDON AND NEW YORK

This edition published 2012
by Routledge
2 Park Square, Milton Park, Abingdon, Oxon, OX14 4RN

Simultaneously published in the USA and Canada
by Routledge
711 Third Avenue, New York, NY 10017

*Routledge is an imprint of the Taylor & Francis Group, an informa
business*

First issued in paperback 2013

British Library Cataloguing in Publication Data
A catalogue record for this book is available from the British Library

Library of Congress Cataloging-in-Publication Data
Destradi, Sandra.

Indian foreign and security policy in South Asia : regional power
strategies / Sandra Destradi.

p. cm. -- (Asian security studies ; 31)

Includes bibliographical references and index.

1. India--Foreign relations--South Asia. 2. South Asia--Foreign relations--
India. 3. National Security--India. 4. Regionalism--South Asia. 5. Security,
International--South Asia. 6. South Asia--Strategic aspects. I. Title.

DS450.S64D47 2011

327.53054--dc23

2011024297

ISBN13: 978–0–415–68078–3 (hbk)
ISBN13: 978–0–203–15274–4 (ebk)
ISBN13: 978–0–415–72124-0 (pbk)

Typeset in Times New Roman by
Fakenham Prepress Solutions, Fakenham, Norfolk NR21 8NN

To Dino

Contents

List of tables and figures

Acknowledgements

During the past years many people have supported me in writing this book, and they all have my deep gratitude. First of all, I would like to thank Prof. Dr. Cord Jakobeit and Prof. Dr. Joachim Betz, who supervised my work on an earlier version of this book, which was submitted as a PhD thesis to the University of Hamburg, Germany, in October 2009. Moreover, I owe sincere thanks to Prof. Dr. Stefan Brüne for having helped me to begin this project.

I am grateful to Prof. Sumit Ganguly for inviting me to publish in the Asian Security Studies series. Thanks to Prof. Len Seabrooke, Prof. Shaun Breslin and the other participants in the Warwick Manuscript Development (MWD) workshop 2010 for their helpful suggestions on how to improve the structure of the book.

Financial support from the Cusanuswerk, which funded this project for the years 2006–2009, is gratefully acknowledged. Institutionally, I am indebted to GIGA German Institute of Global and Area Studies, which has provided a stimulating environment over the past years.

Parts of the book appeared as 'Regional powers and their strategies: Empire, hegemony, and leadership' in the October 2010 issue of *Review of International Studies*, and I thank Cambridge University Press for granting permission to reuse that material in Chapter Two.

I would also like to thank the many people who supported me during my fieldwork in New Delhi, particularly each and every one of the experts I had the opportunity to interview. I wish to extend my gratitude to Prof. Ummu Salma Bava at Jawaharlal Nehru University, who was an invaluable help in arranging contacts for my interviews. She also took the time to share with me her knowledge on India and gave me useful advice about my research. My sincere thanks to Dr. Ash Narain Roy at the Institute of Social Sciences for his support, and for providing me with insights into Indian society. I would also like to thank Marilen Daum and Ulrich Geiger for their wonderful hospitality in Delhi, as well as the whole library team at Max Müller Bhavan for having allowed me to work there.

Furthermore, I am deeply thankful to all those who variously assisted me during the writing and revision stages by reading the manuscript and giving me their invaluable feedback. Among them are my mother Rosemarie Destradi, Teeas Bhattacharya, Cordula Tibi Weber, Annette Büchs, Natalie Hess, Vibhavan Prasad, Johannes Vüllers, Ellinor Zeino-Mahmalat, and Nadine Godehardt. Last but not least, my deep gratitude goes to my partner, Sven j. Olsson, who intellectually, morally and emotionally supported me over the past years and held endless discussions with me on almost every issue addressed in this book.

List of abbreviations

AIADMK	All India Anna Dravida Munnetra Kazhagam
AL	Awami League
APC	Armoured Personal Carrier
APRC	All-Party Representative Committee
ASEAN	Association of Southeast Asian Nations
ATTF	All Tripura Tiger Force
BDR	Bangladesh Rifles
BJP	Bharatiya Janata Party
BNP	Bangladesh Nationalist Party
BRICS	Brazil, Russia, India, China, South Africa
BSF	Border Security Forces
CAMEO	Conflict and Mediation Event Observations
CAQDAS	Computer-Assisted Qualitative Data Analysis Software
CEPA	Comprehensive Economic Partnership Agreement
CFA	Ceasefire Agreement
COPDAB	Conflict and Peace Data Bank
COW	Correlates of War
CPI(M)	Communist Party of India (Marxist)
CPN-M	Communist Party of Nepal (Maoist)
CPN-UML	Communist Party of Nepal – Unified Marxist Leninist
CPR	Centre for Policy Research
CTG	Caretaker government
DGFI	Directorate General Field Intelligence
DMK	Dravida Munnetra Kazhagam
DPI	Dalit Panthers of India
EEZ	Exclusive Economic Zone
FDI	Foreign Direct Investment
HuJI	Harkat-ul-Jihad-al-Islami
ICG	International Crisis Group
ICRIER	Indian Council for Research on International Economic Relations
ICS	Islami Chhatra Shibir
IDEA	Integrated Data for Event Analysis
IDP	Internally Displaced Person

IDSA	Institute for Defence Studies and Analyses
IOJ	Islami Oikya Jote
IPCS	Institute of Peace and Conflict Studies
IPKF	Indian Peace Keeping Force
ISGA	Interim Self-Governing Authority for the North-east
ISI	Inter-Services Intelligence
ISLA	Indo–Sri Lanka Agreement
JAGODAL	Jatiyo Ganotantrik Dal
JHU	Jathika Hela Urumaya
JMB	Jamaat ul Mujahideen Bangladesh
JMJB	Jagrata Muslim Janata Bangladesh
JNU	Jawaharlal Nehru University
JVP	Janathi Vimukti Peramuna
LDC	Least Developed Country
LTTE	Liberation Tigers of Tamil Eelam
MDMK	Marumalarchi Dravida Munnetra Kazhagam
MoU	Memorandum of Understanding
MULTA	Muslim United Liberation Tigers of Assam
NC	Nepali Congress
NC(D)	Nepali Congress (Democratic)
NDA	National Democratic Alliance
NDFB	National Democratic Front of Bodoland
NLFT	National Liberation Front of Tripura
NSCN	National Socialist Council of Nagaland
NSP (A)	Nepal Sadbhavana Party (Anandidevi)
NWPP	Nepal Workers and Peasant Party
ORF	Observer Research Foundation
PANDA	Protocol for the Analysis of Nonviolent Direct Action
PLA	People's Liberation Army
PMK	Pattali Makkal Katchi
POTA	Prevention of Terrorism Act
PPP	Pakistan People's Party
P-TOMS	Post-Tsunami Operational Management Structure
RAB	Rapid Action Battalion
RAW	Research and Analysis Wing
RNA	Royal Nepalese Army
RPP	Rashtriya Prajatantra Party
RSC	Regional Security Complex
SAARC	South Asian Association for Regional Cooperation
SAHRDC	South Asia Human Rights Documentation Centre
SEAC	South East Asia Command
SIPRI	Stockholm International Peace Research Institute
SLFP	Sri Lanka Freedom Party
SLMM	Sri Lanka Monitoring Mission
SPA	Seven Party Alliance

TC	Tamil Congress
TNA	Tamil National Alliance
TUF	Tamil United Front
TULF	Tamil United Liberation Front
TVMP	Tamil Makkal Viduthalai Pulihal
UDMF	United Democratic Madhes Front
ULF	United Left Front
ULFA	United Liberation Front of Asom
UNF	United National Front
UNHRC	United Nations Human Rights Council
UNMIN	United Nations Mission in Nepal
UNP	United National Party
UPA	United Progressive Alliance
UPFA	United People's Freedom Alliance
WEIS	World Event Interaction Survey
YCL	Young Communist League

1   Introduction
India in its troubled neighbourhood

Over the past two decades, India has emerged as a major player on the international stage. The economic liberalization initiated in 1991 paved the way for a period of extraordinary economic development characterized by average growth rates of 7 per cent per year over the past two decades (Mitra 2011: 139). India's 'rise' in the international economy was accompanied by a more pragmatic approach in its foreign policy: India abandoned, de facto, its traditional non-aligned approach and started cooperating with all the major powers. The signing of the 'nuclear deal' with the United States is the most glaring example of its new pragmatism in foreign policy, as well as of the growing international acceptance of India as a power at global level. Moreover, India has come to play a central role in international negotiations such as those on climate change at Copenhagen in 2009, and has established or cooperated in a range of multilateral forums, such as IBSA (India, Brazil, South Africa) or BRICS (Brazil, Russia, India, China, South Africa), through which emerging powers have been coordinating their approach to global affairs.

Whilst such developments in foreign policy can be defined as a success story at a global level, things look very different at a regional level. Despite its clear material power preponderance and its position at the centre of the South Asian region, India has not been able to create a secure and stable environment in which to build upon its growing prosperity and focus on its own rise to great-power status. To paraphrase former U.S. President Clinton, South Asia is still one of the most dangerous places on earth. This is due not only to the intra-state conflicts and insurgencies that have been destabilizing several South Asian countries over the past decades, but also to the tense inter-state relations in the region, which make South Asia one of the least integrated regions in the world. The only distinctively South Asian regional organization, the South Asian Association for Regional Cooperation (SAARC), explicitly excludes any kind of contentious and bilateral issues from its agenda (SAARC 2011). The region lacks cooperative mechanisms of dispute resolution and even substantial trade and infrastructure links.

Besides the long-standing conflict with Pakistan, India's relations with almost all of its smaller neighbours have been equally fraught with difficulties. Threat perceptions, historical animosities, and the fear of losing their own identity and autonomy have shaped the attitude of neighbouring states towards India. As a consequence, the South Asian region can be characterized as being constituted by two 'theatres of conflict', both focused on India (Bajpai 2003b: 209–10): one located in the West, encompassing India and Pakistan, 'where military hostilities are always a distinct possibility'; and one located in the East, including India and its smaller neighbours (Sri Lanka, Nepal, Bangladesh, Bhutan, and the Maldives), defined as a 'theatre of less militarized conflict in which hostilities are virtually ruled out' (ibid.).

This book focuses on India's relations with the main countries in this 'Eastern theatre of conflict': Sri Lanka, Nepal, and Bangladesh. In fact, while the 'Western theatre' is unequivocally characterized by the long-standing conflict between India and Pakistan, India's relations with the smaller neighbours are less unambiguous, as we will see below. This study specifically aims to provide an assessment of the strategies that the regional power India has been pursuing in its interactions with these smaller neighbours in the field of foreign and security policy. Thereby, it contributes to the debate on India's foreign policy at the regional level of analysis, which has been assessed in very different manners. At the same time, it contributes to the burgeoning literature on 'regional powers' – emerging countries that occupy a predominant power position in their respective regions, and which have often been assumed to adopt 'benevolent' foreign policies towards their neighbours and to act as 'leaders' in their regions.

In order to assess India's foreign policy towards Sri Lanka, Nepal, and Bangladesh, we need a suitable analytical framework that allows us to identify to what extent the foreign policy strategies pursued by India have been conflictual or cooperative. To this end, this study resorts to three notions widely employed in the literature on states that dominate a hierarchical system as well as in the literature on regional powers: empire, hegemony, and leadership. Since these notions are often used interchangeably, as synonyms, a theory-led conceptual distinction and clarification of these terms as well as a suitable operationalization is carried out. As a result, we have a continuum of ideal-typical foreign policy strategies that a regional power can pursue. They reach from an imperial strategy based on the use or threat of force, to hard, intermediate, and soft hegemonic strategies based on sanctions, incentives, or persuasion; to leading strategies based on a commonality of goals between leader and followers. The empirical analyses of India's relations with Sri Lanka, Nepal, and Bangladesh will reveal that New Delhi pursued predominantly hegemonic foreign policy strategies over the past decade, thereby refuting assumptions about the necessarily cooperative nature of the foreign policy of regional powers, as well as assumptions about the cooperative nature of India's approach to its Eastern neighbourhood.

Besides assessing the kind of foreign policy strategies pursued by India, the book also discusses the degree to which New Delhi has been successful in pursuing those strategies. As we will see, the analysis reveals that India has not been able to transform its predominance in terms of material power capabilities into actual leverage at the regional level. Through their resistance and the involvement of external powers, India's weaker neighbours have been able to undermine the success of New Delhi's foreign policies and even to substantially constrain its foreign policy options. This is what makes the study of the otherwise neglected smaller South Asian neighbours particularly interesting in comparison to the more extensively studied India—Pakistan relations. While the unequivocally conflictual bilateral relations between India and Pakistan largely correspond to the predictions of neorealist and particularly traditional balance of power approaches in International Relations (IR) theory (Ganguly/Hagerty 2005: 3), India's relations with the smaller South Asian countries provide some fresh insights for the debate on power and influence in IR. The resort to the notions of empire, hegemony, and leadership with their different degrees of legitimacy proves particularly helpful in this regard. As Guzzini (2009: 9) puts it, '[...] with legitimacy, traditional analysis of power and influence become murky, since legitimacy is notoriously not just a function of actor resources, let alone material ones'. The South Asian region offers a particularly extreme imbalance in the distribution of power, with India clearly dominating over the neighbouring countries in geopolitical terms as well as in terms of material power capabilities (see Chapter Three). By building upon empirical evidence from this region in order to develop broader hypotheses on (regional) power relations, this book addresses a gap highlighted by Ganguly and Pardesi (2010), who point out that, so far, 'very few South Asian case materials have been effectively integrated into the mainstream of the foreign and security policy literature [and] only a very small number of scholars have devoted any significant effort in drawing on [the] substantial body of evidence from the region'.

The following sections provide, first, a review of the literature on regional powers and their foreign policies; second, a discussion of the two main – and conflicting – interpretations of the development of India's regional policy over the past two decades; and third, an overview of the structure of the book.

Regional Powers and their Foreign Policy Strategies

So-called 'emerging' or 'rising' powers like India – and also China, Brazil, or South Africa – have attracted a great deal of scholarly attention in recent years. Besides the literature that focuses on their growing role as 'system challengers' or new norm builders at the global level,[1] a recent strand in the literature conceptualizes these countries as 'regional powers'.[2] The basic idea is that these states are not only powerful emerging countries in international relations, but that they also play a central role in their respective regions. In the context of the new regional dynamics unleashed by the end of the Cold War,[3] they are assumed to strongly

---

1 See, for example, Hurrell (2006); Alden/Vieira (2005); Soares de Lima/Hirst (2006). More policy-oriented approaches highlight these countries' natures as 'leading powers' able to shape global governance in single issue areas (Husar/Maihold 2009), or their character as 'anchor countries' having a determining impact on regional economic development (Stamm 2004).
2 See Nolte (2010); Destradi (2010); Frazier/Stewart-Ingersoll (2010); Prys (2010).
3 On the importance and autonomy of the regional level of analysis, see Buzan/Waever (2003).

influence the interactions taking place at the regional level and to contribute to shaping the regional order, or, in other terms, the degree of co-operation or conflict, or the level of institutionalization in their respective regions (Nolte 2010).

However, despite the increasing scholarly interest in these countries, and despite the agreement on the existence of a group of states named 'regional (great) powers',[4] the essential traits of regional powers have long been debated issues (Østerud 1992: 1–3; Nolte 2006: 23). The only aspects on which early studies on regional powers agreed were their geopolitical belonging to a certain region; their relative material preponderance in that region; and their ability to exercise some degree of influence on their regional neighbours.[5] The actual mechanisms of leverage at the regional level and the strategies employed by regional powers have long remained understudied subjects.

Structuralist approaches like those developed by Buzan and Waever (2003) and Lemke (2002), for example, do not explicitly focus on the foreign policy strategies pursued by regional powers. According to Buzan and Waever (2003: 35–7), regional powers differ from great powers because their 'capabilities loom large in their regions, but do not register much in a broad-spectrum way at the global level' (ibid.: 37). Regional powers are conceptualized in terms of the possession of power capabilities as countries that determine the 'polarity' of Regional Security Complexes (RSCs) (ibid.: 55–62). Lemke (2002: 49) similarly conceives of regional powers as 'local dominant state[s] supervising local relations, by establishing and striving to preserve a local status quo', but he does not explicitly deal with the strategies of regional powers, even though he admits the potential usefulness of incorporating strategic considerations into his theory (ibid.: 38–9).

A range of case studies on the foreign policy of single regional powers has led some authors to the assumption that these countries pursue cooperative or 'leading' strategies in dealing with their neighbours – and that their leadership efforts are accepted and legitimized by their regional followers.[6] Accordingly, the essential features of regional powers have been considered to be the adoption of a stabilizing and leading role as well as the assumption of responsibility for the region (Schoeman 2003: 352–3, 362); the influence on rule-making accepted by neighbouring countries (Schirm 2005: 110–2); the resort to soft power (Gratius 2004); and the establishment of 'consensual hegemony' (Burges 2008).

However, this 'leadership hypothesis', which prevailed in the earlier literature on regional powers, lacks wider empirical evidence. Even a superficial look at the empirical reality in different regions reveals that regional powers do not always act as regional leaders. Just to cite some examples, Russia's military intervention in Georgia in 2008 (Allison 2009) shows that regional powers still pursue aggressive

---

4 See, for example, Neumann (1992); Østerud (1992); Hurrell (1992, 2007a: 141); De Silva (1995); Fuller/Arquilla (1996); Buzan/Waever (2003: 24); Soares de Lima/Hirst (2006).
5 See Østerud (1992: 12); Schirm (2005: 111); Nolte (2006: 28).
6 See the conceptualization of regional powers as 'regional leading powers' (*Regionale Führungsmächte*) by Nolte (2006).

strategies in their sphere of influence; the 'simmering rivalry' (Calder 2006) between China and Japan undermines China's 'leadership' in East Asia; South Africa's failed military intervention in Lesotho in 1998 'sparked questions about South Africa's true intentions in the region' (Soko 2008: 58); and even Brazil has encountered an increasing resistance on the part of Argentina to its more assertive regional policy (Hurrell 2006: 9).

As a consequence, some authors (Schirm 2010; Flemes/Wojczewski 2010) have started questioning the assumption that regional powers always adopt leadership strategies and have, instead, highlighted how other regional states may contest the leadership projects of regional powers. This has led to a shift in the debate towards a more systematic identification of the range of 'roles' and 'orientations' of regional powers (Frazier/Stewart-Ingersoll 2010), of the features of 'regional powerhood' (Prys 2010), and of the spectrum of foreign policy strategies these countries can pursue (Destradi 2010).

The latter approach will be taken as a point of reference in this book, which argues that the strategies of regional powers can be arrayed along a continuum ranging from conflict to cooperation. Therefore, we will start by defining a regional power as 'a state which belongs to a region, disposes of superior power capabilities, and exercises an influence on regional neighbours' (ibid.: 930). This implies that we will need to delimitate the region taken as a point of reference; and to identify the country endowed with a dominant share of power capabilities– that is, the regional power. Finally, as a third step, we will carry out an assessment of the foreign policy strategies employed by the regional power in its efforts to influence its neighbours.

As mentioned above, given the extensive use of the notions of leadership and hegemony in the literature on regional powers, these concepts will be employed in this study; they will be complemented by the notion of empire, which has taken centre stage in the debate on the role of the USA as the sole remaining superpower at the global level. The conceptual distinction and clarification of the blurred notions of empire, hegemony, and leadership will serve as the basis for an operationalization of these concepts. The analytical framework thus developed will be employed for the in-depth analysis of India's foreign policy approach to Sri Lanka, Nepal, and Bangladesh.

Cooperative or Unilateralist? Concurring Interpretations of India's Policies in its Eastern Neighbourhood

While India's relations with Pakistan are unequivocally conflictual, different interpretations of India's approach to the smaller states of the 'Eastern theatre of conflict' can be found in literature. On the one hand, some authors (e.g., Ayoob 1999; Wagner 2005a, 2006b; Bajpai 2003a; Mohan 2007) have highlighted that a clear shift has taken place from the unilateralist approach pursued by New Delhi in the 1980s, mainly under Indira Gandhi,[7] to the more cooperative approach initiated in the 1990s and propagated under the label 'Gujral doctrine'. New Delhi's new approach to neighbouring countries enunciated by the Indian prime minister Gujral was based on the following five principles: India would grant non-reciprocal concessions to all neighbours with the exception of Pakistan; no South Asian country should allow its territory to be used for activities detrimental to another country in the region; non-interference in the internal affairs of other countries; mutual respect of territorial integrity and sovereignty; and settlement of disputes through peaceful bilateral negotiations.[8]

Moreover, in the 1990s, a series of bilateral disputes between India and its small Eastern neighbours was solved, for example the Ganges water dispute with Bangladesh (Bajpai 2003a: 198). Wagner (2005a, 2006b: 240) interprets these developments as a clear shift from hard power to soft power in India's regional policy. He considers this shift to have been determined by the failure of India's hegemonic ambitions in the 1980s, which revealed India's inability to influence its neighbours and, instead, contributed to make South Asia 'a region of "chronic instability"' (ibid.: 13). Mohan (2007) attributes the shift to cooperative strategies in India's foreign policy to the adoption of a realist approach on the part of New Delhi – what he calls 'new Indian realism'. This approach is considered to be focused on regional integration, stability, and prosperity as necessary preconditions for India's own growth and development.

On the other hand, there are authors who emphasize that India's relations with its neighbouring countries continue to be characterized by a series of unresolved disputes as well as by a high degree of suspicion and hostility towards India on the part of the smaller neighbours (e.g., Thomas 2002; Buzan 2002; Ghosh 2006). As Dubey (2000: 44) puts it, 'India faces unique problems in dealing with its neighbors all of whom suffer from an identity crisis vis-à-vis India' as well as of a 'big-neighbor-small-neighbor syndrome'. This induces the smaller countries in South Asia in particular to 'view any initiative coming from India with great suspicion' (ibid.). This interpretation of international relations in India's Eastern neighbourhood seems to imply that although India has been changing its rhetoric towards smaller neighbouring states, no significant shift has taken place in India's actual behaviour. As Shukla (2007: 240) puts it,

> the Gujral doctrine cosmetically improved the regional political atmosphere and India's relations with all its neighbours in general terms but the optimism embodied in the Gujral doctrine about unilateral goodwill and generosity did not bring about the desired results in the management of the security problems which remained.

---

7 With what came to be called 'Indira Doctrine', Prime Minister Indira Gandhi clearly affirmed India's desire for a non-intervention of external countries in its neighbourhood in a sort of Indian version of the Monroe Doctrine. For a detailed discussion, see Hagerty (1991).
8 See Embassy of India – Washington D.C. (1997).

In other words, according to this perspective, 'since Gujral's departure, his doctrine has largely been confined to foreign policy debates among commentators and scholars' (Mishra 2004: 645). This interpretation also argues that India's concessions have been of limited relevance only, and have not been considered satisfactory by its neighbouring countries; as a consequence, in the assessment of authors like Mitra (2006: 21), India has not been able to emerge as a benevolent regional power leading South Asia. At the same time, the strong focus of India's regional policy on the conflict with Pakistan has led to the neglect of the rest of the neighbourhood and to the adoption of policies 'in wanton disregard of how they are going to effect [sic] the interests of the small neighbors' (Dubey 2000: 44).

A series of interviews conducted in 2002 among (former) diplomats of the neighbouring countries by an Indian magazine outlines the following main traits of India's policies towards its smaller neighbours (Sudarshan 2002):

- India takes them for granted.
- India displays a big brotherly attitude.
- India insists on the principle of reciprocity.
- India is not willing to go the extra mile and correct its trade imbalances with all its neighbours.

Moreover, some authors from the neighbouring states explicitly term India's policies as imperial, with a reference to India as the successor state of the British colonial empire (Shah 2004). In a nutshell, this second strand in the literature promotes the idea that a shift in India's regional policy has taken place only at the rhetorical level, while India still pursues hard policies towards smaller neighbours.

In summary, these two strands in literature offer competing interpretations of India's foreign policy in its Eastern neighbourhood in South Asia. We can term the two underlying competing hypotheses as 'cooperative' and 'unilateralist', respectively. The interest in determining whether India's foreign policy fits into the cooperative or the unilateralist end of the continuum of possible foreign policy strategies drives the empirical analysis of India's foreign policy approach to Sri Lanka, Nepal, and Bangladesh.

Structure of the Book

The book proceeds as follows: Chapter Two focuses on the development of an analytical framework for the study of the strategies pursued by regional powers. This framework, which is later applied to the study of India's foreign policy towards Sri Lanka, Nepal, and Bangladesh, is based on the elaboration of a continuum of ideal-typical foreign policy strategies. As outlined above, this continuum is based on the notions of empire, hegemony, and leadership. As we will see, the threat or use of force constitutes the central feature of an imperial strategy. Hegemonic strategies can be of three types, according to the means predominantly employed: hard (threats and sanctions), intermediate (incentives, hard persuasion), or soft (soft persuasion, socialization efforts). Leadership is based on a commonality of goals between leader and follower(s). After a theory-led clarification and distinction between the notions of empire, hegemony, and leadership, the chapter develops suitable indicators for the identification of the corresponding strategies. The essential analytical categories are the commonality or divergence of goals between the regional power and the neighbouring state(s), which will be an indicator of leadership; the means employed by the regional power, which will allow for the identification of imperial or hegemonic strategies; and the reactions and perceptions of the neighbouring state(s).

In Chapter Three, India is identified as the regional power in South Asia. To this end, the chapter discusses the delimitation of the South Asian region and outlines the distribution of power capabilities among the states of the region according to some basic power indicators. Finally, the chapter provides a brief overview of India's overall goals for the South Asian region, which serve as a point of reference for the subsequent case studies.

In the following chapters, the book provides an in-depth analysis of India's foreign policy towards the three main countries in India's Eastern neighbourhood – Sri Lanka, Nepal, and Bangladesh. The selection of issues and time frames refers to India's main security concerns with regard to each of these countries in recent years. A diachronic analysis of different phases allows us to assess the changes in India's foreign policy strategies and the dynamics of strategic interaction between India and each of its neighbours. These, in turn, reveal the difficulties that India has been facing in asserting its influence at the regional level.

The empirical chapters all follow the same structure. After a presentation of the historical background, they provide an overview of relevant events in the time frame chosen for analysis. Subsequently, the analytical framework developed in Chapter Two is applied in order to identify the strategies pursued by India and the reactions and perceptions of India's neighbours. Finally, some conclusions are drawn on the success or failure of India's foreign policy strategies with reference to the goals pursued by New Delhi.

Chapter Four deals with India's approach to Sri Lanka in the final years of the civil war, starting from the pullout of the Liberation Tigers of Tamil Eelam (LTTE) from peace negotiations in 2003 and ending with the termination of military hostilities in May 2009. The analysis of the Sri Lankan case reveals that India pursued a mix of soft, intermediate, and hard hegemonic strategies between 2003 and 2009. It failed, however, to achieve its main goal of reaching a peaceful settlement of the ethnic conflict. In fact, India was not able to effectively influence the Sri Lankan government. On the contrary, the latter proved to be successful in 'engaging' India, thereby increasing India's stakes in the situation on the island and inducing New Delhi to implicitly support its fight against the LTTE.

Chapter Five deals with India's foreign policy strategies during the peace and democratization process in Nepal. It analyses the years between the dismissal of the elected prime minister by the Nepalese king in 2002 and the establishment of a democratically elected government under Maoist leadership in 2008. The chapter argues that India's approach to Nepal in the years 2002–2008 can be defined as a partially successful hegemonic strategy with parallel elements of informal leadership. India's historically close relations with Nepal allowed New Delhi to exercise a high degree of influence on domestic developments in this neighbouring country. India played a constructive role in avoiding Nepal's descent into complete anarchy and in fostering a dialogue between the Maoists and the democratic parties, which ultimately led to the signing of the Comprehensive Peace Agreement in 2006. At the same time, however, India's official approach to Nepal was reactive, with New Delhi almost blindsided by events during the popular uprising in April 2006.

Chapter Six assesses India's approach to the problems of Islamist militancy, migration, border security, and anti-India insurgency. The time frame starts with the establishment of a coalition government led by the Bangladesh Nationalist Party (BNP) in 2001 and ends with the re-establishment of democracy after a phase under a military-backed interim government in 2008. Relations with Bangladesh provide an example of a failed hegemonic strategy on the part of India. Given the threat perceptions in Bangladesh and the politicization of any issue related to India, until 2008 New Delhi could not make any progress in achieving its core goals – namely, the solution of the problems of migration, insurgency, and terrorism. At the same time, a limitation of China's influence on Bangladesh was also impossible to realise.

Finally, Chapter Seven accomplishes two main tasks. First, it offers a summary of the empirical findings of the book, highlighting how the fine-grained analysis of India's relations with its three main Eastern neighbours contributes to our understanding of security dynamics in South Asia. These findings provide a fresh view on Indian foreign policy, qualifying assumptions about India's cooperative approach to its small neighbours.

Second, the concluding chapter draws some lessons from the Indian case, which can serve as a basis for further theorizing about regional powers and, more generally, about power and influence in highly asymmetrical relationships. As Ganguly and Pardesi (2010) put it, the study of South Asia and the integration of evidence from this region into 'general studies of foreign, security, and defence policies [...] not only will enable scholars to test existing propositions but also may help generate new hypotheses about questions of war and peace in the global order'. The findings of the empirical analysis reveal that a clearly predominant regional power may not be able to convert its extraordinary endowment with power resources into actual leverage on the region. Paradoxically, the threat perceptions and resistance of small neighbouring states can contribute to keep a regional power entangled in its region, thereby hampering its rise to great-power status at the global level. The book concludes by outlining future avenues of research at the nexus of (Comparative) Area Studies, International Relations, and Foreign Policy Analysis.

2 Empire, Hegemony, and Leadership

Assessing the strategies of regional powers

To address the question regarding the nature of India's foreign policy in its inter-actions with the countries of its 'Eastern neighbourhood', this chapter develops an analytical framework for the assessment of regional power strategies. Towards this end, it develops a conceptual distinction and clarification among the notions of *empire*, *hegemony*, and *leadership*.[1] These three concepts have been widely employed in the literature on the role of powerful states at the global level of analysis – particularly of the USA as the sole superpower after the end of the Cold War – and can equally be fruitfully employed to study the foreign policy of dominant states at the regional level.

A conceptual distinction between the notions of empire, hegemony, and leadership is necessary because these concepts have often been used inter-changeably, as synonyms, leading to an almost inextricable confusion about their usage. Just to cite some examples, hegemony has been defined by Wallerstein (1984: 38) as an imbalance in power distribution that enables the unilateral assertion of the dominant state. Other authors, as will be discussed below, would term this approach as 'imperial'. The use of the term 'hegemony' as 'necessarily coercive and based on the exercise of power' (Lake 1993: 469) contrasts sharply with widespread conceptions of hegemony as benevolent leadership or provision of public goods (e.g., Kindleberger 1973). To complicate things further, other terms are often employed to characterize the behaviour of strong states, among them the notion of 'dominance', defined as the ability to get others to act by threat-ening them with the prospect of 'external coercion' and the use of violence (Triepel 1938: 39).

In his seminal work on concepts in the social sciences, Goertz (2006: 1–2) points out that 'concepts are a central part of our theories, yet researchers, apart from Sartori and Collier, have focused very little attention on social science concepts per se'. Goertz (ibid.: 27–67) identifies three levels making up the structure of concepts that allow for a sound theoretical discussion and for a viable

1 Parts of this chapter have been published as: Destradi, Sandra (2010) 'Regional powers and their strategies: empire, hegemony, and leadership', *Review of International Studies* 36 (4): 903–30 © Cambridge Journals, reproduced with permission.

operationalization of concepts. At the basic level, concepts are approached theoretically in a general fashion, and this is what will be done in the section within this chapter on 'Contested Concepts', which is devoted to the theory-led discussion of the main traits of empire, hegemony, and leadership. At the secondary level, the 'constitutive dimensions' of concepts are outlined, thereby going more into detail and specifying the basic level concepts. This step will be approached with the application of empire, hegemony, and leadership to the discussion of possible strategies adopted by regional powers, and the further diversification of the notions of hegemony (hard, intermediate, and soft) and leadership (leader-initiated and follower-initiated).

Finally, at the indicator/data level, concepts are specified through an operationalization allowing for the collection of data, 'which permits us to categorize [...] whether or not a specific phenomenon, individual, or event falls under a concept' (ibid.: 6). This will be undertaken in the section devoted to the operationalization of empire, hegemony, and leadership for the analysis of regional powers' strategies. Finally, appropriate methodological tools for empirical analysis will be discussed, and the sources used for the empirical analysis of India's foreign policy will be presented.

Contested Concepts: Empire, Hegemony, and Leadership

As Goertz (ibid.: 16) puts it, '[t]o focus on concepts is to think about the nature of the phenomenon being conceptualized', that is, '[t]o develop a concept is more than providing a definition: it is deciding what is important about an entity' (ibid.: 27). The 'basic level' approach to empire, hegemony, and leadership is therefore based on a discussion of different theorizations about these concepts and looks for both the distinguishing features and the 'boundaries' among the three concepts under scrutiny.

Empire

The term 'empire' suffers from a lack of juridical or political science-based specification, thereby assuming a diffuse character, leading to different normative interpretations and abuses in its usage (Münkler 2005b: 44; Ferguson 2008: 272–7). This section will look for the essential features of the notion of empire as they emerge from the debate in the discipline of International Relations (IR). Moreover, it will discuss the problems of setting a 'threshold' for the definition of empire. The resort to military force or to the threat of it will be identified as the distinguishing feature of empire.

In recent years, especially after the terrorist attacks of 9/11, the war in Afghanistan, and the invasion of Iraq, the notion of empire has gained an unprecedented momentum in the media and in scholarly debates on the role of the United States as the sole remaining superpower. Innumerable authors, dealing with US foreign policy in more or less valuable literature, have employed the term 'empire' as a synonym for the current world order dominated by the USA (e.g., Cohen 2005;

Layne/Thayer 2007; Colás/Saull 2006; Ferguson 2004; Sandschneider 2007).[2] The concept is used to denote the United States' global pre-eminence as well as the attributes of the current US-centred unipolar world (Ikenberry 2001). Interestingly, the notion of empire was adopted by the American neo-conservative establishment to define a foreign policy strategy based on a (militarily sustained) unilateralism as a means for the enforcement of US interests and values (Schrader 2005: 102). This breaking of the 'taboo' of defining the United States – which because of their anti-imperial struggle have always perceived themselves as anti-imperialist par excellence – as an empire was possible only thanks to re-conceptualizations of empire as benevolent, informal empire, or 'empire by invitation' (Lundestad 2003).

In the heated debate on the 'empire USA', its advocates propagate the US-centred world order as clearly power-based, but 'benevolent' (Kagan 1998) unilateralism. In this unilateral system, the USA not only has a right to exercise a global ordering role, but even considers it a duty to guarantee security, prosperity and freedom at the global level, resorting to military power if necessary (*Pax Americana*)[3]. The opponents of the 'empire USA', on the contrary, consider it as a greedy system of subordination based on militarism (e.g., Johnson 2000, 2004; Mann 2003; Boggs 2005) and global dominance (e.g., Chomsky 2003). Interestingly, the conceptual confusion between empire, hegemony, and at times also leadership, was determined to a large extent by the need to adopt euphemisms for empire in the debate on the United State's role in the post-Cold War world (Ferguson 2003). As Sterling-Folker (2008: 326) puts it:

> The terms we IR scholars have used to describe U.S. behavior have also been part of the niceties that have made our power projection palatable. [Therefore] it is no surprise that we prefer to use the terms "unipolarity," "great power," "superpower," or "hegemon" instead. Such terms shield us from accepting that the United States continually behaves in a very nasty, imperialistic manner toward the rest of the world. The term "hegemony," for example, is used to suggest "leadership" or "authority." In the hegemonic stability literature, our hegemony is deemed to be necessary not because we are bad imperialists but because leadership or authority is required for all economic exchange to occur efficiently. We are not imposing an empire, we are producing a world order, so the story goes.

If we leave aside the concrete reference to US policy, what emerges from this debate is, besides the confirmation of the controversial nature of the term 'empire', the fact that both advocates and opponents of the 'empire USA' associate this term with unilateralism and the use of military power.

---

2 Even before the 'empire USA' debate, the study of the rise and fall of empires had taken centre stage after the dissolution of the USSR. See, for example, Motyl (2001) or Dawisha/Parrott (1997).

3 On the notion of *Pax Americana*, see Parchami (2009).

This assessment corresponds to the conclusions of other authors, who deal with the conceptualization of empire in greater detail. Münkler (2005a) contributes to the debate on the 'empire USA' by trying to clarify the notion of empire through an assessment of the common traits of all great empires of the past. He conceives of empire as of a form of international order that has remained unchanged across time. Even though in the current 'post-imperial' age (ibid.: 219) nation-states predominate and classic territorial empires have disappeared, the USA can be considered as an empire based on the control over flows of capital, information, goods, services, and, more generally, globalization processes (ibid.: 182, 231). However, Münkler does not sufficiently explain how this control takes place and what foreign policy instruments the imperial power uses in its relations with other states. Nevertheless, Münkler gives us some important insights into other basic features of empire. All great empires in the course of history have had a 'pretence of exclusiveness' in their 'world' (which always corresponded to the whole known or reachable world), thereby not admitting any competitors. Given the extreme power disparity between the centre and the other entities, in every empire the subordinate entities become client states or satellites dependent on the centre (ibid.: 18). If an entity does not comply with the wishes of the centre, the imperial power is forced to resort to the threat of military intervention, otherwise it risks losing its dominant position (ibid.: 30). Moreover, the attitude of empires and their rhetoric – often articulated in religious terms, implying a self-sacralization of the centre and a demonization of all the 'others' (in the ancient world, the 'barbarians') – has always led to anti-imperial reactions and to different forms of resistance against the imperial power (ibid.: 149–57; 168–212).

In the contemporary nation-state based international system, the notion of empire becomes a designation for a particular kind of hierarchical inter-state relationship. According to Doyle (1986: 19), empires can therefore be defined as

> [...] relationships of political control imposed by some political societies over the effective sovereignty of other political societies. They include more than just formally annexed territories, but they encompass less than the sum of all forms of international inequality.

While in the traditional, territorially based, formal empires the policy course adopted by the metropolis was implemented either directly or through governors, in informal empires we find de jure independent, but de facto subordinated governments, which implement the prescribed policies (ibid.: 37). Wendt and Friedheim (1995: 695) elaborate a similar definition of informal empires, characterized as 'structures of transnational political authority that combine an egalitarian principle of de jure sovereignty with a hierarchical principle of de facto control'.

But how can empires be distinguished from other kinds of hierarchical inter-state relations? '[T]he task of pinpointing the "essence of empire" is daunting' (Ferguson 2008: 274). Even though the notion of hegemony will be analysed later in greater detail, a brief overview of the debate about the distinction between empire and hegemony helps identify the traits peculiar to empire.

Doyle (1986: 54–81) takes Thucydides' narration of the Peloponnesian War as a point of reference, and considers the intervention in other entities' domestic affairs as the essential distinguishing factor between empire and hegemony. Not only did Athens control the foreign policy of its smaller allies, but it also intervened in their internal affairs, thereby acting imperially. Sparta, on the contrary, limited its interference to foreign policy issues and should therefore be defined as a hegemonic power.

Other authors look for less simplistic, though not always satisfying, solutions. Münkler (2005a: 77) affirms that one of the discriminating features of empire is the huge power difference between the imperial centre and the subordinated entities, a divide so big that it cannot be bridged by 'equality fictions'. However, he does not specify further how extreme this power disparity must be. Given the impossibility of unequivocally demarcating a threshold of power capabilities necessary to identify an empire, this criterion needs to be abandoned (Rapkin 2005: 393). Similarly, if we define informal empire as a 'political relationship' (Lake 1997: 32), it is difficult to identify the threshold in the degree of relational hierarchy that allows for the identification of informal empire. Neither Wendt/Friedheim (1995: 695) nor Lake (1997) are able to determine to what extent the sovereignty of subordinate states has to be curtailed in order to talk about informal empire.

The best solution seems to lie in the analysis of the actors' behaviour – that is, of the *means* employed in the exercise of imperial power (Take 2005: 117). In the case of strong limitations to sovereignty, these means are sometimes considered to be coercion and imposition (Krasner 2001: 18). While coercion, as will be discussed later, constitutes a possible feature of hegemony, empire is characterized by the resort to physical violence or to its threat. 'Imposition entails forcing the target to do something that it would not otherwise do. Physical force, or the threat thereof, matters' (ibid.: 31). The ultimate distinctive feature of imperial behaviour is therefore represented by military intervention or its threat:

> The depth and objects of centralized control vary. Within a given issue-area control can range from proscribing a particular policy while still permitting significant local autonomy, to prescribing one, in effect vetoing all others [...]. It is difficult to define how much centralization is required for informal empire, but this is less important than the expectation of intervention when rules are violated.
>
> (Wendt/Friedheim 1995: 697).[4]

The use or threat of physical, military force has also been highlighted by Münkler (2005a: 30), who underlines that powers adopting an imperial strategy are forced

---

4 Ikenberry (2001: 196) proposes a similar understanding of what he calls 'highly imperial hegemonic order' (one more example of terminological ambiguity), which is based on the exercise of 'coercive domination' that the subordinate states cannot counter through a strategy of balancing.

to resort to the threat of military intervention in order to maintain their dominant position if subordinate states do not comply with their will.

On the basis of the reviewed literature, the essential features of empire can therefore be summarized as follows:

- In an international system composed of nation-states, empire cannot be considered as a territorial unit formed through conquest and expansion. Instead, empire represents a particular form of political relationship or, as will be outlined later, a strategy that can be adopted by dominant powers;
- Imperial relations can be established between states that are equal de jure. However, the asymmetry in the distribution of power is so extreme that, de facto, a hierarchical relationship emerges;
- The imperial power pursues its *own* goals and interests, if necessary by imposing them on the other states involved;
- Imperial relationships imply a substantial limitation of the sovereignty of subordinate states. The imperial power considers itself to be entitled to impose its wishes on the others;
- In order to keep its predominant power position, the imperial power is 'compelled' to intervene to repress insubordination;
- The distinguishing feature of empire is represented by the resort to military intervention or to the threat of it: as a last option, a military attack is always impending.

Hegemony

While the identification of the essential features of empire is relatively simple, since a sort of basic consensus on some central elements – the resort to force or its threat – exists in the above-mentioned literature, the meaning of hegemony is more difficult to grasp. This can be traced back to several reasons: firstly, 'hegemony' is often used as a synonym for both 'leadership' (e.g., Kindleberger 1973; Rapkin 2005) as well as 'empire' (e.g., Wallerstein 1984: 38; Lake 1993: 469); secondly, it is employed by authors belonging to extremely different schools of thought with sometimes radically diverging research interests; thirdly, like 'empire', 'hegemony' has become a normatively loaded term, especially in the context of the US debate on the alleged transition of the USA from a cooperative and benevolent hegemony to an egoistic and greedy empire (e.g., Rapkin 1990a: 3–4; Münkler 2005a: 11–16).

Hegemony, it is argued in this study, is a form of power exercised through strategies that are more subtle than those employed by states behaving as imperial powers. The *means* through which hegemonic power is exercised – and here the distinction between hegemony and empire becomes evident – can vary from threats and the exertion of pressure to the provision of material incentives, to the discursive propagation of the hegemon's norms and values. The *end* of hegemonic behaviour – and this, as we shall see, is the main difference between hegemony and leadership – is always primarily the realization of the hegemon's own goals.

One of the most significant contributions to the notion of hegemony comes from Antonio Gramsci (1975), who analysed this concept with reference to the realm of social relations in his *Prison Notebooks*. A social class, he argues, acts hegemonically if it tries to establish a new order by formulating a universal ideology that brings the interests of subordinate classes in line with its own interests, or presents and affirms its own interests as general interests for the whole society. Hegemony implies the ability of the hegemon to let subordinates believe that power rests upon the consensus of the majority (ibid.: 1638). In this process, ideational and material power resources are always operating together and influencing each other. According to Gramsci, hegemony is and remains a form of dominance, even though it abstains from the use of force. To represent power, Gramsci (ibid.: 1576) takes over Machiavelli's metaphor of the centaur: like the centaur, which is half human and half animal, power is always twofold, encompassing the use of force and coercion on the one hand, and consensus and hegemony on the other.

> To the extent that the consensual aspect of power is in the forefront, hegemony prevails. Coercion is always latent but is only applied in marginal, deviant cases. Hegemony is enough to ensure the conformity of behaviour in most people most of the time.
>
> (Cox 1983: 164)

Another 'classic' but widely neglected approach is that of Heinrich Triepel (1938). Triepel considers hegemony as a form of power situated at an intermediate level on a continuum reaching from mere influence to domination (ibid.: 140). As opposed to domination, hegemony is not based on coercion; instead, it is a tamed form of power, characterized by a high degree of self-restraint on the part of the hegemon (ibid.: 39–40, 148–149). Triepel considers hegemony to be a particular kind of leadership, but he underlines that in international relations subservience to a hegemon will never be based on 'joyful devotion' as in the field of social relations. It will rather depend on the cost-benefit calculations of the weaker states as well as on their recognition of their own weakness (ibid.: 144).

The contributions by Gramsci and Triepel embody the salient aspects later discussed in different strands of the debate on hegemony in the discipline of IR. These essentially revolve around two interrelated points: around the very nature of hegemony, which is supposed to be either benevolent or coercive (or, in other words, 'altruistic' or 'egoistic')[5], and around the means employed to exercise hegemony, which are considered to be either material power resources (sanctions,

---

5 'Benevolent' and 'coercive' or 'altruistic' and 'egoistic' are normative terms. However, since they have marked a broad debate, they will be adopted: 'If it is impossible [...] to purge concepts of their contested appraisive dimension, it is crucial that this dimension be explicitly acknowledged rather than swept under the illusory carpet of objective neutrality' (Rapkin 1990a: 4).

rewards, incentives) or 'ideational' factors (persuasion to accept norms and values).

The origins of the debate on the benevolent versus coercive nature of hegemony lie in the theory of hegemonic stability, originally formulated by Kindleberger (1973) in the context of a perceived decline in US influence on world affairs. In his analysis of the economic crisis of the 1930s, Kindleberger argues that the establishment of a stable economic system depends on the existence of a single state, which dominates in terms of material capabilities and bears the costs of the opening of markets: '[F]or the world economy to be stable, it needs a stabilizer' (Kindleberger 1981: 247). The largest state in a group is the one most interested in the maintenance of the status quo, since it would suffer most from a lack of stability. Moving from an initially egoistic imperative – the creation of a stable environment for its own development – the hegemon invests its resources to stabilize the system. These stabilization efforts correspond to the provision of public goods to the other states, which will act as free-riders and take advantage of the stability created by the hegemon without sharing the costs (Snidal 1985: 581). The hegemon's behaviour, which leads to advantages for all the states in the system, is considered to be 'benevolent' by one strand in the theory of hegemonic stability. The interpretation of hegemony as a beneficial condition for the international system – as the only condition able to provide stability – has contributed to the conceptual confusion between hegemony and leadership.

The introduction of a 'negative' connotation of hegemony is due to Gilpin (1981), who transposes the theory from the analysis of international economy to the broader study of international relations. Gilpin frees hegemony from its benevolent stance and associates it more closely with the pursuit of national interests. While the hegemonic state provides public goods, in this case stability and peace, it imposes a sort of 'tax' on subordinate states, obliging them to contribute to the costs of provision. Since the other states are too weak to exercise effective opposition, they will be forced to comply. However, possible benefits deriving from the public goods provided could induce subordinate states to accept hegemony and legitimize it. Herein lies the reason for the 'egoistic' provision of public goods by the hegemon: a cost/benefit calculation tells the hegemon that it is 'cheaper' to pursue its interests by establishing an order acceptable to others than by resorting to the use of force (Snidal 1985: 587).

Gilpin's contribution marked the beginning of a debate, in which a clearer discrimination of the concepts of 'hegemony' and 'leadership' was attempted, and the ambiguous nature of hegemony was highlighted (ibid.; Lake 1993). Snidal (1985: 614) comes to the conclusion that hegemony can be 'benevolent, coercive but still beneficial, or simply exploitative'. Lake (1993: 460–2, 469–78), on his part, tries for a broader distinction between 'leadership theory' and 'hegemony theory', which he believes are separate components in the theory of hegemonic stability; however, both include elements of coercion. Hegemony theory, he argues, concerns the hegemon's efforts to create economic openness by manipulating the trade policies of other states, which could prefer a closed system: '[t]hus, hegemony is necessarily coercive and based on the exercise of power; the hegemon must effectively change the policies of other states to satisfy its own goals' (ibid.: 469).

Somewhere between these benevolent and coercive interpretations of hegemony lies the more explicitly egoistic account of hegemony provided by power transition theory. This approach is based on the idea of a hierarchical international system in which the dominant state is supposed to be satisfied and interested in maintaining the status quo. In order to realize its main interest, the maintenance of stability, the dominant state 'co-opts the aid of powerful allies and distributes to them *private goods* – benefits it denies to rivals and states too weak to affect the international balance of power' (Bussmann/Oneal 2007: 89, emphasis added).

To summarize, the debate on the coercive versus benevolent nature of hegemony reveals, firstly, the great heterogeneity of interpretations of hegemony, which has contributed to the conceptual confusion with empire and leadership; secondly, and more interestingly, all approaches outlined above highlight the self-interested nature of hegemony. Also, in the case of the provision of public goods, the hegemon's primary aim is the establishment of a stable environment *for itself*. The benefits that are derived from this provision for the subordinate states are essentially a sort of by-product. This insight corresponds to the assumptions made by neo-Gramscian authors such as Cox (1996: 421), who argues that hegemony constitutes a subtle form of domination:

> In the hegemonic consensus, the dominant groups make some concessions to satisfy the subordinate groups, but not such as to endanger their dominance. The language of consensus is a language of common interest expressed in universalist terms, though the structure of power underlying it is skewed in favor of the dominant groups.

While the debate about the benevolent versus coercive character of hegemony takes place within rationalist approaches to IR, the other great debate around the concept of hegemony sees an opposition between rationalist and constructivist approaches. This debate concerns the kind of power resources – material versus ideational – required for and employed in the exercise of hegemony.

For rationalist authors, the central problem concerns the conversion of military and economic power resources into political power, since a hegemonic state is supposed to be predominant in terms of material power capabilities. Realists assume that hegemonic states provide material incentives to their weaker counter-parts in order to establish a stable international order. Both hegemonic stability theory, with its emphasis on the provision of public goods, and power transition theory, which concentrates on the provision of private goods, focus on the role of material incentives. Other realists, however, recognize the importance of moral and normative factors in the successful establishment of hegemony (Ikenberry/ Kupchan 1990a: 50–1). Thus, Gilpin (1981: 29) states that the distribution of power, which represents the 'principal form of control', is not the only factor necessary for the maintenance of international order; prestige ('the probability that a command with a given specific content will be obeyed', even without the direct exercise of power, ibid.: 31) as well as the rules imposed by the hegemon in order to advance its interests also count (ibid.: 36).

Similarly, according to Mastanduno (2002: 185–6),

> [a] hegemonic state has the power to shape the rules of the international game in accordance with its own values and interests. An important implication is that a hegemonic distribution of power will not always produce the same international outcomes; outcomes depend on the particular priorities and purposes of whatever state happens to dominate.

In opposition to realist theories emphasizing material power resources, post-structuralist accounts highlight the role of norms and ideas in the establishment of international hegemony. Nabers (2010: 932) argues that hegemony (or, in his terminology, leadership) is based on the 'inter-subjective internalisation of ideas, norms, and identities' by subordinate states. According to this perspective, the distribution of material capabilities is thought to influence other states' ideas about the world, but material power factors have no intrinsic significance by themselves. Hegemony is therefore characterized as 'discursive hegemony' (ibid.): the hegemon 'exercises power over another state by influencing, shaping, or deter-mining his wants, beliefs, and understandings about the world' (Nabers 2008: 8).

To summarize, the insight derived from the debate on the means employed by hegemonic powers, is that most theoretical approaches assume that material and ideational factors interact in the exercise of hegemony. 'These two ways of exercising hegemonic power are mutually reinforcing and frequently difficult to disentangle' (Ikenberry/Kupchan 1990b: 286). In this case we can again refer back to Gramsci and the neo-Gramscians, who underline the interplay between material and ideational power resources 'to found and protect a world order [...] universal in conception, i.e. not an order in which one state directly exploits others but an order which most other states [...] find compatible with their interests' (Cox 1983: 171). While the employment of material resources implies altering the incentives – that is, the costs and benefits of following different courses of action for other states (Ikenberry/Kupchan 1990b: 287) – the use of ideational power resources is considered necessary in order to gain acceptance of the hegemonic state's pre-eminent position, and thereby to establish some degree of consensus (Cronin 2001: 112; Hurrell 2005: 172–3; Hurrell 2004: xxix; Ikenberry/Kupchan 1990b: 285–6).

This brief analysis of the main debates about hegemony highlights two essential features of this concept:

- Hegemony is essentially self-interested and aims primarily at the realization of the hegemon's goals, which, however, are mostly presented to subordinate states as collective goals;
- Hegemons operate by employing a combination of material power resources and incentives as well as 'ideational' power instruments (the changing or

reshaping of norms and values in the subordinate states) in order to gain consensus in the subordinate states.

For this reason, '[...] hegemony rests on a delicate balance between coercion and consensus, between the exercise of the direct and indirect power of the hegemonic state and the provision of a degree of respect for the interests of the weaker states' (Hurrell 2004: xxix).

Leadership

Like hegemony and, to a lesser extent, empire, leadership is a controversial concept in IR theory. What is especially confusing is the occasionally undifferentiated usage of hegemony and leadership. This terminological ambiguity has its roots in the theory of hegemonic stability and its assumption that only a 'hegemonic' state that possesses predominant resources can 'lead' by providing public goods.[6]

In this study it is argued that there is a fundamental difference between hegemony and leadership, which lies in the goals pursued by the dominant state: while the hegemon aims to realize its own 'egoistic' goals by presenting them as common with those of subordinate states, the leader guides – 'leads' – a group of states towards the realization of common objectives.

Theories from social psychology and political science, the fields in which the study of leadership began, are particularly helpful in grasping this meaning of leadership.[7] While early studies were devoted to an identification of the character traits of great public figures, from the 1960s various management theories began to deal with the relationship between leaders and followers, and with the need for leaders to recognize the needs of their team (Northouse 1997: 32–73; Kogler Hill 1997). On the basis of Burns' (1978) work, the ability of leaders to influence their followers became a central object of study in the 1980s, thereby implying that leadership excludes the exercise of power and coercion since great significance is attributed to the followers' needs (Northouse 1997: 130–58). Leadership was therefore conceived of as 'transformational': leaders are able to alter the motives and preferences of followers, but they in turn are influenced by them. Therefore, the leader and the followers 'share a common cause' (Goethals et al. 2004: 870). Northouse (1997: 3) summarizes the salient aspects of this range of social psychological leadership theories as follows: '[...] (a) leadership is a process, (b) leadership involves influence, (c) leadership occurs within a group context, and (d) leadership involves goal attainment'. From these points, the following definition is derived: 'Leadership is a process whereby an individual influences a group of individuals to achieve a common goal' (ibid.).

The aim of this brief digression is to underline how various theories outside

---

6 For a critique of this aspect of the theory of hegemonic stability, see Wiener (1995b: 1–19).

7 For an overview on this early literature, see Paige (1977, especially ch. 3); Stogdill (1974); Goethals et al. (2004); Northouse (1997).

the discipline of IR have conceptualized leadership as an interaction between leader and followers on the basis of common goals. This conception is radically different from the materialistic assumptions made by the theory of hegemonic stability, which originally equated the provision of public goods with leadership, thereby conflating hegemony with leadership (Kindleberger 1973).[8] With the end of the Bretton Woods system, the failure of the war in Vietnam and the oil crisis, the 1970s brought about a debate on the international role of the United States which came to be framed in terms of 'hegemonic decline' (Rapkin 1990a: 1). In the so-called 'declinist-renewalist' debate, 'declinists' argued that the USA had lost their hegemonic position in the international economy and was therefore no longer able to exercise a leadership function. 'Renewalists', in contrast, stressed not only the ability, but also the duty of the USA to exercise leadership, since no other international actor had access to sufficient resources to fulfil this role. In both cases leadership was considered merely as a function of hegemony.[9]

As mentioned above, it was with the application of the theory of hegemonic stability to the field of international relations undertaken by Gilpin (1981), and later by Snidal (1985) and Lake (1993), that hegemony became associated with a 'negative', 'egoistic' behaviour. Ultimately, these attempts to disentangle the concepts of hegemony and leadership led to an ambiguous characterization of hegemony (between benevolent and coercive), while leadership mostly retained a more explicit association with benevolence.

'Transactional' accounts of leadership focus on the achievement of mutual gains and benefits through the exercise of leadership. According to Knorr (1975: 24–5), the essential features of leadership in international relations are the absence of coercion and the reciprocal flow of benefits: '[...] one actor gives something of value to another without condition, without any stipulated payment, now or later' (ibid.: 311). Fitting examples are the creation of customs unions, 'from the establishment of which all participants would gain – not one from the other, but all from sharing newly created values, in this case, of an economic nature' (ibid.); or the case in which 'A acts as a successful mediary in bringing conflict between B and C to a conclusion that is acceptable to both, and preferable to continued conflict' (ibid.). According to this perspective, as Young (1991: 285) puts it in his article on institutional bargaining, '[l]eadership [...] refers to the actions of individuals who endeavor to solve or circumvent the collective action problems that plague the efforts of parties seeking to reap joint gains in a process of institutional bargaining'.

The transactional approach, focused on an exchange of benefits, might be of importance for leadership, but we should go a step further and conceive of leadership as being characterized by the pursuit of common objectives and,

---

8 According to Kindleberger (1973: 296–8), the outbreak of the Great Depression was determined by a lack of leadership on the part of the USA and Great Britain.
9 For a discussion on this debate, see Wiener (1995b: 1–19). For a critique of declinist positions, see Strange (1987).

therefore, by a commonality of interests between leader and followers. Instead of focusing on common gains, we should therefore focus on common goals.[10] This point is particularly relevant when it comes to a distinction between leadership and hegemony. In fact, the focus on a commonality of gains between leaders and followers could be misleading in defining leadership: as will be outlined later in greater detail, a state adopting an intermediate or soft hegemonic strategy might also reap joint gains with its subordinates. Moreover, as the theory of hegemonic stability tells us, subordinate states take advantage of the collective goods provided by the hegemon – and thereby gain even more than the hegemon itself, since they act as free riders. But this does not necessarily mean that they willingly follow the leader in the effort to reach common goals.

The notion of a commonality of goals, developed by social psychological theories, has been taken over by some authors in the field of IR. For a long time, however, the interests and motivations of followers and, correspondingly, the dynamics of followership have been ignored (Cooper et al. 1991). If we look at the followers, we find, for example, that the US did not exercise 'real' leadership in the second Gulf War; even though its allies seemed to 'follow', their interests and goals did not correspond to those of the US (ibid.). '[I]n order to give leadership concrete meaning, a leader must have followers, those willing to buy into a broad vision of collective goals articulated by a leader in whom both legitimacy and trust are placed' (ibid.: 408). In other words, as Schirm (2010: 216) puts it with reference to emerging powers, 'leadership […] gains followership only if it is credibly framed as a project also representing the goals of others even to the point of changing one's own goals and thus blurring the distinction between the goals of the emerging power and those of followers'.

As Wiener (1995a) underlines, international leadership should be studied from a behavioural perspective, independently of the possession of material power resources by the leader. More generally, we can affirm that leadership does not imply, in a strict sense, the exercise of power by the leader since the followers' participation is voluntary and in their own interest. Therefore, the provision of incentives or side-payments is not relevant for understanding leadership. On the contrary, to sum up the position assumed in this study, leadership implies '[…] leaders inducing followers to act for certain goals that represent the values and motivations – the wants and the needs, the aspirations and the expectations – of *both* leader and followers' (Burns 1978: 19, emphasis added).

Therefore, if we take a closer look at existing theories, we come to the following conceptual clarification and distinction between empire, hegemony, and leadership:

- The ultimate distinguishing feature of empire is represented by the use or the threat of physical violence/military intervention;
- Hegemony is characterized by the hegemon pursuing its *own* 'egoistic' goals. It relies on a variety of more or less coercive or cooperative means and entails the

---

10 On the distinction between 'transactional' and 'transformational' leadership, see Goethals et al. (2004: 870).

effort to make the hegemon's goals, interests, and notions of order be perceived as the most desirable or the only appropriate ones;

- Leadership is characterized by a commonality of goals between leader and followers. The provision of material benefits is not central to the understanding of leadership.

Imperial, Hegemonic, and Leading Strategies

Having delineated the salient features of the debates surrounding the notions of empire, hegemony, and leadership, and having clarified the meaning of these terms, we now need to make them applicable to the study of regional powers' strategies. In this context, attention will also be paid to the degree of legitimacy of imperial, hegemonic, and leading strategies as well as to the expected reactions and perceptions of subordinate states. This specification of the notions of empire, hegemony, and leadership will, in turn, serve as the basis for the subsequent operationalization.

When we talk about *strategy*, this term, regardless of the field in which it is employed (be it military, business, or politics), 'at its most fundamental, signifies a means of achieving one's own aims whilst frustrating those of the opposition' (Grattan 2002: 22). Goals and means are, therefore, the two fundamental aspects of strategy.

In the present study, the term 'strategy' refers to the integration of political, economic, and military aims for the preservation and realization of states' long-term interests – that is, what is commonly named 'grand strategy' in order to distinguish it from the purely military art of using battles to win a war (Kennedy 1991: 1–7).[11] In fact, while traditionally military and diplomatic tools repre- sented the exclusive objects of strategic analyses, the notion of strategy has been broadened; it incorporates different issue areas in which 'a state's theory about its international role and about how best to fulfil or defend that role' (Pedersen 1998: 18, emphasis removed) is put into practice.

The focus on state strategies is typical of foreign policy analysis and has the advantage of combining a clearly actor-centred perspective, which deals with domestic factors influencing the development of grand strategies (Rosecrance/ Stein 1993: 12–21), with the consideration of structural constraints (Pedersen 1998: 16–18). At the same time, strategy always entails the notion of interplay between actors. In other terms, strategy constitutes an interactive process based on a continuous re-adaptation and revision of behaviour on the basis of the (expected) behaviour of the other actors involved: 'each actor's ability to further its ends depends on how other actors behave, and therefore each actor must take the actions of others into account' (Lake/Powell 1999: 3).

---

11   For a 'classical' but more restrictive view of grand strategy, see Liddell Hart (1991: 321–2).

Imperial Strategy

The distinctive feature of an *imperial strategy* – the recourse to military inter-vention or to an explicit threat to use force – has already been outlined in the section on the definition of empire. Some additional aspects related to the behaviour of imperial actors as well as to the reactions of subordinate actors need to be acknowledged.

Analysing an assumed change of US policy from hegemony to empire, Rapkin (2005: 398–400) adds two further elements typical of an empire to those already mentioned above: a preference for *unilateral* problem solving and actions; and a *sense of exemptionalism* implying the imposition of one's own rules on others as well as the rejection of rules contrasting with one's interests (an oft-cited example is the US response to the Kyoto Protocol). An imperial strategy therefore implies that the state implementing it will 'use its power unilaterally to get what it wants, in spite of everyone else's preferences' (Sterling-Folker 2008: 325). As a consequence, we can affirm that an imperial strategy is always illegitimate, if we conceive of legitimacy according to Habermas (1973): in a hierarchical interstate relationship the dominant position of the stronger state is legitimated if the weaker states share its values and goals – that is, if a 'consensual normative order that binds ruler and ruled' is established (Ikenberry/Kupchan 1990b: 289). As Hurrell (2007b: 90) puts it, '[l]egitimacy is about providing persuasive reasons as to why a course of action, a rule, or a political order is right and appropriate'. As a conse-quence, if empire represents a system in which the imperial power unilaterally imposes its own rules, clearly rejects all rules contrasting with its own interests, without justifying or explaining its policies 'in the light of principles that are held in common' (ibid.), then imperial rule is always illegitimate in a Habermasian sense.

The decisive distinguishing factor of an imperial strategy – the threat or use of military power – implies that imperial domination is always accompanied by a great dissatisfaction in subordinate states. This can lead to forms of resistance (Münkler 2005a: 149, 189–200; Rapkin 2005: 396; Doyle 1986: 40) or simply to inescapable subjugation if subordinate states are too weak to resist.

Moreover, the notion of empire is mostly associated with highly aggressive, intimidating rhetoric on the part of the imperial power. A typical example of such an 'imperial' foreign policy approach can be seen in the diplomatic style adopted by the Bush administration with the announcement of a pre-emptive war doctrine in the US national security strategy of September 2002 (Rapkin 2005: 396). Accordingly, one further difference between empire and hegemony needs to be highlighted: both imperial and hegemonic powers possess superior power capabilities, and both want to preserve their predominant position. However, hegemonic powers do not explicitly declare their intentions, while imperial powers adopt an intimidating and threatening discourse, revealing their readiness to resort to military power to implement their imperial projects.

Hegemonic Strategies

While imperial strategies do not address subordinate states' preferences, hegemonic strategies always imply, as we have seen, some degree of consensus. What makes the concept of hegemony so difficult to define and to analyse is the wide range of policy options and strategies that a state defined as 'hegemonic' can pursue. The literature on hegemony tells us that 'some degree of consensus' is required and that hegemons can utilize a whole range of power resources, reaching from the imposition of sanctions to the 'normative persuasion' (Ikenberry/Kupchan 1990a: 55) of subordinate states. The awareness of a variation in the exercise of hegemonic power gives rise to a widespread assumption that hegemony can assume different, more or less unilateral versus cooperative, or coercive versus benevolent, forms, and that the different characters of these hegemonic strategies depend upon the kind of power resources employed.

As a consequence, a further specification and differentiation of forms of hegemony is necessary in order to make the concept of hegemony suitable for empirical analysis. This specification should go beyond the outlined benevolent/coercive and material/ideational divides and should combine these analytical categories into new subtypes, otherwise the fuzzy concept of hegemony can hardly be employed to study state strategies in international relations. Only a few attempts to go beyond mere assumptions of the existence of different kinds of hegemony, if not to build a taxonomy of hegemonic strategies or behaviour, have been made so far in IR theory.[12] This study proposes a division of hegemony into three broad subtypes, which will be labelled as 'hard', 'intermediate' and 'soft' hegemony. The differentiation among these types of hegemonic strategy will be carried out according to the power instruments employed by the dominant power. Besides Nye's (2004) classic distinction between military, economic, and soft power, a further guiding framework for this differentiation will be Ikenberry and Kupchan's (1990a, 1990b) work on the legitimation of hegemony, since the more or less effective 'manufacturing of consent' (Wendt/Friedheim 1995: 700) and the consequent degree of legitimation depend on the hegemonic strategies used.

If we exclude the use of military power or the threat of intervention, which are typical of an imperial strategy, the first form of hegemonic strategy, *hard hegemony*, can be conceived of as a system of domination based on coercion but exercised, as Gramsci suggests, in a more subtle way than an imperial strategy. This means that the hegemonic state primarily aims to realize its own goals and to satisfy its own interests, but seeks to hide this aspiration by emphasizing, to some extent, a commonality of interests with subordinate states. This kind of hegemonic strategy

---

12 Among them are Snidal (1985: 579–95), who highlights that hegemony can be 'benevolent, coercive but still beneficial, or simply exploitative' (ibid.: 614); and Ikenberry (2001), Pedersen (2002), and Hurrell (2004), who focus on the degree of coercion employed by the hegemonic power. However, these approaches to (regional) hegemony are somewhat confusing given the overlapping of their different sub-categories and the lack of extensive operationalization efforts.

is based on a discrepancy between the stated, rhetorical commitment to common goals by the hegemon and the intention to act unilaterally and establish a sort of dominance over subordinate states. Secondary states are forced to change their practices through sanctions and (non-military) threats. This has been suggested by Ikenberry and Kupchan (1990a: 56) in their 'coercion' model of hegemonic power, and by Pedersen (2002: 682) in his 'unilateral hegemony' model, as well as by most realist accounts. Another element, which most authors do not explicitly mention, but which fits into this kind of hegemonic strategy, is the exercise of political and diplomatic pressure on subordinate states to induce them to comply with the hegemon's hierarchical conception of order.

If a regional power follows a hard hegemonic strategy, the compliant behaviour of subordinates will derive mainly from the fact that 'secondary states make rational calculations about the expected costs of noncompliance' (Ikenberry/ Kupchan 1990b: 287). This implies that there is no real change in their normative orientation and that the legitimation of hegemonic power is compromised. In fact, instead of real legitimation based on the adoption of the norms and values promoted by the hegemon, in hard hegemony we find something that could be called 'pseudo-legitimation'. This may lead to different forms of non-violent resistance ranging from diplomatic protests and counter-accusations to the refusal to conform to the hegemon's wishes, or to the simple disregard of the hegemon's pressures. Even if subordinate states comply with the wishes of the hard hegemon – that is, in the case of a successfully employed hard hegemonic strategy – this change in their behaviour will not imply an internalization of the values and norms promoted by the hegemon.

While hard hegemony is based on coercion, *intermediate hegemony* works through the provision of material benefits and rewards (as suggested by hegemonic stability theory), as well as through the promise of future incentives aimed at making subordinate states acquiescent. In this case too, the hegemon pursues its narrow interests and goals, even though it emphasizes the existence of common interests and objectives. However, in the case of intermediate hegemony the discrepancy between rhetorical commitment and actual behaviour is less blatant than in hard hegemony, since the hegemon renounces the use of threats and sanctions. This form of hegemonic strategy is based on what Knorr (1975: 7), in his distinction of forms of power, defines as 'reward power': '[i]t is influence based on A's promise of some sort of goal gratification to B *on condition* that B will supply something of value to A'. Besides incentives and promises, it is argued in this study that 'hard' persuasion efforts are typical tools of intermediate hegemony. This particular form of 'verbal behaviour' will be dealt with later in more detail.

As far as legitimacy is concerned, the absence of threats and pressures makes the intermediate hegemonic strategy more acceptable for subordinate states than the hard one. As pinpointed by Knorr (ibid.:8): '[p]romises are commonly taken as less unfriendly than threats as a way of manipulating relationships. B feels less put upon and is less likely to defy the influence attempt. He receives something of value even if he also loses something of value'. For this reason we can speak of a 'partial legitimation' of intermediate hegemony. Open resistance to the hegemon does not take place as a reaction to an intermediate hegemonic strategy. In the case of a successful implementation of this kind of strategy, the subordinate states will react with compliance. However, their compliant behaviour will not be based on the adoption of the hegemon's norms and values, but on rational cost-benefit calculations about the incentives provided. Despite compliance, some limited forms of verbal resistance, for example more or less disguised critical comments on the hegemon, might take place – even though subordinate states are happy to accept the incentives provided to them.

Moving towards the cooperative end of the continuum of foreign policy strategies, we find *soft hegemony*, a strategy that does not encompass coercion or incentives and, therefore, strongly resembles leadership. However, in contrast to leadership, in soft hegemony the goals and interests of the hegemon are still at the forefront. A soft hegemonic strategy is therefore based on one-sided non-coercive influence aimed at modifying and reshaping the norms and values of subordinate states. Ikenberry and Kupchan (1990a: 57) delineate this kind of approach in their 'normative persuasion' model:

> the hegemon is able to alter the normative orientation and practices of secondary elites without sanctions, inducements, or manipulation. Rather, the hegemon engages in a process of socialization and ideological persuasion in which legitimacy emerges through the osmosis of norms and values from dominant to secondary elites [...].

The complex socialization process also leads to a redefinition of the subordinate state's national interests in terms of the hegemon's normative order and to a transformation in its policies corresponding to the hegemon's values and principles (ibid.). As will be outlined later in greater detail, among the soft hegemonic foreign policy means are: instruments of normative persuasion, like contacts with elites within secondary states (Ikenberry/Kupchan 1990b: 290), verbal 'soft persuasion' tools, and different cooperative forms of diplomatic interaction. Concerning the reactions of subordinate states, in soft hegemony we should talk about consent rather than compliance. Consent, in fact, does not derive from utilitarian calculations but is rather a result of the convergence of norms and values. For this reason, soft hegemony is the only form of hegemonic strategy that can obtain a full legitimation by subordinate states in a Habermasian sense (Ikenberry/Kupchan 1990a: 57).

The three forms of hegemony outlined above can be conceived of as different specifications of the same concept. A transition from one form of hegemonic strategy to the other is possible, if not highly probable. In fact, as Ikenberry and Kupchan (ibid.: 57–8, 65–8; 1990b: 290–2) have highlighted, the projection of norms and values (soft hegemonic strategy) can follow a coercive moment (hard hegemonic strategy) or the provision of material incentives (intermediate hegemonic strategy or, in their terminology, 'external' or 'positive' inducement).

The authors argue that policy coercion and different forms of pressure represent a sort of 'first stage' in the process of establishing and legitimating international hegemony: the hegemon first forces subordinate states to change their policies, and later, gradually, the elites in subordinate states adopt the hegemon's norms and values. This is what the authors call 'acts before beliefs' (Ikenberry/Kupchan 1990a: 58). The final objective of a hegemonic state is the establishment of an accepted, uncontested, and legitimated international order fixing hierarchical asymmetries. Such an order is, in fact, much 'cheaper' to manage because no use of force or side-payments is necessary, but the attainment of such an uncontested order may first require the employment of 'harder' strategies.

Another caveat is required at this point: the proposed distinction between these three forms of hegemony is, of course, ideal-typical. As we will see, (regionally) dominant states follow strategies lying somewhere between the three kinds outlined above. What will be relevant for the empirical analysis of foreign policy strategies, therefore, is a 'prevalence' in the use of coercive/threatening/sanctioning/pressurizing, co-opting/rewarding/inducing/persuading, or convincing/persuading foreign policy means.

Leadership Strategy

At the cooperative end of the continuum of foreign policy strategies, we find *leadership*, defined as a relationship between leader and followers in which common goals are pursued. These goals represent the values, motivations, and expectations of both leaders and followers.

But how does international leadership occur concretely? On the basis of the relevant literature, it is argued that two kinds of leadership exist, depending on who initiates the leadership relationship. Also in this case, Ikenberry and Kupchan's (ibid.: 55–8) models of 'hegemonic' order are helpful. On the one hand, in the 'normative persuasion' model presented above, the 'hegemon' (in this case, the leader) 'engages in a process of socialization and ideological persuasion in which legitimacy emerges through the osmosis of norms and values from dominant to secondary elites' (ibid.: 57). On the other hand, the authors develop two legitimation models based on the voluntary participation of followers: the first, named 'endogenous learning', is based on the development of identical norms and values in different states due to coincidence or to a common reaction to structural conditions.[13] The second, the 'emulation' model, is focused on the adoption of the dominant state's norms and policies by the followers in an effort to imitate its success, but without attempts by the leader to influence their normative orientations or policies.

The first possible way of establishing international leadership originates from

13   Instead of endogenous 'learning' we should, however, talk about endogenous 'adaptation'. Learning implies an active, conscious process, while in this case we are dealing with an almost automatic and unconscious reaction to a given situation or context.

the initiative of the leader and will therefore be called *leader-initiated leadership*. In this case, the leader's strategy is based on its engagement in a socialization process with the aim of creating shared norms and values, and generating 'true' followership.

> The leader may have to consult, to explain, to persuade, even on occasion to cajole. But because followership involves followers intertwining their own interests with those of a leader in whom they place confidence and trust, these followers are likely not simply to defer and acquiesce to the leader, but to willingly follow that leader.
>
> (Cooper et al. 1991: 398)

This model corresponds to the 'normative persuasion' process outlined by Ikenberry and Kupchan. The means employed by a 'leading' regional power correspond, therefore, to those of soft hegemony and consist in 'soft' persuasion, socialization of elites, and cooperative diplomatic statements. The difference between this leader-initiated leadership and hegemonic normative persuasion lies, as specified above, in the goals pursued: in soft hegemony, the hegemon promotes its own norms and values for the realization of its own interests and objectives, while in leadership the goals striven for are collective. It is also possible that the socialization process initiated by the leader makes followers aware of their group interests or of an existing commonality of interest with the leading state. In this context, it is hypothesized that soft hegemony and leadership can represent different strategies in an ongoing process: the hegemon may initiate a socialization process with the aim of realizing its own objectives, but in a second stage the adoption of its norms and values by subordinate states may lead to a commonality of ends and interests, thereby transforming subordinates into followers.

Besides leader-initiated leadership, we could also imagine that the followers give the impetus for the establishment of a leadership—followership relation. Although this *follower-initiated leadership* does not amount to a strategy that a regional power could adopt, briefly dealing with it is useful to highlight the active role smaller states in the region can play if they need a leader to achieve their common goals. This particular impulse for leadership is derived as a logical consequence from the adoption of a 'bottom-up' perspective, which not only focuses on the leader but also places the followers in the centre of the analysis. A group of states can be too heterogeneous or simply too weak to reach a collective goal – and therefore may need a leader to become capable of acting. This might happen, following Tucker's (1981: 15–18) reflections on political leadership, in two different cases: in crisis situations or, more specifically, if the group is threatened from outside; or in the 'everyday business' of international relations. In the first case, the leader will help the group to achieve the common goal of defending itself or of reacting to the crisis situation by assuming a 'directive' function. The followers will ask the leading state for help or, at least, for support in terms of coordination: '[a] leader is one who gives direction to a collective's activities' (ibid.: 15). In the second case, the leader will be induced by followers to adopt a 'managerial' function, helping them 'organizing action' (Wiener 1995a: 223) in order to reach their objectives. This implies that common norms and values, and especially shared goals, already exist among the group of states constituted by leader and followers – the aspect outlined in Ikenberry and Kupchan's 'endogenous learning' model described above. The leader therefore does not have to launch a socialization process, but just has to bundle the interests of the group and 'lead' its followers towards their realization.

Regardless of the initiator of leadership, we can affirm (and this is one of the few points on which most approaches to leadership agree)[14] that international leadership is always legitimated given the commonality of goals and the convergence of norms and values between leader and followers: 'followers see the leader as legitimately placed to make decisions on their behalf' (Cooper et al. 1991: 398). By hypothesizing the existence of truly 'benevolent' leadership strategies, however, we do not intend to assume that states act completely 'altruistically' or against their own interests. This is simply not imaginable. Nevertheless, the pursuit of common goals is not that unusual, at least in certain policy areas. Hence the inclusion of leadership in this discussion about the ideal-typical strategies of regional powers appears to be adequate and helpful.

At this point, however, a fundamental question emerges. To what extent do goals have to be shared between leader and followers in order to talk about leader-initiated leadership? A divergence in goals would, in fact, be an indicator of hegemony while a complete identity of goals would represent the precondition for follower-initiated leadership. For the regional power to adopt a leadership strategy, it is argued that its *core goals* in a given issue area need to be shared, while some differences may exist on secondary goals. Moreover, the objectives pursued by leader and followers need to have a character of 'common good' and not to represent an exclusive interest of the 'leader'; in the latter case, the regional power's approach should be termed 'hegemonic'. This qualification on the commonality of goals is of central importance and will be assumed every time we talk about 'common goals' in the present study.

Table 2.1 recapitulates the main findings of the theory-led conceptual clarification and distinction among empire, hegemony, and leadership and of the identification of ideal-typical strategies pursued by regional powers. Several dimensions are relevant in this regard, from the commonality or divergence of goals to the change of subordinate states' normative orientations. Since follower-initiated leadership originates from the initiative of the regional power's smaller neighbouring states, it is not considered to be a strategy pursued by the regional power. The fields marked in grey in Table 2.1 therefore represent the possible strategies regional powers can adopt.

14 See, for example, Wiener (1995a: 225–6); Cooper et al. (1991: 398); Rapkin (1990b: 196).

Table 2.1. Main features of Empire, Hegemony, and Leadership

	Empire	Hegemony			Leadership	
		Hard	*Intermediate*	*Soft*	*Leader-initiated*	*Follower-initiated*
Goals	Self-interested	Self-interested	Self-interested	Self-interested	Common	Common
Means	Military intervention, threat of intervention	Coercion: non-military threats, sanctions, diplomatic pressure	Material benefits/incentives, 'hard' promises, persuasion efforts	'Soft' persuasion, socialization efforts, diplomatic praise, cooperative diplomatic statements	'Soft' persuasion, socialization efforts, diplomatic praise, cooperative diplomatic statements	Acceptance of directive or managerial function
Self-representation	Aggressive, threatening, compelling subordination	Cooperative	Cooperative	Cooperative	Cooperative	Cooperative
Discrepancy between self-representation and actual behaviour	Low	High	Middle	Low	Low	Low
Legitimation	No legitimation	Pseudo-legitimation	Partial legitimation	Legitimation	Legitimation	Legitimation
Subordinate states' strategies	Resistance or subordination	Resistance. If hegemonic strategy successful: compliance based on rational calculations about the costs of non-compliance	(Resistance.) If hegemonic strategy successful: compliance based on rational cost-benefit calculations	Consent based on redefinition of norms and values	Willing followership	Initiation of leadership as reaction to a threat/crisis or because of lack of coordination
Change in subordinate states' normative orientation due to dominant state's policy	No	No	No	Yes	Yes	No

Source: Destradi (2010). © Cambridge Journals, reproduced with permission.

The notions of empire, hegemony, and leadership are particularly useful for characterizing a *continuum* of strategies employed by powerful regional states.[15] In fact, not only does the multidimensional nature of these concepts allow for a classification of observed behaviours; it also takes into account a broader range of dimensions related to the interaction of the regional power with its neighbours within the region, such as the strategies of these subordinate states, the degree to which they confer legitimacy to the regional power, and possible alterations in their normative orientation. When it comes to operationalizing these concepts for empirical research, however, we need to reduce the number of dimensions considered, as will be outlined in the following section.

Operationalizing Empire, Hegemony, and Leadership

What is striking in the almost inextricable body of literature regarding empire, hegemony, and leadership is the scarcity of attempts to operationalize these concepts.[16] So far, these notions have mostly been analysed singularly – and in most cases without reference to specific state *strategies*. For this reason, referring back to the extensive literature on foreign policy analysis, we need to determine specific indicators for the ideal-typical strategies identified above.

Empire, hegemony, and leadership are concepts that have been developed with a clear reference to the global level of analysis, and particularly to the USA as a great power or, later, as the sole superpower in the post-Cold War era. In order to analyse the possible strategies pursued by regional powers, the notions of empire, hegemony, and leadership have to be broken down to the regional level of analysis. As Lake and Morgan (1997: 7, emphasis removed) argue, 'regions are not simply "little" international systems that behave in ways identical to their "larger" counterparts. Nor are they sui generis, understandable only through unique theories. We need general theories that incorporate regional relations'. While some authors argue that global-level notions cannot simply be 'transposed' to the regional level (Prys 2010), it is assumed in this study that the concepts of empire,

---

15 For similar forms of continuum with hegemony in the middle, see Triepel (1938); Bull (1977); Prys (2010).

16 As outlined above, some efforts were made to distinguish hegemony from empire, but a complete operationalization is still lacking. As far as hegemony at the *regional* level is concerned, Myers (1991: 5) defines regional hegemons as 'states which possess power sufficient to dominate a subordinate state system'. The approach to regional hegemony developed by Prys (2010) is more satisfying as it goes beyond the predominance of power resources and includes other dimensions: self-perception, regional perceptions, provision of public goods, and the projection of preferences and values. However, by making the provision of public goods a necessary condition for regional hegemony, this approach ignores the more coercive forms hegemony can take. One of the most complete and useful operationalization attempts of the concept of hegemony was developed by Triepel (1938), who took into consideration both hard and soft tools of hegemony and incorporated verbal diplomatic means in these categories. Some of these indicators, such as admonitions (cajoling, admonishing, instructing, and counselling) (ibid.: 236–9), were used in the empirical analysis in this study.

hegemony, and leadership as well as their interpretation in terms of strategy do not change in their very nature with a change in level of analysis. For example, the main features of an imperial strategy, the resort to (or threat of) military force and the resistance or subjugation of subordinate countries, do not change whether the imperial strategy is employed inside the region or beyond it. The target state's belonging to the region or, conversely, being placed in another region or continent might have an impact on the actual implementation of a military campaign or on the evaluation of its feasibility, but not on the strategy per se, namely that a military attack is carried out or an ultimatum is posed and the target state resists or succumbs to it. Similarly, leadership is always based on a commonality of goals between leader and followers, irrespective of whether it takes place between the global superpower and its allied countries in remote regions on other continents, or between a powerful regional state and its neighbours. As Schirm (2010: 214) puts it, 'leading a group of country apparently requires the same strategies independent of geography'.

On the basis of the theory-led discussion developed above, it is argued that two elements are central for distinguishing among imperial, hard/intermediate/soft hegemonic, and leading strategies. These two essential discriminating factors are a) the commonality or divergence of the *goals* pursued by the regional power and neighbouring countries, and b) the *means* employed by the regional power in its relations with these countries.

Proceeding by exclusion, an analysis of the commonality or divergence of goals allows one to identify (or exclude) a leadership strategy. That is, if the core goals are the same and if their content implies a 'common good' for the actors involved, these constitute necessary and sufficient conditions for leadership. Therefore, a divergence of core goals would allow us to rule out a leadership strategy on the part of the regional power. Having identified or ruled out leadership, an analysis of the means employed by the regional power helps us identify an imperial or hegemonic strategy, be it hard, intermediate, or soft.

The adoption of an ends-means approach is almost 'classic' in foreign policy analysis, particularly when it comes to the study of state strategies: '[s]trategies imply particular means to an end' (Frieden 1999: 45). An actor operating strategically would specify its objectives, plan how to achieve them, and choose the instruments to do so (Byman/Waxman 2002: 27). However, an exclusive focus on goals and means bears two analytical difficulties. First, empire, hegemony, and leadership are normative concepts and their conceptualization, as developed in this study, is based on a benevolent-coercive continuum. Nevertheless, the benevolent or coercive character of, for example, hegemony, is not an intrinsic quality of hegemony itself. It derives, instead, from the perceptions of subordinate states affected by the hegemonic strategy. The provision of foreign aid, for example, can be welcomed by a subordinate state, but it can, at the same time, be perceived as an affront and rejected by another. The nature of foreign aid as an incentive to induce policy changes depends, therefore, both on the intentions of the state providing it and the manner in which this aid is perceived by the recipient country.

Second, the identification of clear causal relations between the dominant state's behaviour and the subordinate state's reactions is extremely difficult. In the case of trade concessions, for example, it is problematic to find out whether a change in the subordinate state's behaviour in another issue area (for example, security) was a reaction to the concessions or not. Moreover, it is difficult to determine the rationale behind the dominant state's behaviour. Is the goal always the achievement of a change in the normative orientation of subordinates, or can there be cases in which the dominant state 'merely' pursues more immediate goals? To continue with the example of trade concessions: were they made as incentives to change the subordinate state's behaviour, or were they simply aimed at strengthening the dominant state's economy or at increasing its control over the subordinate's economy?

These two problems make an ends-means approach to the study of regional powers' strategies insufficient. For this reason, we need to take into consideration the strategies and perceptions of the subordinate states in order to reach a better assessment of the strategies pursued by the regional power.

For example, the analysis of the *subordinate states' strategies* or, more simply, of their foreign policy behaviour is useful for the identification of resistance; according to its intensity, resistance would be an indicator of an imperial, or of a hard or intermediate hegemonic strategy pursued by the regional power. Moreover, the *subordinate states' perceptions* about the dominant state influence the degree of legitimacy the latter enjoys. As was outlined in the previous sections, in the case

Table 2.2   Analytical categories

	Empire	*Hard Hegemony*	*Intermediate Hegemony*	*Soft Hegemony*	*Leadership*
Commonality of goals	No	No	No	No	Yes
Means	Military intervention, threat of intervention	Coercion: non-military threats, sanctions, diplomatic pressure	Material benefits/ incentives, promises, 'hard' persuasion efforts	'Soft' persuasion, socialization efforts, diplomatic praise, cooperative diplomatic statements	'Soft' persuasion, socialization efforts, diplomatic praise, cooperative diplomatic statements
Subordinate states' actions/reactions	Resistance or subordination	Resistance. If hegemonic strategy successful: compliance based on rational calculations about the costs of non-compliance	(Resistance). If hegemonic strategy successful: compliance based on rational cost-benefit calculations / tactical concessions	Consent based on redefinition of norms and values	Willing followership
Perceptions -> Legitimation	Entirely negative -> No legitimation	Negative -> Pseudo-legitimation	Mixed -> Partial legitimation	Positive -> Legitimation	Positive -> Legitimation

Source: Author's compilation, based on Destradi (2010). © Cambridge Journals, reproduced with permission.

of entirely negative perceptions determined by imperial behaviour, the regional power will not be legitimated at all; hard hegemony will provoke negative perceptions which, in turn, lead to a 'pseudo-legitimation' of the regional power; mixed (positive and negative) perceptions will imply a partial legitimation in the case of intermediate hegemony; and positive perceptions will correspond to a full legitimation of the regional power, which is achieved in the case of soft hegemonic or leading strategies.

Therefore, the inclusion of the behaviour and perceptions of the regional power's counterpart(s) is helpful to complement and to validate the results of the ends-means analysis. Table 2.2 summarizes the main analytical categories needed for the identification of regional powers' foreign policy strategies. In the following sections, operational indicators will be developed and discussed for each of these categories.

Commonality or Divergence of Goals

The determination of a commonality or divergence in *core goals* between the regional power and subordinate states represents the main indicator of a leadership strategy – or, in the absence of common goals, for the exclusion of this kind of strategy. However, strategic choice approaches underline several difficulties inherent in the identification of state preferences or goals, the main methodological problem being the impossibility to directly observe them:

> Like participants, scholars of international politics observe only the behavior of states and their leaders; we cannot know their true motivations. And while the observed behavior might perfectly reflect an actor's preferences, it might just as well be powerfully affected by uncertainty, institutions, and other features of the strategic setting.
>
> (Frieden 1999: 40)

An exclusive inference of goals from observed behaviour would therefore commit 'the logical fallacy of asserting that the preferences of those most favored by an outcome must have determined the outcome itself, ignoring the possibility that strategic interaction might have fundamentally transformed the process and its end point' (ibid.: 52). Such an approach bears the risk of circular reasoning – that is, of inferring the actor's goals from the outcome, and afterwards arguing that the outcome was determined by the actor's goals (Patchen 1988: 343). For this reason, the determination of actors' goals represents 'one of the most daunting problems in social sciences' (Frieden 1999: 53).

A possible solution entails the identification, as a first step, of *declared* goals enunciated in official statements and documents and, as a second step, the *induction* of goals from state behaviour. This allows us to assess discrepancies between stated and assumed 'real' goals.[17] Induction represents the most practicable method to validate the determination of state goals for the purpose of this analysis.[18] As Lukes (2005a: 81) puts it, so-called 'covert' preferences ('half-articulated or unarticulated grievances or aspirations which, because of the bias of the dominant political agenda or the prevailing culture, are not heard and may not even be voiced', ibid.) can be inferred from 'choice behaviour' or from 'a close observation of what [actors] say and do, what they would choose were choices available that are currently unavailable' (ibid.). Moreover, as will be discussed later in more detail, some solutions can be found to further increase the validity of the results reached – notably a triangulation of data. Beyond this, according to the analytical framework developed above, the induction of goals and the identification of commonalities or divergences are complemented and validated by the analysis of subordinate states' reactions and perceptions. Therefore, if the subordinate state displays a certain degree of resistance towards or negative perceptions of the regional power, then the fact would refute the hypothesis of leadership and, instead, hint at a hegemonic strategy; even if the analysis of stated goals, and perhaps even the induction of non-stated goals, lead to the identification of common core goals between a regional power and a subordinate state.

Foreign Policy Means

The volume of literature dealing with different foreign policy means – from interventions, to sanctions, threats, incentives, and socialization efforts – is impressive (Bemelmans-Videc 1998: 1). From this body of literature in the field of IR and in the sub-discipline of foreign policy analysis, we will now derive a range of indicators that will allow us to identify the means employed by India as a regional power.

The typical means characterizing the exercise of imperial power is represented by the use or threat of military force. The Correlates of War (COW) project has elaborated a set of extremely useful definitions of militarized incidents, which can be adopted here to outline the means typical of an imperial strategy (Jones et al. 1996). A militarized incident is defined as 'a single military action involving an explicit threat, display, or use of force by one system member state towards another system member state' (ibid.: 169). This implies that militarized actions provided for by treaty or taking place at the invitation of the target state are not taken into consideration. Moreover, the military action has to be explicit, non-routine, governmentally authorized, and carried out by the official military

---

17 On the problems of assuming the existence of 'real' goals, see Lukes (2005a).

18 Further methods to specify state preferences, their assumption and their deduction (Frieden 1999: 53–66), appear inadequate. The assumption of preferences ignores the multiplicity of actors, issues, and dimensions typical of international relations. The deduction of preferences from theory would represent the most satisfying solution, if it was not for two problems: first, such theories are not always in place – or not at the necessary level of aggregation; second, 'the preferences deduced from preexisting theories are only as good as the theories themselves' (ibid.: 65).

forces or government representatives of a state. In ambiguous cases (vague and non-specific actions, or actions carried out by regular forces disguised as irregular forces, covert operations, etc.), the militarized action is taken into consideration only if the subordinate state reacts to that specific action militarily or diplomatically (or if the action is verified by an impartial observer) (ibid.). The COW project proposes the following indicators, which can be adopted to identify an imperial strategy:[19]

- Uses of force: use of chemical, biological, and radiological (CBR) weapons, declaration of war, raid, seizure (of material or personnel), occupation of territory, blockade[20];
- Displays of force: border violation, nuclear alert, fortify border, show of planes/ships/troops, mobilization, alert;
- Threats of force: threat to use nuclear weapons, to declare war, to occupy territory, to blockade, to use force (ibid.: 171–3).

While the detailed COW categories provide a good set of indicators for imperial foreign policy means, it is almost impossible to formulate a comprehensive list of indicators for all conceivable foreign policy instruments typical of hard, intermediate, and soft hegemonic strategies as well as of leadership.[21] Therefore, the following sections will focus on providing appropriate examples and on discussing possible interpretations of observable events and diplomatic interactions, but without any pretence of exhaustiveness. An important distinction to be made is between non-verbal and verbal foreign policy means. 'Verbal behaviour [...] – as opposed to "substantive" physical or legal actions' (Davies/McDaniel 1994: 68) is particularly important for the assessment of diplomatic interactions – that is, for the analysis of the level at which a large part of inter-state interactions take place.

The essential feature of a *hard* hegemonic strategy is coercion, which can be exercised through non-military threats, sanctions, and diplomatic pressure.[22] As Byman and Waxman (2002: 3) put it,

---

19 For details on coding, see Jones et al. (1996: 171–3).
20 'Clash' has been removed as an indicator since it is not suitable for the actor-centred approach to strategy adopted in this study. In fact, 'clash' is defined as the 'outbreak of military hostilities between regular armed forces of two or more system members, in which the initiator may or may not be clearly identified' (ibid.: 173).
21 Among the datasets collecting event data on a conflict–cooperation continuum, the Conflict and Peace Data Bank (COPDAB), and the Conflict and Mediation Event Observations (CAMEO) were used as points of reference for some indicators and for the elaboration of codes in the qualitative content analysis. See CAMEO (2009); Azar (1993: 26) .
22 The literature on coercion and sanctions is huge. The former was widely studied in the context of the Cold War (e.g., Schelling 1966; Pennock/Chapman 1972; George et al. 1971), while the latter gained momentum after the increase in the use of sanctions by the US and the UN in the 1990s (e.g., Doxey 1996; Cortright/Lopez 2002).

[c]oercion is not destruction. Coercive strategies are most successful when threats need not even be carried out. [...] Coercion may be thought of, then, as getting the adversary to act a certain way via anything short of brute force; the adversary must still have the capacity for organized violence but *choose* not to exercise it.

The goal of coercion consists of inducing another actor to change its behaviour or, in other words, to manipulate its decision-making (ibid.: 1; 18). So-called 'dispositional' coercion specifically implies that one actor threatens another with a sanction if the latter does not act as requested (Bayles 1972: 17). [23]

Threats are the central element on which coercion is based. While military threats are indicators of an imperial strategy, *non-military threats* refer to a hard hegemonic strategy. However, not all threats involve coercion. In order to be indicators for a hard hegemonic strategy, threats must imply the agent's intention to get the target to act in a specific manner and to impose a sanction if it does not (ibid.: 21). In any case, therefore, threats are *verbal* coercive moves implying 'a demand on another party, plus a sanction that will be inflicted if the demand is not met' (Snyder/Diesing 1977: 213). Threats may be more or less explicit or ambiguous, according to the degree of credibility and commitment they need to convey (ibid.: 216–8). As Knorr (1975: 10) puts it, threats may be 'substantive', which means specific and precise (for example, an ultimatum), or 'inferential', that is, more vague and implicit: 'For example, to put some pressure on B, who presumably knows what A wants, A may make vague domestic statements about increasing military expenditure' (ibid.). As far as the content of threats is concerned, non-military threats may involve a wide range of issue areas, from economic relations to culture and diplomacy or, for example, the exclusion from established international (or regional) institutions (Pedersen 1999: 91). The threat to break or reduce diplomatic relations is probably the hardest threat in the field of diplomacy. *Blackmailing* is a particular form of threat 'employed offensively to get the opponent to do something he has not done and does not want to do – to make him pay a price, give up territory – in order to avoid the threatened sanctions' (George et al. 1971: 24).

Sanctions or, more precisely, negative sanctions, are 'efforts to place [...] pressure on an adversary' (Byman/Waxman 2002: 106). They differ from threats since they try to change the target's behaviour not through a verbal demand but though concrete action. Sanctions are therefore often employed as a consequence of failed threats.[24] Mostly, sanctions are of an economic nature. They can be aimed at weakening the target's economy; at creating popular discontent and

---

23 Byman and Waxman (2002: 6–7) propose, moreover, a distinction between compellence and deterrence, but '[b]oth actions ultimately boil down to inducing the adversary to choose a different policy than it otherwise would' (ibid.: 7).
24 Sanctions as coercive tools of political pressure are defined more broadly than international, formal sanctions imposed upon actors violating international norms (Doxey 1996: 9).

thereby destabilizing the existing regime; or at creating disadvantages for single groups of actors or sectors of the economy (for example, financial assets), which constitute the regime's power base. Among the examples of economic sanctions listed by Baldwin (1985: 41) and Mastanduno (2008: 173–4) are the following: embargo, boycott, tariff increase/discrimination, withdrawal of most favourite nation (MFN)-treatment, blacklist, quota, license denial, dumping, preclusive buying, freezing assets, control on import/export of capital, aid suspension, expropriation, discriminatory taxation, and monetary sanctions.

Besides these economic sanctions, military sanctions not involving threat, display, or use of force also are possible hard hegemonic means, e.g. a weapons embargo or an interruption of military assistance or cooperation. While sanctions normally are deprivations or harm (Bayles 1972: 22), the cutting of incentives – or, more precisely, of 'legitimately expected benefits' (ibid.: 23) – also corresponds to imposing sanctions, if this cut is tied to a request.

In the fields of culture and communication, some sanctioning measures could be the following, as listed by Doxey (1996: 14):

- Restriction or withdrawal of visa privileges;
- Restriction or cancellation of telephone, cable, postal links;
- Restriction, suspension, or withdrawal of landing and overflight privileges, of water transit, docking, and port privileges, or of land transit privileges;
- Curtailment or cancellation of cultural exchanges, scientific cooperation, educational ties, sports contacts, tourism.

Importantly, sanctions might be used in combination with other coercive instruments in order to increase pressure on the subordinate state in the context of a hard hegemonic strategy (Byman/Waxman 2002: 114).

The third central element of coercion is *diplomatic pressure*. This can entail different kinds of *verbal coercive declarations* (Snyder/Diesing 1977: 220), which belong to the typical set of tools of hard hegemonic diplomacy. In this regard, the 'degree of bellicosity of the language' (ibid.) matters; and so does its perception by the affected states. Frequently used forms of verbal pressure are, for example, *condemnations* of specific actions or policies, *denunciations* of leaders, systems, or ideologies, *accusations*, *criticism*, the *denial* of support, as well as imperative *orders*, etc.[25]

Apart from verbal utterances, diplomatic pressure can be exercised through the following actions:

25 Many of these indicators are listed in the COPDAB codebook as 'strong verbal expressions displaying hostility' (Azar 1993: 26). Among the verbs belonging to this category are: denounce, accuse, demand, protest, condemn, reject, blame, charge, oppose, and challenge. Some of them were adopted to develop the codes for qualitative content analysis employed in the empirical chapters.

- The summoning of diplomatic representatives to convey a protest;
- The postponement or cancellation of official visits, meetings, or negotiations (Doxey 1996: 14);
- The reduction of the diplomatic representation affecting diplomatic personnel, consular offices, etc. (ibid.);
- The political isolation of the subordinate state (Byman/Waxman 2002: 114–17). This can take place through the adoption of resolutions condemning the target state, for example at the United Nations or in other international organizations, as well as through other forms of political protest (ibid.: 115). Isolation, in particular, 'can play a major role in [...] neutralizing the adversary's options for counter-coercion' (ibid.) and therefore constitutes a typical strategic foreign policy instrument;
- The severance of diplomatic relations (Doxey 1996: 14).

Political Intervention is another relevant but often ignored instrument of coercive policy-making. The hardest form of political intervention is represented by the backing of insurgent movements in the target state (Byman/Waxman 2002: 117–20). This aspect is not considered as an imperial strategy tool in the present work. This is because the support for insurgent movements does not correspond to the imperial means outlined above – that is, to an explicit, overt, and 'official' threat, display, or use of force; instead, it works indirectly. However, the affinity to imperial means is huge. Besides the support for insurgent movements, other forms of political intervention designed to destabilize another state's government can also be considered as indicators of hard hegemony. Examples of this kind of intervention include the targeted erosion of the regime's power base; the creation of unrest and popular dissatisfaction with the regime (subversion); or the 'decapitation' of the leadership, that is, the jeopardizing of its personal security (ibid.: 59–78; Brighi/Hill 2008: 132).

While hard hegemonic strategies are based on different forms of coercion, in the case of *intermediate hegemony*, the essential indicators are *inducements*. According to Cortright (1997: 6), *incentives* can be defined as 'the granting of a political or economic benefit in exchange for a specified policy adjustment by the recipient nation'. In other terms, incentives are 'transfers of positively valued resources, such as money, technology, know-how, from one actor to another with the aim of driving the behavior of the recipient in a direction that is desirable from the point of view of the provider' (Bernauer/Ruloff 1999: 2). This implies that the offer or provision of incentives or concessions has the objective of obtaining the compliance with one's wishes or wants. As Byman and Waxman (2002: 9) point out, inducements are the 'flipside' of coercion. Therefore, the goals of the state exercising pressure or providing inducements are in the forefront – hegemony is always focused on the hegemon's own goals. However, due to their lesser intrusion into subordinate states' sovereignty compared to coercive tools, incentives are more likely to be accepted and the state providing them is more likely to obtain legitimacy. In fact, while threats and sanctions normally produce resistance and resentment in the target state, incentives have the advantage of raising hope, encouraging the government of the target state to cooperate or conform with the wishes of the state providing the incentives (Mastanduno 2008: 184; Cortright 1997: 10–11). Even though a certain degree of resistance may persist, the probability of inducing cooperation is higher.[26] Moreover, coercion and inducements can be mixed and combined in order to maximize the success of a policy. Inducements can contribute, for example, to allow the adversary to 'save face', 'enabling leaders to claim victory even in defeat' (Byman/Waxman 2002: 9).

Incentives can vary according to their 'immediateness' versus 'continuity' and to their degree of conditionality. Mastanduno (2008: 182) distinguishes between immediate incentives ('tactical linkage') and long-term engagement ('structural linkage'). While immediate incentives are usually more explicitly conditional and directly targeted at specific policy changes, long-term engagement is usually unconditional and works at a deeper level with the goal of gradually transforming the interests and goals of the target state.

Also in the case of incentives, in the absence of a comprehensive database of possible incentives (ibid.), a non-exhaustive series of examples is provided. In his classic work on sanctions and inducements, Baldwin (1985: 42) lists several examples of 'positive sanctions' in the economic field: favourable tariff discrimination, granting MFN treatment, tariff reduction, direct purchase (payment for services or goods), subsidies to exports/imports, granting licences, aid provision, investment guarantees, encouragement of private capital exports/imports, and favourable taxation of foreign capital investment. Beyond the field of economy and trade, possible incentives include granting access to advanced technology, offering diplomatic and political support, military cooperation, environmental and social cooperation, debt relief, security assurances, and granting membership in international organizations or security alliances (Cortright 1997: 7).

Promises are also important intermediate hegemonic foreign policy tools. As threats constitute a possible verbal precursor of sanctions, promises represent their 'benevolent' counterpart: they imply holding out the provision of incentives if the target state complies with the hegemon's wishes (Mastanduno 2008: 182; Baldwin 1985: 42). An interesting case located between incentives and promises is that of *bribery*, which constitutes a 'prepaid reward' (Knorr 1975: 7) for compliant behaviour.

Besides the provision of incentives, intermediate hegemony is assumed to be characterized by *verbal* efforts directed at generating compliance with the hegemon's wishes. In the present study, these efforts are labelled as '*hard persuasion*'. In particular, *admonitions*, *exhortations*, *requests*, and *expressions of concern* are taken as indicators of this kind of strategy given their 'imperative'

---

26 However, incentives, especially economic ones, can also have negative repercussions on the state providing them. For example, states offering incentives become vulnerable to future extortion attempts, and it is almost impossible to bribe a state into making compromises on such vital issues as its security (Dorussen 2001: 253).

character. Their goal, in fact, is not a change in the normative orientation of the target but a change in its behaviour. However, it is important to note that hard persuasion efforts are clearly distinct from incentives or threats. '[P]ersuasion consists in the use of arguments rather than incentives to convince the target of the appropriateness of [...] rules' (Schimmelfennig et al. 2006: 7). Therefore, the admonitions, exhortations, requests, etc. must be free, on the one hand, of explicit threats and, on the other, of promises of rewards.

The main tool of a *soft hegemonic strategy* is represented by *normative persuasion* efforts employed as part of a socialization process. If we define international socialization as 'a process in which states are induced to adopt the constitutive rules of an international community' (ibid.: 2), then the content being transmitted will consist of identities, beliefs, values, roles, norms, or rules (ibid.: 3). In a bilateral relationship between a dominant and a subordinate state, socialization can be conceived of as the adoption of the beliefs and behaviour promoted by a 'norm entrepreneur' on the part of a norm follower (Finnemore/Sikkink 1998: 902). Norm entrepreneurs make 'detailed ends-means calculations to maximize their utilities, but the utilities they want to maximize involve changing the other players' utility function in ways that reflect the normative commitments of the norm entrepreneurs' (ibid.: 910). In this case, socialization attempts are clearly part of a hegemonic strategy since the hegemon's goals stand in the forefront.

   Among possible forms of strategic interaction aimed at norm diffusion are the following:

- *Education of elites.* If we look at socialization attempts by a dominant state, efforts at influencing foreign elites are represented, for example, by the education of subordinate states' elites in the dominant country, the provision of scholarships, etc;
- *Cultural diplomacy.* An important and 'observable' tool of socialization is represented by the effort to spread one's own culture as a way of promoting one's norms and values. All activities related to cultural diplomacy in foreign countries may be interpreted as indicators of soft hegemony;
- *'Soft' Persuasion.* Like coercion and 'hard' persuasion, soft persuasion has the goal of inducing the target to accept one's demands – the crucial difference is that 'it does not involve threatening harm to the other party if he does not concede' (Snyder/Diesing 1977: 198) nor does it involve addressing the counterpart in an 'imperative' tone. Persuasion may take place through milder verbal moves, such as *cajoling, instructing,* and *counselling* (Triepel 1938: 236–9), through *expressions of wishes and preferences, expressions of commitment, hope, and confidence* as well as through *argumentation* or *arguing* (Finnemore/Sikkink 1998: 915). 'Actors rely on a variety of techniques to persuade, including appeals to emotion, evoking symbols, as well as the use and extension of logical arguments' (Risse/Sikkink 1999: 14);
- *Diplomatic praise.* The praise for behaviour that conforms to certain norms represents a further tool of socialization. At the international level, praise is

exercised by diplomatic representatives (Finnemore/Sikkink 1998: 902) and can take the form of *expressions of appreciation* or *satisfaction, commendation, or congratulation*;

- Similarly, *cooperative verbal diplomatic statements* such as invitations of representatives of the target state, accepting invitations, expressions of condolences and sorrow about tragedies in the target country, etc. are assumed to be tools of a soft hegemonic foreign policy strategy if paired with diverging core goals.

These soft hegemonic means resemble the tools typically employed by countries adopting a *leadership strategy*. The main difference between hegemony and leadership consists in whose goals are being pursued, with the essential trait of leadership being the commonality of core goals between leader and followers. The leader's approach may include efforts at socialization similar to those pursued by a state that follows a soft hegemonic strategy. Therefore, as far as the socialization process is concerned, the means employed will be the same as in soft hegemony. The difference lies in the *content* of the goals being promoted, which are supposed to be oriented towards something like a 'common good'. If socialization takes place, this implies that some norms are being transmitted, that is, that the goals of leader and followers will not be entirely identical (otherwise efforts at norm diffusion would most probably be superfluous). Therefore, the best research strategy to identify leadership will be to look, first, at the regional power's and the subordinate states' goals in order to assess the existence of commonalities on *core* goals and possible differences in secondary goals; second, at the existence of means indicating the pursuit of a leadership strategy on the part of the regional power.

To summarize, in order to identify a leadership strategy, the following three necessary conditions apply:

- A commonality of core goals sufficient to induce us to assume that subordinate states would be willing to 'follow' the leader, that is, to adapt their secondary goals to those of the leader;
- The goals promoted by the leader are directed to the advantage of both leader and follower(s); that is, they are not the 'egoistic' goals of the regional power;
- The regional power employs foreign policy means directed at a socialization of the subordinate state(s).

Table 2.3 provides an overview of the above-mentioned means typical of imperial, hard, intermediate, and soft hegemonic, as well as of leading strategies. The indicators in the right column are to be understood as a non-exhaustive list of examples of possible means employed in the different categories. Coercion, incentives, socialization, and persuasion are broader categories encompassing different means subsequently listed. Moreover, a distinction is made in table 2.3, between non-verbal means, that is, actual behaviour, represented by the white fields; and verbal means in the grey fields. This distinction becomes relevant when it comes to the problem of selecting the sources to analyse in empirical studies.

Table 2.3   Overview of means

Strategy	Specification	Means (examples)
Imperial Strategy	Uses of force	Use of CBR weapons, raid, seizure, occupation of territory, blockade
		Declaration of war
	Displays of force	Border violation, nuclear alert, fortify border, show of planes, show of ships, show of troops, mobilization, alert
	Threats of force	Threat to use nuclear weapons, threat to declare war / ultimatum, threat to occupy territory, threat to blockade, threat to use force
Hard Hegemonic Strategy	*Coercion*	
	Non-military Threats	
	Sanctions	Embargo, boycott, tariff increase, tariff discrimination, withdrawal of MFN treatment, blacklist, quotas, licence denial, dumping, preclusive buying, freezing assets, control on import or export of capital, aid suspension, expropriation, taxation, monetary sanctions
		Weapons embargo, interruption of military assistance, interruption of military cooperation
		Curtailment/cancellation of cultural exchanges, scientific cooperation, educational ties, sports contacts, tourism; restriction of travel/withdrawal of visa privileges; restriction/cancellation of telephone, cable, postal links; restriction/ suspension/cancellation of landing/ overflight/water transit/docking/port/land transit privileges
	Diplomatic Pressure	Verbal coercive declarations: condemnation, denunciation, accusation, criticism, denial of support, order
		Summoning of diplomatic representatives; postponement/cancellation of official visits, meetings, negotiations, etc.; reduction of diplomatic representation; political isolation; severing diplomatic relations
	Political Intervention	Support for insurgent movements
		Subversion
		'Decapitation' of leadership

Strategy	Specification	Means (examples)
Intermediate Hegemonic Strategy	*Incentives*	Favourable tariff discrimination, granting MFN treatment, tariff reduction, direct purchase, subsidies to exports or imports, granting licences, providing aid, investment guarantees, encouragement of private capital exports or imports, taxation, granting access to advanced technology, debt relief
		Granting membership in international organizations or security alliances; military cooperation
		Offer of political support, security assurances
	Promises / Bribery	
	'Hard' Persuasion Efforts	Admonitions, exhortations, requests, expressions of concern (but no explicit threats or promises)
Soft Hegemonic Strategy		Education of elites, cultural diplomacy
	'Soft' Persuasion	Cajoling , instructing, counselling, arguing, expressions of wishes and preferences, expressions of commitment or support, hope, and confidence
Efforts at socialization (hegemon's goals and	Diplomatic praise	Expressions of appreciation/satisfaction, commendation, congratulation
interests in the forefront)	Cooperative verbal diplomatic statements	Invitations, accepting invitations
Leadership Strategy		Education of elites, cultural diplomacy
Efforts at socialization (common goals and	'Soft' Persuasion	Cajoling , instructing, counselling, arguing, expressions of wishes and preferences, expressions of commitment, support, hope, or confidence
interests in the forefront)	Diplomatic praise	Expressions of appreciation/satisfaction, commendation, congratulation
	Cooperative verbal diplomatic statements	Invitations, accepting invitations

Source: Author's composition, based on Jones et al. (1996: 171–3); Baldwin (1985: 41–2); Mastanduno (2008: 173–4); Doxey (1996: 14); Azar (1993); Byman/Waxman (2002: 59–78, 117–20); Cortright (1997: 7); Triepel (1938: 236–9); Finnemore/Sikkink (1998: 915).

The analysis of the foreign policy means used by the regional power, and of the commonality or divergence between the goals of the regional power and those of its small neighbours, needs to be complemented by an assessment of the strategies and perceptions of subordinate states.

The typical reactions to an imperial strategy are represented by resistance or, if the subordinate state is too weak to react, by subordination. On the one hand, as Münkler (2005a: 172–212) highlights, imperial domination leads to anti-imperial strategies by subordinate actors. These can be asymmetrical forms of violent rebellion or, in international relations, (hard) balancing strategies. On the other hand, as Lukes (2005a: 74) points out, domination is usually met by 'subordination, subjugation […], conformism, acquiescence and docility'. This kind of subordination will take place because of an impossibility to resist. However, it does neither imply an acceptance or internalization of the dominant state's norms and values, nor the establishment of common goals. At the level of perceptions, the aggressive policy style and rhetoric of the imperial power will automatically produce threat perceptions among subordinate states (Rapkin 2005: 396). The lack of a consensual normative understanding between imperial power and subordinate states, together with their threat perceptions, in turn, determine the lack of legitimacy of imperial power.

The reactions to a hard hegemonic strategy will mainly consist of 'counter-coercive strategies' (Byman/Waxman 2002: 19). For example, the imposition of sanctions will provoke diplomatic protests of various kinds, reaching from the summoning of diplomatic representatives to the issuing of protest notes, etc. Another form of resistance against sanctions perceived as unjust might be the formation of coalitions of subordinate states (balancing) but also, for example, the mobilization of the international public opinion against the hegemonic state. 'Adversaries generally avoid exposing themselves to the coercer's strengths. They employ weapons of the weak […] and try to exploit the humanitarian conscience or political sensitivities of the coercing powers in an effort to fracture public opinion' (ibid.: 18–19). In the case of economic sanctions, to cite another example, the target state may react by trying to undermine them through the black market, the diversion of investments from unsanctioned sectors to sanctioned ones, etc. (ibid.: 109–10).

In most cases, the resistance to the hegemonic power will not take place in the form of armed resistance, given the lack of a military component in the threats and the sanctions imposed. It is assumed, in fact, that a high degree of concomitance exists between the kind of means adopted by the regional power and those adopted by subordinate states.[27]

In the very specific case of political intervention (support for insurgents, subversion, 'decapitation' of leadership), that is, of the covert manipulation of another country's political development, the risk of backfiring and provoking strong resistance is much higher than in the case of overtly coercive means. As Hill

---

27 Intriguingly, however, threats sometimes may not even need to be formulated – for example, past uses of coercive power or the sheer superiority in terms of power capabilities may induce a smaller state to engage in self-censorship (Lukes 2005a: 78).

(2003: 145) points out, '[i]t is likely that in the long run subversion breeds even more antagonism and resistance than invasion and occupation, which do at least clarify the nature of the enemy'. In the case of subversion, therefore, the reactions of subordinate states are more likely to take violent forms. Perceptions about a state adopting a hard hegemonic strategy will most likely be negative. However, a high degree of hostility on the part of the smaller countries, determined for example by fear or by historical animosities, may also induce the dominant state to follow a hard hegemonic strategy on the basis that a softer form of influence would not be effective.

Reactions to an intermediate hegemonic strategy are expected to be characterized by compliance due to rational cost-benefit calculations related to the acceptance of incentives. However, this compliance might be complemented by verbal expressions of resistance, albeit only moderate ones (e.g., critique). Correspondingly, perceptions about the state adopting an intermediate hegemonic strategy are mixed – positive because of the benefits deriving from incentives, and negative because of the existing divergence of goals. Given the lack of a successful socialization process, in fact, the subordinate country (or, at least, a considerable part of its elite) is aware of the 'egoistic' character of the hegemon's moves.

The reactions to a soft hegemonic strategy, on the contrary, will be based on a genuine *consent* (as opposed to compliance) on the part of subordinate states. The process of socialization and persuasion may 'convince' subordinate states of the desirability and appropriateness of the norms propagated by the hegemon. This corresponds to hegemony as Gramsci conceived it. However, some elements of resignation and quiescence may still persist in subordinate states. As Lukes (2005a: 132) points out, 'consent' and 'resignation' can take place at the same time and do not have to be treated as entirely opposed and mutually excluding concepts. Overall, however, in the case of soft hegemony, subordinate states' perceptions about the hegemon are mainly positive and the predominant position of the state acting as a soft hegemon is fully legitimated by the subordinate countries.

Finally, given the commonality of goals between leader and followers, the reactions to a leadership strategy will be determined by the voluntary adoption of a 'consensus-oriented foreign policy' aligned with that of the leader (Breuning 2007: 152). As has been discussed above, followership constitutes a central element in the definition of leadership and the followers' positive perceptions about the leader contribute to a full legitimation of the leader's role. Therefore, in the case of leadership strategies, the role of the small neighbours of a regional power is particularly relevant and deserves special attention.

Some Notes on Methods and Sources

Having discussed the conceptual boundaries between the notions of empire, hegemony, and leadership, as well as the operationalization of these notions for the analysis of regional power strategies, the sequence of analytical steps and the methods most suitable for empirical analysis need to be outlined. Moreover, some general remarks will be made on possible sources and data, and the specific sources employed in the subsequent empirical chapters for the study of India's strategies in its eastern neighbourhood will be briefly discussed.

The first indicator to be taken into consideration is the commonality or divergence of goals between the regional power and neighbouring states. As mentioned above, the identification of goals has to be based, as a first step, on the *stated* goals enunciated in official statements and documents. As a second step, it should be complemented by the *induction* of goals from state behaviour in order to assess discrepancies between stated and 'real' goals.

A suitable method to identify the goals enunciated by governments is represented by a summarizing qualitative content analysis (Mayring 2003). Qualitative content analysis is a procedure to 'extract meaning from communication' (Hermann 2008: 151). Its goal consists of 'making inferences by objectively and systematically identifying specified characteristics of messages' (Holsti 1969: 14, emphasis removed).[28] The advantages of content analysis in comparison to other forms of textual analysis are, among others, the following:

- Analysis is systematic: it follows a fixed and traceable procedure and a pre-determined set of rules. Thereby, content analysis meets social science methodological standards, which require an inter-subjective verifiability of the results. Free interpretations, as those typical of hermeneutic approaches, are rejected. Moreover, the material to be analysed has to be 'fixed' (put on record) in order to make any analytical step traceable and comprehensible;
- Analysis is theory-led: the material is analysed according to a research question rooted in theory. The results are interpreted in a theoretical framework and the single analytical steps are also guided by theory. For example, in our case this means that the necessity to identify the goals pursued by the regional power is derived from the theoretical considerations that 1) goals are an essential element of strategy, and 2) goals are essential indicators to distinguish imperial, hegemonic, or leading state strategies;.
- The aim of content analysis consists of making inferences about particular aspects of communication, for example about the 'sender' or its intentions, interests, and goals (exactly what is required in the present work), or about the effects of the communication on the 'receiver' (Mayring 2003: 12–13).

Content analysis can be carried out in many different ways according to the research question and the theoretical framework adopted. A synthesis of two of the most detailed guides to qualitative content analysis (Mayring 2003; Hermann 2008) entails the following fundamental steps:

1. Direction of the analysis and diversification of the research questions;
2. Compilation of a text corpus;

---

28   The 'objectivity' mentioned by Holsti is what is now called 'inter-subjectivity', that is, the fact that the statements made by the researcher can be tested by other researchers (Roller et al. 1995: 167).

3. Contextualization. This step implies reflections about the kind of material used: who is speaking, on what occasion, can the speaker be spontaneous, who are the target audience, etc.? Moreover, some reflections are needed about formal traits of the collected material. In the present study, for example, a differentiation was made between press statements, which are usually more considered in their tone and content, and question and answer sessions with the press, in which the government officials interviewed sometimes express themselves more freely. Further types of material were the speeches of government representatives and joint statements (which are supposed to reflect a common understanding of two countries);

4. Definition of the sequence of analytical steps. In this regard, Mayring's (2003) work is particularly helpful since it distinguishes three procedures for content analysis (summarizing, explicating, and structuring), which serve different purposes.[29] In any case, a system of categories is needed in order to extract passages from the text corpus;

5. Definition of the units of analysis or recording units (Roller et al. 1995: 170), that is, of those parts of the text that are to be classified. These can be words, phrases, sentences, paragraphs, or whole documents (Hermann 2008: 157)[30];

6. The analysis itself, preceded by the definition of *categories*, *coding rules*, and *key examples*. A system of categories can be derived from theory or, inductively, from the text corpus itself, according to the procedure chosen;

7. Interpretation of results;

8. Determination of the reliability of results;

9. Ascertainment of validity.[31]

The summarizing qualitative content analysis technique is particularly helpful when it comes to the identification of officially stated foreign policy goals. The advantage of this technique is that one can approach the text corpus without a set of pre-formulated categories of analysis. A possibly 'open', highly inductive approach to the texts allows to reduce the bias deriving from previous knowledge of the cases and to reach a possibly 'naturalistic' mapping of an object (Mayring 2003: 74–5).[32]

---

29 A discussion on the summarizing and structuring techniques is carried out below.

30 The importance of determining the unit of analysis becomes evident when quantitative elements are introduced into the analysis. In fact, if we take the whole document as the recording unit, each code appears only once per document even though the coded issue may be mentioned several times in the document. Conversely, choosing the paragraph as the unit of analysis will increase the number of codes attributed to a given issue if this is mentioned in different paragraphs across the document.

31 On different kinds of validity, see Holsti (1969: 143–8).

32 In this study, content analysis was carried out with the support of the software Atlas.ti. On the advantages of Computer-Assisted Qualitative Data Analysis Software (CAQDAS), see Kelle (1995), Fielding/Lee (1998).

Having identified the main goals stated in official documents through this inductive approach, these goals need to be validated and complemented through the inference of non-stated goals from actual state behaviour. Moreover, a triangulation of sources with expert interviews and the secondary literature helps to further increase the validity of results.

For the identification of India's foreign policy goals, three text corpuses were created for the content analysis, one for each of the countries analysed. All bilateral documents, speeches, statements, and parliament (Lok Sabha and Rajya Sabha) proceedings available on the homepage of the Indian Ministry of External Affairs (MEA) concerning the three countries under scrutiny in the period analysed were selected. Each corpus was, moreover, chronologically subdivided into two to four different 'primary documents' corresponding to the phases analysed. The MEA was chosen for the selection of sources since it constitutes the main ministry involved in foreign policy decision-making in India.[33]

The unit of analysis for the identification of goals was set to be the whole document – that is, an entire speech, statement, or Q&A proceeding from parliament. The categories – in this case, the foreign policy goals – were elaborated inductively on the basis of the text material, and the whole corpus was coded accordingly. Codes referring to specific goals were later grouped into 'code families' of broader goals (in the case of Bangladesh, for example, 'limitation of spill-over effects' or 'economic issues'). Subsequently, a quantitative element was added to the analysis by taking into consideration the relative frequency of the occurrence of codes for each phase under scrutiny. This allowed some inferences to be drawn about the importance of goals, keeping in mind, however, that the most frequently *stated* goals do not necessarily need to be a country's core or primary goals. In fact, the latter may be mentioned only rarely in official documents or, conversely, the frequency of stated goals may just depend on their topicality but may not reveal anything about their actual importance.[34]

As a further step, the results from the content analysis were triangulated with analyses in the secondary literature and with India's observable behaviour as reported by the press. This allowed qualification of the weight of the stated goals analysed on the basis of official documents, thereby submitting them to a 'reality check', and the identification of other important non-stated goals. A triangulation of data is helpful to overcome the intrinsic biases related to single-source and single-method studies, and thereby increase the validity of the results (Webb 1970; Denzin 1978: 294–307).

33 Even though Indian foreign policy making has long been characterized by a centrality of the prime minister and a small circle of advisors (Thomas 2002: 191; Wagner 2006b: 237), these informal consultation processes cannot be appropriately documented. The prime ministers' speeches referring to the single countries analysed are contained in the MEA's online archives and therefore taken into appropriate consideration.
34 Just to cite an example, the protection of minority rights in Bangladesh was cited very frequently in Q&A sessions in parliament as a consequence of frequent reports of episodes of violence, but did not constitute one of the *core* goals of India in its relations with Bangladesh in the period analysed.

Twenty-nine semi-structured expert interviews carried out in New Delhi in November–December 2008 served as further sources for triangulation. Given the research topic, experts dealing with India's relations with neighbouring South Asian countries, particularly with Sri Lanka, Nepal, and Bangladesh, were interviewed. The interviewees were selected through a mix of cold calling and snowball sampling (Goldstein 2002), and comprised:

- Government officials: five officials at the Ministry of External Affairs, three of whom at the Joint Secretary level;
- Experts: five retired diplomats or army generals, and one senior politician directly involved in the events in one of the countries analysed; moreover, 11 scholars from the following institutions: School of International Studies at Jawaharlal Nehru University (JNU), Institute for Defence Studies and Analyses (IDSA), Indian Council for Research on International Economic Relations (ICRIER), Observer Research Foundation (ORF), and Centre for Policy Research (CPR);
- Journalists: three journalists, one each from *The Hindu, The Hindustan Times,* and *Mail Today*;
- Diplomats: three diplomats from the neighbouring countries assigned to India.[35]

While the main objective of the expert interviews was the collection of additional data about India's foreign policy goals and those of the neighbouring countries, the interviews were also used to gather insider information about the foreign policy means employed by New Delhi and about the perceptions about India held by diplomats of the neighbouring countries.

To better understand and classify India's foreign policy goals identified in the analysis, their compatibility with India's overarching goals for South Asia as a whole was also assessed. In the absence of programmatic governmental documents outlining Indian foreign policy – what Neumann (2008: 67) calls 'monuments'; for example, white papers – other sources providing an overview of India's regional policy needed to be identified. Therefore, reference was made to some particularly relevant speeches given by important government representatives selected, as Neumann (ibid.) suggests, on the basis of the frequent references to them in the secondary literature. The analysis was carried out according to the summarizing qualitative content analysis technique illustrated above. In order to identify the goals of each of the neighbouring countries analysed, the interviews with the

---

35 The interviews were anonymized. Unfortunately, it was not possible to carry out interviews with diplomatic representatives from Nepal since in October–December 2008 the new government under Maoist leadership had not yet replaced the old diplomats with new representatives. The majority of the interviews carried out with scholars, journalists, and former diplomats were recorded and entirely transcribed. In the case of government officials and diplomatic representatives, recording was replaced by note taking and subsequent memory protocols. This pragmatic approach is justified by the complementary function of the interviews in the overall research design.

neighbour states' diplomats were used as sources, together with newspaper articles and secondary literature.

The second fundamental step in the identification of regional power strategies is the analysis of the means employed, that is, of the country's observable foreign policy behaviour. As outlined above, this consists of verbal behaviour and non-verbal actions.

In order to analyse the verbal behaviour of the regional power's representatives, a structuring qualitative content analysis of official documents can be carried out (Mayring 2003: 82–5). This kind of content analysis is particularly suitable if the categories are deduced from theory. In the case of our analysis of means, the main categories for verbal means (the grey fields in Table 2.3) are: threat; pressures (with the subcategories: condemnations, denunciations, accusations, criticism, denial of support, orders); promises; 'hard persuasion' (with the subcategories: admonitions, exhortations, requests, expressions of concern); 'soft persuasion' (with the subcategories: cajoling, instructing, counselling, arguing). In a nutshell, the structuring qualitative content analysis aims to identify particular topics – particular foreign policy means – in the text. In the empirical analysis, the unit of analysis was set at the level of single propositions and, more specifically, of all utterances directly addressing the target state (Sri Lanka, Nepal, Bangladesh) or containing a verb having India (or the Indian government, the government official speaking, etc.) as the subject and referring to the country analysed. Definitions and coding rules were elaborated on the basis of theory, and further adapted and integrated in the course of the analysis. This is an essential feature of qualitative approaches, which allow for an inductive integration (if not for a complete generation) of categories from the source itself. A quantitative assessment of the relative frequency of the occurrence of codes is particularly helpful to identify what kind of verbal means is predominantly employed. This also allows for comparisons across time phases and cases.

The assessment of verbal behaviour needs to be complemented by the analysis of non-verbal foreign policy means. Faced with the problem of choosing which events to analyse and how to make sure that no relevant events are excluded from the analysis, a viable solution is to focus only on those actions of the regional power that are related (in a broad sense) to its goals. This choice is based on the conception of strategy as an ends-means approach and allows for the exclusion of facts and events irrelevant for analysis.

As far as the problem of selection bias in the choice of primary sources is concerned, it can be addressed through a diversification of sources. In the empirical analysis of India's foreign policy, particular weight was given to the English language press in India, which extensively covers topics related to India's relations with neighbouring states. In particular, *The Hindu,* a daily, and *Frontline,* a magazine, offer an extensive coverage on the South Asian region.[36] Additional

---

36 *Frontline* provided good coverage on the war in Sri Lanka for several years, and was therefore widely used as a primary source.

sources include the international press, as well as the press from the neighbouring states. Further, the transcripts and notes of the expert interviews carried out in New Delhi were important primary sources for the identification (and, at times, for the interpretation) of the foreign policy means adopted by India. Finally, the assessments of means carried out on the basis of these primary sources were supplemented by secondary sources like the International Crisis Group (ICG) reports; reports by Indian think tanks; and academic literature. The indicators elaborated above and outlined in Table 2.3 served as a reference frame to assess the foreign policy means employed by India as reported in these sources.

The assessment of the behaviour and perceptions of India's neighbouring countries was based on a broad range of sources, mainly newspaper articles and secondary literature. Moreover, the interviews carried out with diplomats of the neighbouring countries assigned to India allowed for the collection of primary data about the official assessments of India's foreign policy by these countries.

3 India

The regional power in South Asia

Before applying the analytical framework developed in Chapter Two to the case of South Asia, some brief general remarks on India as a 'regional power' are needed. As previously mentioned, a country can be defined as a regional power if it belongs to a certain region and possesses a relative superiority in terms of material power capabilities within the regional context. In order to define India as the South Asian regional power, we therefore need to define the region to which India belongs in the first place. As a second step, India's relative power capabilities will be assessed according to some basic power indicators. As a final step, this chapter provides an assessment of India's overall foreign policy goals for the region. This will serve as a point of reference for the empirical analyses of India's relations with Sri Lanka, Nepal, and Bangladesh.

Which Region? Delimitating South Asia

Like so many concepts in International Relations, that of 'region' is contested (Buzan 1998: 69) and has been defined in innumerable ways across theoretical approaches as well as across disciplines.[1] One of the less contested aspects in the characterization of regions is the geographical adjacency of their component parts. However, '[o]ne cannot simply take any collection of adjacent states and label them a region' (ibid.: 69–70) since 'geographic regions in themselves show nothing' (Fawn 2009: 17). Moreover, the problem of identifying the borders of regions remains in place: where does geographic contiguity end?

A common approach takes into consideration, besides geographic proximity, 'one or more common traits, such as level of development, culture, or political institutions' (Lake/Morgan 1997: 11), while a more specific approach to the delimitation of regions focuses on existing regional institutions. However, '[t]he existence of institutions in themselves can be misleading' (Fawn 2009: 19) since the mere formal existence of international bodies does not imply that they are effective in their functioning. Moreover, in the case of multiple and overlapping institutions, it might become difficult to choose the one according to which the region is to be defined.

---

1 For an excellent overview of the state-of-the-art, see Fawn (2009).

A functionalist approach is represented by the definition of regions as Regional Security Complexes (RSCs). Buzan and Waever (2003: 44) define an RSC as 'a set of units whose major processes of securitisation, desecuritisation, or both are so interlinked that their security problems cannot reasonably by analysed or resolved apart from one another [emphasis removed]'. This explicit reference to security issues has the advantage of providing a specific definition of the region driven by the research question.

Finally, constructivist approaches to regions focus on issues of identity – 'the flipside of geography' (Fawn 2009: 17). Here, perceptions and representations of the region matter. In his 'region-building' approach, Neumann (2003) considers regions as 'imagined communities', socially constructed by 'region builders'. These political actors – societal actors, scholars, or states – 'as part of some political project, see it in their interest to imagine a certain spatial and chronological identity for a region, and to disseminate this imagination to a maximum number of other people' (ibid.: 161).[2] These actors may be part of the region or be external to it. That is, according to this approach we would need to look at self-perceptions in the region as well as at external constructions of the region by other actors.

Given the absence of an agreement on the issue of defining and delimitating regions, a solution that attempts to identify commensurabilities among the different approaches outlined above is adopted here to draw the boundaries of the South Asian region. Since the focus of analysis is on security issues, Buzan and Waever's definition of the South Asian RSC is taken as the starting point. As a second step, the region thus identified is compared to institutionalist and constructivist delimitations of South Asia with reference to the time span analysed.[3] An overlapping of the three (or more, given possible divergences in perceptions) 'regions' would be the best indicator for a reliable delimitation. Possible divergences – cases in which one country, for example, belongs to a region in terms of security interactions but is not integrated in an existing institutional arrangement or does not perceive itself/is not perceived as part of the region – should then be analysed in more detail on a case-by-case basis.

While the fact that India belongs to the region called 'South Asia' is almost universally accepted, some discrepancies exist as far as the actual delimitation of this region is concerned.[4] If we take Buzan and Waever's definition of the South

2 This approach is particularly interesting when it comes to the study of regional powers as the most powerful states in the region, which can be assumed to have an interest in shaping and consolidating their spheres of influence through discursive means. In the present study, however, the delimitation of the region precedes the identification of the regional power. A potential construction of the region by the regional power will therefore not be taken into consideration as a separate issue.

3 This temporal dimension is of great relevance since regions are not static entities. As Fawn (2009: 33) puts it, 'regions are ongoing projects'.

4 However, at times there are even inconsistencies in the region's nomenclature. For example, the World Bank (2011b) defines 'South Asia' as composed by Afghanistan, Bangladesh, Bhutan, India, the Maldives, Nepal, Pakistan, and Sri Lanka, while the United Nations (2008b) consider 'South-central Asia' as a 'macro-region' composed of Afghanistan, Bangladesh, Bhutan, India, Iran, Kazakhstan, Kyrgyzstan, the Maldives, Nepal, Pakistan, Sri Lanka, Tajikistan, Turkmenistan, and Uzbekistan.

Asian RSC as the starting point for our discussion on the definition of South Asia, we should include the following countries: India, Pakistan, Nepal, Bhutan, Bangladesh, Sri Lanka, and the Maldives (Buzan/Waever 2003: 102). According to the authors' functionalist, security-oriented perspective, the South Asian security complex is centred on the rivalry between India and Pakistan, while the smaller states of the region are tied to the RSC due to their economic and societal links to India. Myanmar/Burma and Afghanistan are not considered to be part of the region; instead, they are defined as insulators, which separate the South Asian RSC from other security complexes (ibid.: 103).

Coming to an institutionalist perspective, the only distinctively South Asian international organization is the South Asian Association for Regional Cooperation (SAARC). Despite SAARC's limited operability due to the exclusion of any kind of contentious and bilateral issues from the agenda, the sum of its member states has often been equated with South Asia (e.g., Basrur 2000: 82; Wagner 2005b: 2; Ghosh 2006). The Indian prime minister Manmohan Singh himself talked about 'SAARC as a region' in 2005 (MEA 2005o). Until 2007, when Afghanistan became a member of SAARC, the countries participating in it were the same as those identified by Buzan and Waever as members of the South Asian RSC: India, Pakistan, Nepal, Bhutan, Bangladesh, Sri Lanka, and the Maldives. According to this approach, Afghanistan would not be considered as a part of the region until 2007, while Myanmar/Burma would not belong to the region at all and, instead, would be part of South-east Asia given its membership in ASEAN.

From a constructivist perspective, we would focus on collective regional identities and common perceptions of 'regionness' in the identification of regions. The region-building approach highlights how 'multiple [...] interpretations of the region struggle, clash, deconstruct, and displace one another [...]' (Neumann 2003: 176) until a hegemonic discourse prevails – and is challenged again by new counter-hegemonic discourses. According to Sinderpal Singh (2001), who applies this kind of approach to the study of South Asia, the currently predominant definition of this region is the result of a hegemonic discourse established by different actors across time: by the British colonial rulers, by the US-led Western alliance during World War II, and by the Republic of India. According to this interpretation, Afghanistan and Myanmar/Burma do not belong to the region. In fact, Afghanistan was excluded from what was presented as the 'natural' South Asia during the colonial period because the British rulers wanted to conceal their inability to expand their empire to Afghanistan (ibid: 17–18). Myanmar/Burma, on its part, was excluded from the dominant framings of South Asia because, being occupied by the Japanese during World War II, it was incorporated in the Western Alliance's South East Asia Command (SEAC) and thereby came to be part of 'South-east Asia' (ibid.: 26–27). With the so-called 'Indira Doctrine',[5] India acted as region-builder by stating its claim for hegemony in a region comprising Pakistan, Bangladesh, Nepal, Bhutan, Sri Lanka, and the Maldives: 'the "regional

5 See, among others, Cohen (2002: 137–8).

hegemony" discourse has been used by the Indian state to spatially frame and culturally essentialise South Asia so as to show the Indian domination of South Asia as "natural hegemony", as a [sic] inevitable state of affairs' (ibid.: 25).

This approach seems to have remained in place till the present time. In fact, an analysis of more recent speeches by representatives of the Indian government confirms Singh's assessment. The region is often defined as India's 'neighbourhood', as the Indian 'subcontinent', or as India's 'periphery' – thereby underlining the centrality of India (e.g, MEA 2007a). As far as its concrete delimitation is concerned, Indian government representatives have usually implicitly equated South Asia with SAARC (e.g., MEA 2005b, 2006d).[6]

In conclusion, if we look for overlaps of the three above-cited delimitations of the region, all approaches agree on the following countries belonging to South Asia: India, Pakistan, Nepal, Bangladesh, Bhutan, Sri Lanka, and the Maldives. The case of Afghanistan, on the contrary, is ambiguous.[7] In this study, Afghanistan is not considered to be part of the region given its exclusion from the South Asian security complex by Buzan and Waever, and because it was not a member of SAARC for the largest part of the time span analysed. Had the analysis been predominantly focused on the years after 2007, this decision would have been different. Myanmar/Burma can be excluded from the analysis of the South Asian region since it has not been classified as a member of the region by neither the RSC approach, nor by the institutionalist and constructivist approaches.[8]

India's Power Position in South Asia

Having outlined the delimitation of the region, we now need to assess India's power preponderance in South Asia in order to define this country as a regional power. As Treverton and Jones (2005: 1) put it, '[t]he starting point for thinking about, and developing metrics for, national power is to view states as "capabilities containers"'. However, the measurement of relative power is not without its problems: on the one hand, different IR approaches conceive of power in different ways;[9] on the other hand, the possession of material power resources does not

---

6 At times, Indian government officials have defined India's region in broader terms, highlighting that India's 'political, security and economic interests span in particular the area from the Gulf to South East Asia' (MEA 2002a). Myanmar/Burma does not seem to strictly belong to South Asia from the Indian perspective, as outlined in the following statement by the Indian foreign secretary in 2006: 'We believe that with the entry of Afghanistan into SAARC, we have now completed the identity of SAARC in this region' (MEA 2006h).
7 For a discussion arguing in favour of the inclusion of Afghanistan in the South Asian region, see Hanif (2009).
8 For a critique on the exclusion of Myanmar/Burma from typical definitions of South Asia, see Sibal (2009).
9 On different conceptualizations of power, see, among many others, Lukes (2005a); Barnett/Duvall (2005); Guzzini (2009).

Table 3.1   Power distribution in South Asia

	Surface area (thousand sq. km)	*Total population (millions), 2009*	*GDP nominal (US$ billion at current prices), 2008*	*Military expenditure (US$ m. at constant (2009) prices), 2009*	*Total armed forces (thousands), 2005*
India	3,287.3	1,155.3	1,206.684	35,819	1,190
Pakistan	796.1	169.7	164.557	5,039	590
Bangladesh	144.0	162.2	84.196	1,024	140
Sri Lanka	65.6	20.3	39.604	1,480	150
Nepal	147.2	29.3	12.283	210	90
Bhutan	38.4	0.7	1.389	9[a]	8
Maldives	0.3	0.3	1.261	56[b]	n.a.

[a] 2005 at constant (2005) prices. Source: U.S. Department of State (2005).

[b] 2006 at current prices. Source: IISS (2008).

Sources: surface area and total population: World Bank (2011a); GDP: IMF (2009); military expenditure: SIPRI (2011b); total armed forces: U.S. Department of State (2005).

reveal anything about the convertibility of these resources into actual political leverage or about the resulting behaviour of states. Since the latter point – the identification of the strategies adopted by India as a regional power and the evaluation of their success – represents the main object of the present study, some very basic power indicators will suffice for the identification of the regional power. The following indicators are suggested as points of reference:[10]

- Demographic and geographic indicators: total population; surface area
- Economic capabilities: GDP (nominal)
- Military capabilities: military expenditure; total armed forces.

It is argued that, in order to be classified as a regional power, a state should possess the largest share of power capabilities in each of these categories. In ambiguous cases, a case-specific discussion is required, which could be carried out according to several other indicators like pretension (that is, leadership claims), leverage (that is, actual influence on the region), and recognition (that is, acknowledgement of the regional power's status by other actors) (Shim 2009: 8–9).

In the case of South Asia, however, the predominance of India is unequivocal. As outlined in Table 3.1 and in Figure 3.1, India accounts for 75 per cent of South Asia's total population; 73 per cent of the region's total area; and 79 per cent of

---

10 These indicators have been chosen because of their nature as aggregates, which allows for the determination and comparison of shares of total capabilities.

Surface area

Bangladesh 3% Sri Lanka 2% Nepal 3% Bhutan 1% Maldives 0%
Pakistan 18%
India 73%

Total population (2009)

Bangladesh 11% Sri Lanka 2% Nepal 1% Bhutan 0% Maldives 0%
Pakistan 11%
India 75%

GDP nominal current prices (2008)

Bangladesh 6% Sri Lanka 3% Nepal 1% Bhutan 0% Maldives 0%
Pakistan 11%
India 79%

Military expenditure (2009)

Sri Lanka 3% Nepal 0% Bhutan 0%
Bangladesh 2%
Maldives 0%
Pakistan 12%
India 83%

Total armed forces (2005)

Sri Lanka 7% Nepal 4% Bhutan 0% Maldives n.a.
Bangladesh 7%
Pakistan 27%
India 55%

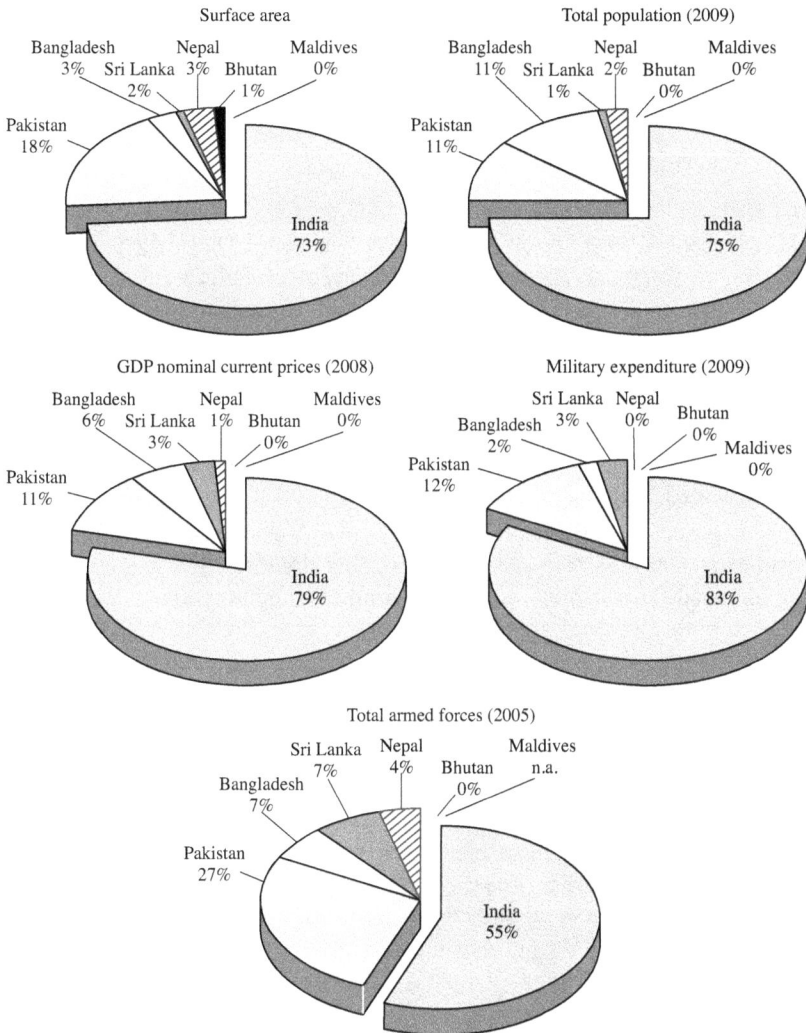

Figure 3.1 India's share of power capabilities in South Asia

the total gross domestic product. At the military level, the nuclear status of both India and Pakistan contributes to qualify India's position. However, if we consider nuclear weapons as having a primarily deterrent function, the military capabilities of India, whose military expenditures correspond to 83 per cent of the regional total and which accounts for 55 per cent of the region's total armed forces, confirm India's standing as the South Asian 'regional power'. The geographical situation in South Asia, where none of India's smaller neighbouring countries borders another, provides for a hub-and-spokes geopolitical setting centred on India. This further reinforces India's predominance.[11] As Ghosh (2006: 35) puts it, '[n]o other regional grouping in the world has a comparable one-state dominant profile'. All these conditions allow us to define India as the regional power in South Asia.

India's Overall Goals for the Region

In the context of the South Asian region, India pursues a range of foreign policy goals, which need to be briefly outlined at this stage. They will prove helpful as a point of reference for the in-depth analyses of India's relations with Sri Lanka, Nepal, and Bangladesh carried out in the following chapters. Since the Indian government does not publish 'white papers' or other official documents outlining its foreign policy objectives, the assessment of these goals was carried out through a qualitative content analysis of several 'key' speeches (Neumann 2008, see Chapter Two);[12] several expert interviews carried out in New Delhi served as complementary sources. This analysis has revealed that the main foreign policy objective India has been pursuing in South Asia is stability. The idea of having a 'peaceful and tranquil periphery' (MEA 2005b) is related to India's need to concentrate its resources on its own development (MEA 2007a) without being hindered by instability emanating from neighbouring countries. Since the borders to these countries are porous, India has often been affected by negative security externalities coming from its South Asian neighbours. We will discuss these aspects later in greater detail since each of the countries analysed presents examples of spill-over effects to India – be it in the form of refugee flows, trans-national activities of insurgent groups, or migration. At the same time, over the past years a growing awareness has emerged among Indian foreign policy makers that domestic threats may matter even more than external ones (GOI 2006) – and some of these threats are considered to be connected to India's regional neighbours, among them terrorism and the activities of rebel groups. For these reasons the South Asian region is of great importance to India. As Feigenbaum (2010: 85) puts it, 'even as India's interests increasingly reach beyond South Asia, these dangers [emanating from the region] may force New Delhi to focus less on global issues than on priorities closer to home'. The limitation of spill over effects can therefore be considered to have been the second main goal of India for the South Asian region as a whole.

Among the stated objectives of the Indian government, the goal of 'collective prosperity' (MEA 2005o) for South Asia figures prominently in the sources analysed. In this discourse, India is presented as the economic driving force of the region, and the whole of South Asia is expected to take advantage of India's economic growth (GOI 2005). The idea of strengthening 'connectivity' among

---

11 Almost all of the Indian experts interviewed highlighted this peculiarity of the South Asian regional setting.
12 The following speeches were selected as 'key' texts since reference to them was made in other sources, as suggested by Neumann (2008: 67): MEA (2002a, 2005b, 2005o, 2006d, 2007a).

the countries of South Asia further complements this vision.[13] However, as one of the interviewees aptly put it, 'development is more a national goal than a goal for the region'.[14] While economic interdependence might be helpful, security issues clearly remain in the forefront.

A similar assessment needs to be made for the fourth major goal outlined by Indian foreign policy makers: democracy, seen as a precondition for the establishment of 'an edifice of peace and cooperation in our sub-continent' (MEA 2005b). However, Indian government representatives made it clear that this goal would not be pursued through an aggressive policy of democracy promotion on the part of New Delhi. As Foreign Secretary Shyam Saran put it, '[a]s a flourishing democracy, India would certainly welcome more democracy in our neighbourhood, but that too is something that we may encourage and promote; it is not something that we can impose upon others' (MEA 2005b). Therefore, the goal of democracy does not appear to have been a central foreign policy objective of New Delhi, despite its mention in key documents.

In addition to these objectives stated in the key documents analysed, we need to take into account another objective highlighted by the interviewees: the preservation of India's influence on the South Asian neighbourhood and, corresponding to that, the limitation of the role of external actors. As one of the interviewees put it, 'India wants to have its say in the region'.[15] One of the government officials interviewed paraphrased India's attitude as follows: 'external involvement has generally complicated the problems [in the region] and is often motivated by these [the intervening] countries' own goals. The lack of knowledge of the local conditions has often led to failures'.[16] As we will see in the empirical chapters, the objective of limiting external actors' influence on the neighbourhood significantly influenced India's foreign policy strategies.

---

13 The notion of connectivity was prominently outlined by Prime Minister Manmohan Singh in his speech at the 13th SAARC Summit (MEA 2005o).
14 Interview with expert, New Delhi, 18 November 2008.
15 Interview with expert, New Delhi, 26 November 2008.
16 Interview with government official, New Delhi, 20 November 2008.

4 The Civil War in Sri Lanka and India's Unsuccessful Hegemonic Strategy

Over the past decades, Sri Lanka's history has been shaped by the ethnic conflict between the Sinhalese majority of the population and the Tamil minority, who has been asking for greater autonomy and self-determination. This ethnic conflict turned into a full-fledged civil war between government forces and the Liberation Tigers of Tamil Eelam (LTTE), a rebel organization which claimed to be the sole representative of Sri Lankan Tamils and fought for secession and the formation of a Tamil state in Sri Lanka. The armed conflict, which ended with the military defeat of the LTTE and the killing of its leader, Velupillai Prabhakaran, in May 2009, represented the major cause of concern for India in its relations with Sri Lanka over the past decades. In fact, it constituted a serious source of instability within the region, and for India in particular it bore the risk of spill-over effects and of internal destabilization in single states, especially in Tamil Nadu. Moreover, the conflict in Sri Lanka had an international, extra-regional security dimension for New Delhi since external parties were involved in it to varying extents over the past decades.

Against this background, this chapter provides a detailed assessment of India's foreign policy strategies in dealing with the Sri Lankan crisis between 2003, when the peace process mediated by Norway broke down, and the end of the military conflict in May 2009. India's foreign and security policy strategy in the years 2003–9 can be defined as predominantly hegemonic. Across different phases, and according to the means employed by India, we can observe the implementation of a soft hegemonic strategy in the years 2003–6, and of an intermediate hegemonic strategy entailing 'hard' elements in the years 2006–9. Overall, given India's inability to achieve its goals with reference to the war in Sri Lanka, we can classify India's hegemonic strategy as unsuccessful.

The Civil War in Sri Lanka: Historical Background

Sri Lankan society has been defined as 'one of the most complex plural societies in the world' (de Silva 1986: 2). According to estimates, 74.6 per cent of the population is represented by Sinhalese, 18.1 per cent by Tamils (12.6 per cent Sri

Lankan Tamils and 5.5 per cent Tamils of Indian origin)[1] and 7 per cent by Arabs. Along religious lines, the majority of the population, coinciding broadly with the Sinhalese majority, is Buddhist (69.3 per cent), and there are Hindu (15.5 per cent), a Muslim (7.5 per cent), and a Christian (7.6 per cent) minorities (Federal Foreign Office – Germany 2009).[2] Along language divides, the two main languages spoken on the island are Sinhalese (81 per cent) and Tamil, spoken by about 18 per cent of the population – comprising Sri Lankan Tamils, Indian Tamils and Muslims (Sambandan 2004b).

As soon as Ceylon[3] gained its independence in 1948 through a peaceful transfer of power from the British, the ethnic tensions between the Sinhalese majority and Tamil minority, which had been held in check during the colonial period, exploded. The Sinhalese, who had been indirectly discriminated against by the colonial administration, immediately sought a dominant position of power. This was a consequence of their 'reverse psychology of superiority' (Bouffard/Carment 2006: 152): despite being a majority on the island, the Sinhalese have perceived themselves as a minority in a Tamil-dominated area comprising South India. Very soon, ethnicity became the main instrument of political mobilization and, starting from the 1950s, Sri Lanka was gradually turned into a Sinhalese Buddhist state. With the 'Official Language Act' of 1956, Sinhala was declared the only official language of the country, while the new constitution of 1972 conferred a special status to Buddhism. Ethnic tensions in the country were further exacerbated when, in the 1970s, changes in the admission policies of universities led to a heavy discrimination against Tamil applicants (ibid.: 153; Khosla 2008: 46).

Since the early years of Sri Lanka's independence, some efforts were made to find a solution allowing for a fairer distribution of power between Sinhalese and Tamils (Bouffard/Carment 2006: 155–6). However, not only did their failure contribute to a political reorganization, but also to a progressive radicalization of the Tamils. In 1974, several Tamil parties merged into the Tamil United Front (TUF), which in 1976 changed its name to Tamil United Liberation Front (TULF) as it started demanding a separate state for the Tamils in Sri Lanka (ibid.: 157). The 1970s and 1980s also saw the formation of several Tamil armed rebel groups. This included one militant group in particular, called the Tamil New Tigers, which was formed in 1972. The group changed its name in 1976 to Liberation Tigers of Tamil Eelam (LTTE) under the leadership of Velupillai Prabhakaran.

By 1983, the Tamil guerrilla groups were 'well-trained, well-equipped and large enough to pose a threat to the national army' (ibid.). After the killing of 13 Sri

---

1 The Tamils of Indian origin had been resettled from South India by the British to work in the plantations in Sri Lanka.

2 Federal Foreign Office – Germany (2009). Data about the ethnic and religious composition of the Sri Lankan population vary greatly according to the source consulted. The CIA World Factbook (2011) resorts to provisional data derived from the 2001 census, which are, however, highly distorted since the Tamil areas of Jaffna, Mullaitivu, and Killinochchi were excluded from it (dos Santos 2007: 170).

3 The name Ceylon was changed into Sri Lanka in 1972. From now on, however, reference will also be made to the island as 'Sri Lanka' for events preceding this date.

Lankan soldiers by Tamil rebels, in July 1983 anti-Tamil riots spread in Sri Lanka (ibid.). In little more than a week, over 3,000 Tamils were killed and a further 150,000 were left homeless. The riots turned out to be well-planned, full-fledged pogroms, in which government forces were actively involved (dos Santos 2007: 49–52). At the same time, the government promoted a massive crackdown on Tamils on the northern peninsula of Jaffna, which led to a large-scale migration of Tamils to not only Tamil Nadu, but all over the world. These migrants, together with the refugees who fled the island in the following decades, contributed to the creation of an almost worldwide network, which significantly supported the armed struggle of the LTTE financially, logistically, and at times also politically.

Until this phase of the ethnic conflict, India had not been strongly involved in Sri Lanka. However, things changed when Indira Gandhi became prime minister and, in 1983, the conflict turned into a civil war. Several factors led to India's involvement: on the one hand, issues related to the activities of external powers in what India's government perceived to be its own sphere of influence; on the other hand, internal tensions in India, particularly between the central government and the government of Tamil Nadu.

In fact, Indira Gandhi began to perceive the instability in Sri Lanka and the policies adopted by its leaders as a threat to India's predominance in the region when, during the 1983 riots, Sri Lankan president Jayewardene sought military assistance from the USA, Britain, Pakistan, Bangladesh, and Israel for suppressing the agitation (Bouffard/Carment 2006: 158). Jayewardene also signed several agreements with the USA (Dixit 2003: 54), which were perceived as considerable threats by India, and more generally, he displayed a pro-Western foreign policy attitude. In reaction, the Indian prime minister announced her 'Indira Doctrine', which underlined India's unwillingness to tolerate any intervention by outside powers in the region, and stated that South Asian states should first request assistance, if needed, from within the region – that is, from India.

On the domestic level, the Indian government feared a spread of the Tamil demand for greater autonomy to the state of Tamil Nadu, which had already displayed a high degree of resistance towards Delhi.[4] At the same time, the government of Tamil Nadu, led by the Dravida Munnetra Kazhagam (DMK), started providing Sri Lankan Tamils with political support and the rebel groups with military assistance (de Silva 1991: 77–8; 83).[5]

As a consequence of these international and domestic pressures, New Delhi tried to promote, on the one hand, a mediated solution to the crisis in 1984 (Rao 1988),

---

4 In 1965, as the central government had tried to impose Hindi as the only official language of the country, strong resistance came from Tamil Nadu, which threatened to secede from the Union (Dixit 2003: 59).

5 The DMK had its origin in the Dravidar Kazhagam, a political organization founded during the colonial period with the goal of creating an independent Dravidian state in the South of India. In the 1970s, the All India Anna Dravida Munnetra Kazhagam (AIADMK), and in the 1990s the Marumalarchi Dravida Munnetra Kazhagam (MDMK), split from the DMK. The DMK and the AIADMK have been alternating as governing parties in Tamil Nadu since the 1960s.

while on the other hand, it had started supporting Tamil rebel groups through its intelligence agency, the Research and Analysis Wing (RAW). This support also entailed military training, carried out on Indian territory (Dixit 2003: 55).

Very soon, however, India was confronted with what one of the interviewees defined as the 'monsters' it had created itself.[6] With the assassination of Indira Gandhi in October 1984 and the succession of her son Rajiv Gandhi, India's engagement in Sri Lanka continued and even increased, even though New Delhi started to distance itself from the Tamil rebels and to take a more neutral approach. In 1986, Rajiv Gandhi told the government in Tamil Nadu that he was no longer willing to allow Indian territory to be used for the training of the Tamil Tigers (Sanchez Nieto 2008: 579), and the Indian government acted as a mediator by promoting several rounds of peace talks, which ultimately failed (de Silva 1991: 85; Rao 1988). The conflict escalated again when the Sri Lankan government imposed a blockade on fuel supplies to the northern peninsula of Jaffna, since the LTTE had declared that it planned to establish a separate administration there – a decision that was widely understood as a first step towards secession (Rajagopalan 2008: 85).

Fearing a crackdown on Tamils by Sri Lankan government troops and its potential implications on stability in Tamil Nadu (ibid.: 88), India broke the blockade against Jaffna on 4 June 1987 by dropping air supplies to the isolated city (Dixit 2003: 64). Thus, India contributed towards preventing the Sri Lankan military from capturing Jaffna – an 'unmistakable demonstration of Indian support for the Tamil separatist movement in Sri Lanka' (de Silva 1991: 90).

The clear show of force inherent in this violation of Sri Lanka's sovereignty induced the Sri Lankan government to subsequently accept India's conflict management efforts: some weeks later, on 29 July 1987, secret negotiations between the Indian and Sri Lankan governments led to the signing of the Indo–Sri Lanka Agreement (ISLA) from which, however, the LTTE and other Tamil representatives were excluded (Hennayake 1989: 408). Basically, this agreement provided for a certain degree of devolution of powers to the Tamil minority through the creation of provincial councils and the merger of the Eastern and Northern provinces and, in return, for the disarmament of the LTTE and the abdication of its armed fight. Even though the agreement did not entail any provision concerning the deployment of a peacekeeping force, India, as the guarantor of the agreement, shortly thereafter sent the Indian Peace Keeping Force (IPKF) into the Northern and Eastern provinces of Sri Lanka with the aim of supervising the ceasefire and disarming the LTTE.[7]

The IPKF operations in Sri Lanka represent one of the worst moments in India's foreign policy in the past few decades – a moment that radically changed India's attitude in regional affairs and, as we will see, its policy options in dealing with Sri

---

6 Interview with expert, New Delhi, 3 November 2008.
7 In addition to the surrender of weapons by the LTTE, the Agreement provided for a withdrawal of the Sri Lankan army into its camps in Tamil areas (Rajagopalan 2008: 89).

Lanka. Very soon, the IPKF got involved in intra-Tamil conflicts, lost its support among the Sri Lankan Tamil population (Rajagopalan 2008: 91), and encountered the opposition of Sinhalese nationalists (Biswas 2006: 53). Since violence did not cease through the Indian presence, the IPKF had ultimately no alternative to disarming the LTTE by force (Bouffard/Carment 2006: 162). A paradoxical situation emerged: India, which originally had supported the LTTE and contributed to its training, ended up fighting against it under an agreement in which the LTTE itself was not even part. In the years 1988–1990, '[t]he IPKF's role changed from a security guarantor to an enemy force, hated by both sides to the conflict' (Biswas 2006: 53). As the failure of the IPKF became increasingly evident, India and Sri Lanka started looking for solutions to gradually withdraw the Indian troops from the island. Domestic political changes in both countries ultimately facilitated the termination of the IPKF mission, which concluded in March 1990.

Shortly thereafter another event took place, which radically changed India's approach to the Sri Lankan issue. On 21 May 1991, former Prime Minister Rajiv Gandhi, who had remained president of the Congress Party after his electoral defeat in 1989, was assassinated by a suicide bomber while campaigning in Tamil Nadu. The LTTE was held responsible for the assassination and was consequently classified as a terrorist organization by India.

Since the proscription of the LTTE impeded the Indian government to have any direct contact to the Tamil Tigers, starting from 1991 India refused any kind of involvement in Sri Lankan affairs, adopting a 'hands-off' policy.[8] The approach of subsequent Congress-led governments to Sri Lanka, especially the Manmohan Singh government in the period to be analysed, was shaped to a considerable extent by the assassination of Rajiv Gandhi – if for no other reason than his widow Sonia Gandhi has been the leader of the Congress Party since 1998.

The following years were marked by a continuation of violence and a proliferation of terrorist attacks on the part of the LTTE. The civil war flared up in several phases, which came to be called Eelam War I (June 1983-July 1987), Eelam War II (June 1990-January 1995), Eelam War III (April 1995-February 2002), and Eelam War IV (July 2006-May 2009). Time and again a negotiated solution was sought, but in the end all peace efforts failed because of the 'policy of ethnic outbidding' (Biswas 2006: 54) by the major Sinhalese parties and of the LTTE's reluctance to abandon armed struggle and, instead, its continued efforts at rearming, even while peace talks were underway (ibid.).

Finally, in 2001 domestic political changes in Sri Lanka favoured a resumption of the peace process under the newly elected United National Front (UNF) government led by Ranil Wickremasinghe (Wagner 2004: 14). Starting from the second half of 2000, the Norwegian government had begun acting as a facilitator between the Sri Lankan government and the LTTE (Dixit 2003: 88–9). On 22 February 2002 the two parties separately signed a Ceasefire Agreement (CFA) as a first step towards the initiation of peace talks. As provided by the agreement,

---

8 Interview with expert, New Delhi, 25 November 2008.

the Sri Lanka Monitoring Mission (SLMM), led by Norway and composed of observers from Norway, Sweden, Denmark, Iceland, and Finland, was installed with the goal of monitoring the ceasefire, particularly the decommissioning of weapons.

The CFA, which formally survived until 2008, marked a significant moment in the peace process in Sri Lanka. By recognizing the LTTE as an equitable actor in the peace process and by acknowledging the LTTE's state-like competencies in the north and east, the agreement provided for a political upgrading of the Tamil Tigers (Wagner 2004: 19). During the first rounds of negotiations between the LTTE and the government, the prospects for a resolution of the crisis seemed promising, and in December 2002 the two parties even declared their willingness to 'explore' the possibility of a federal solution. However, the great expectations raised by this possible federal compromise did not last long: in January 2003 the first serious differences between the parties emerged over the LTTE's unwillingness to decommission its weapons. However, the event that most significantly undermined the peace process was the exclusion of the LTTE from a preparatory meeting for a donor conference in April 2003. Since this meeting was convened in Washington, the LTTE was not invited to take part in it given its status in the US as a proscribed terrorist organization (Jeyaraj 2003a). Interpreting this exclusion as proof that the international community did not perceive them as an equitable international actor and the sole representatives of the Sri Lankan Tamil people (TamilNet 2003),[9] the Tigers refused to participate in the Tokyo conference and, more importantly, on 21 April 2003 announced their unilateral withdrawal from the negotiations, thereby suspending the peace process.

Eelam War IV

The LTTE's withdrawal from the peace process is taken as the point of departure for analysis. In fact, even though later the LTTE joined peace negotiations again, it was from this moment that the peace process facilitated by Norway began to crumble, leading to an escalation of violence and the eventual outbreak of Eelam War IV. The final point of the analysis is represented by the military defeat of the LTTE on 19 May 2009, which, for the time being, constitutes the end of the 26 year civil war in Sri Lanka. Before starting the analysis of India's foreign policy strategies, the main events that took place in this period in Sri Lanka need to be briefly presented as a point of reference. Two main phases can be identified between 2003 and the end of the war in 2009. The first phase entails the escalation of tensions between the Sri Lankan government and the LTTE from the preparatory seminar in Washington in April 2003 until the actual beginning of Eelam War IV. Since the hostilities started despite the continued existence of the 2002 ceasefire agreement,

9 The LTTE had been fighting for many years to become the sole representatives of the Tamils. In an extremely ruthless way, the Tigers had been eliminating not only rival rebel groups, but they had also been selectively removing moderate Tamil leaders.

we do not have an 'official' date for the beginning of Eelam War IV. However, it was the blockade of the Mavil Aru waterway by the LTTE that unleashed full-scale military operations in July 2006 and can, therefore, be taken as the starting point of the second phase to be analysed.

2003–6: Escalating Violence

Despite its withdrawal from the peace process in April 2003, the LTTE initially declared that it continued to be committed to a negotiated political solution of the conflict. Therefore, even though the LTTE did not participate in the donor conference that took place in Tokyo in June 2003, communication between the conflict parties was kept alive (Bouffard/Carment 2006: 170). However, in October–November 2003, the persisting disagreements over the future administrative structure of the country reached their height. On 1 November, the LTTE submitted its first ever proposal for an interim arrangement within a united Sri Lanka, the so-called Interim Self-Governing Authority for the north-east (ISGA), which called for political autonomy and administrative independence of the Northern and Eastern districts (LTTE 2003). This maximalist statement, whose implementation would have corresponded to the de facto establishment of Eelam in the north-east, was unacceptable to the government and led not only to a serious crisis in the ongoing informal negotiations, but also to a domestic political crisis in the South (ICG 2007b: 19; Wagner 2004: 17). On 4 November 2003, President Kumaratunga suspended the parliament and took over, among others, the defence portfolio. The subsequent row between her and Prime Minister Wickremasinghe induced the Norwegians to suspend their mediation until it became clear who was in charge in Colombo (ibid.: 17–18). The SLMM, however, remained stationed in Sri Lanka and continued its monitoring of the CFA.

In the end, the political crisis in Colombo, which was solved with the call for new elections in April 2004, led to an outcome that proved to be detrimental to the peace process. In fact, in January 2004 Kumaratunga's SLFP and the 'rabidly anti-LTTE' (Smith 2008: 84) Sinhalese nationalist party Janathi Vimukti Peramuna (JVP) had formed a coalition called the United People's Freedom Alliance (UPFA). This new coalition won the elections and the 'more hawkish' (ibid.) Mahinda Rajapaksa became the new prime minister.

In 2004, two further events, the defection of 'Col.' Karuna in March and the tsunami in December, contributed to an increased tension between the conflict parties. Vinayagamoorthi Muralitharan, alias Karuna, was the LTTE's special commander for the Eastern districts of Batticaloa and Amparai and 'number two' in the LTTE after Prabhakaran. When he declared his dissatisfaction with the LTTE's discrimination of the East and demanded greater autonomy from Prabhakaran, the 'northern leadership' accused him of treason. As a reaction, Karuna defected, taking with him approximately 6,000–8,000 well-trained troops

(Sambandan 2004a). This represented a considerable blow to the LTTE, which ultimately lost the East in 2007.[10]

The tsunami that hit the Sri Lankan coast on 26 December 2004 constituted a missed chance for the Sri Lankan government and the LTTE to start cooperating. President Kumaratunga proposed the establishment of a joint mechanism to rebuild the devastated north and east and to jointly manage the resources available for reconstruction, the so-called Post-Tsunami Operational Management Structure (P-TOMS) (ICG 2007b: 20). However, the P-TOMS was never implemented and, instead of promoting cooperation between the conflict parties, it provoked a serious fracture in the governing coalition and a further radicalization in Sinhalese politics. In particular, Buddhist monks protested forcefully against the perceived upgrading of the Tigers to an equal partner of the Sri Lankan state (Sambandan 2005b). Even though the ceasefire agreement of 2002 was still in place, the mounting tension between the conflict parties in 2004 led to the outbreak of a 'shadow war' between the LTTE and government forces (Sambandan 2005c). In particular, a wave of killings of key individuals and hundreds of abductions took place, mostly carried out by the LTTE. The apex of the series of political assassinations was the killing of the Sri Lankan Foreign Minister Lakshman Kadirgamar, a moderate Tamil active in the peace process, on 12 August 2005. Since Kadirgamar was well-known and respected at the international level, his assassination produced a wave of shock among international diplomats and further damaged the international image of the LTTE, who were held responsible for the assassination (Smith 2008: 85).

The most relevant factor in the escalation towards a new phase of armed hostilities was, however, a change in domestic political alliances in Sri Lanka. After the Sri Lankan Supreme Court ruled that President Kumaratunga's tenure ended in December 2005 and that presidential elections would have to take place, Prime Minister Mahinda Rajapaksa started signing poll pacts with hard line Sinhalese parties, notably the JVP and the Jathika Hela Urumaya (JHU), the all-Buddhist clergy parliamentary party. Both parties were committed to the unity of the Sri Lankan state and opposed to any concessions to the LTTE, holding the position that what existed in Sri Lanka was 'not an ethnic problem but a terrorist threat to the territorial unity and sovereignty of the Sri Lankan state' (Uyangoda 2009). Therefore, Rajapaksa contested elections 'on a tough and nationalistic manifesto' (Smith 2008: 86) and the electorate came to be polarized along a unitarist (Rajapaksa)/federalist (Wickremasinghe) divide (Sambandan 2005a).

Ultimately, Rajapaksa won the November 2005 presidential elections by a narrow margin of 2 per cent, getting 51 per cent of the votes. Although indirectly,

---

10 The LTTE and Karuna reached an agreement in order to avoid an internal conflict between the two LTTE factions (Jeyaraj 2004). Later, however, Karuna militarily supported the Sri Lankan government against the LTTE and entered politics heading a political party, the Tamil Makkal Viduthalai Pulikal (TVMP), which allied itself with Rajapaksa's ruling coalition. In October 2008, Karuna was sworn in as a Member of Parliament in Sri Lanka, and in March 2009 Rajapaksa appointed him as Minister of National Integration (BBC News 2008).

his victory was made possible by the LTTE itself, which had called for a boycott of elections in the areas of the country under its control. Had the Tamils voted, Wickremasinghe would certainly have turned out to be the winner (Smith 2008: 86).[11] On 21 November, Ratnasiri Wickremanayake, known for his radical and hard line Sinhala positions, was appointed prime minister. Rajapaksa's electoral victory therefore seemed to be a clear mandate 'to tear up the terms and conditions of the peace process, which is exactly what he did, though he was also shrewd enough to keep alive the vocabulary of peace and with it its apparent continuing commitment to the CFA and the peace process' (ibid.). The mounting tension between the Sri Lankan government and the LTTE throughout 2005, in combination with the internal political changes in Sri Lanka, led to the outbreak of Eelam War IV against the LTTE in 2006. Despite a formal continuation of the CFA, the LTTE's attacks on the Sri Lankan security forces grew in number during 2005 – according to some analysts, 'with the clear intention of provoking war' (ICG 2008e: 2). Ultimately, two events led to the resumption of a full-fledged war between the LTTE and the government forces. The first was a suicide attack on Lieutenant-General Sarath Fonseka, the Commander of the Sri Lankan Army, in April 2006. Even though Fonseka survived, the attack, carried out on the premises of the Army Headquarters, revealed the vulnerability of the Sri Lankan establishment. For the first time since the 2002 CFA, the government reacted by carrying out targeted air strikes against the LTTE in the east of the island. By July 2006, the number of violations of the ceasefire increased, especially on the part of the LTTE, and full-scale fighting began in the Eastern province. The second event was the blockade of the Mavil Aru waterway by the LTTE in July 2006, which deprived about 15,000 families of water. The government reacted by bombing selected LTTE targets around the waterway. Despite mediation efforts by the Norwegian Special Envoy, Jon Hanssan-Bauer, who succeeded in convincing the LTTE to conditionally lift the waterway blockade, the government rejected the proposed deal and continued its military operation. Apparently, neither the LTTE nor the government were interested in an agreement.

2006–2009: Eelam War IV

Despite the formal continuation of the ceasefire, we can talk about the start of Eelam War IV with the escalation of violence that followed the Mavil Aru waterway blockade in July 2006. Even though the civil war in Sri Lanka had already seen several bloody combat phases, this renewed Eelam War was characterized by an unprecedented determination on the part of the government to defeat the Tigers. At the same time, the government continued to declare its commitment

---

11 According to some observers (e.g., Sambandan 2006), the apparently inconsequential action by the LTTE had a clear rationale: the LTTE wanted Rajapaksa to win the elections in order to have a justification for resuming its armed struggle. A victory of Wickremasinghe, on the contrary, would have 'forced' the Tigers to go back to the negotiating table and give up the idea of secession.

to the political resolution of the ethnic conflict. However, Rajapaksa's limited interest in accommodating moderate Tamil demands became evident in October 2006, when the Sri Lankan Supreme Court nullified the temporary merger of the Northern and Eastern provinces realized under the Indo-Sri Lanka Accord of 1987 (Reddy 2006c). Since this verdict was based only on procedural failures, the government could have easily taken the initiative to promote a renewed merger of the north and east, thereby accommodating a long-standing demand of moderate Tamils. However, this did not happen.

A last, unsuccessful attempt to find a negotiated solution to the conflict was made by the co-chairs of the peace process – the EU, the United States, Norway, and Japan, representing Sri Lanka's 58 donor countries – in October 2006. The LTTE intensified its attacks in 2007, carrying out several bus bombings across the country and showing its ability to hit even the capital with a suicide bombing at Colombo railway station in February 2008 (ICG 2008e: 2). In the meantime, the government had launched a full-scale military campaign. In the first half of 2007, in part thanks to the collaboration of Karuna (Reddy 2007b), the Sri Lankan military managed to regain control of the entire Eastern province, which had been under LTTE control for 13 years.

Several factors enabled the Sri Lankan Army to carry out its military offensive so swiftly. First, Rajapaksa dramatically increased military spending – in 2006, Sri Lanka's defence expenditure as a percentage of the GDP was the second-highest in South Asia (IISS 2008). At the same time, the strength of the Sri Lankan army increased dramatically – from only 15,000 soldiers in the 1970s (Reddy 2006a), it had grown to 150,000 by 2005 (U.S. Department of State 2005). The Sri Lankan government also improved and diversified the equipment of its security forces through arms supplies from different countries. At the same time, Rajapaksa increasingly concentrated power in his family's hands. While he held the most important portfolios – Finance, Defence, and Nation Building – himself, he placed three of his brothers in key government positions.[12] In general, the situation in Sri Lanka was marked by a decline in governance, a spread of corruption and, especially starting from 2008, a decline in standards of human rights and civil liberties (Smith 2008: 89).[13]

The second main factor that contributed to the strengthening of the government's position and to its military successes was the weakening of the LTTE's image at the international level. President Rajapaksa was very able in playing the 'terrorism card' with the international community, framing the civil war in terms of a terrorist threat. In the context of the global war on terrorism, this led to the ban of the LTTE in over 20 countries, and to a weakening of the Tigers' international

---

12 President Rajapaksa's brother Gotabhaya Rajapaksa became defence secretary; another brother, Chamal Rajapaksa, became Minister for Fisheries, Water Resources and Ports, and Aviation; and a third brother, Basil Rajapaksa, became the President's 'chief strategist and deal maker' (ICG 2007b: 21).

13 On the authoritarian developments in Sri Lanka after the end of the war, see DeVotta (2011).

fundraising network (Jeyaraj 2007).[14] Besides the terrorism factor, however, it was also the Tigers' intransigent attitude, their repeated attempts to use ceasefires for rearming, and their unwillingness to give up the goal of Eelam that alienated the international community. In January 2008, confident that it would be able to defeat the LTTE militarily within a short time, the government of Sri Lanka formally withdrew from the 2002 ceasefire agreement. At that moment, however, the war 'was already at a point of no return' (Uyangoda 2009). Rajapaksa's declared attitude towards the war had gradually changed over the previous months and years. Whilst the government has previously still claimed that it was willing to hold talks with the Tigers, by the second half of 2007 it began to explicitly state its goal: to defeat the LTTE militarily and to win back the territories that the LTTE had conquered (ICG 2008e: 3).

At the same time, the government continued to claim that it wanted a 'political solution' to the ethnic conflict and the devolution of powers to Tamils. On 23 January 2008, the government announced proposals for the implementation of the existing 13th Amendment to the Constitution, which had been envisaged in the ISLA of 1987 but had not been implemented up to that point.[15] Some months after coming into office, Rajapaksa had announced the formation of an All-Party Representative Committee (APRC), which should develop a power-sharing formula agreed upon by all parties (ICG 2007b: 22–5).[16] However, the APRC was merely a committee of the governing majority since the pro-LTTE Tamil National Alliance had not even been invited to participate, and both the JVP and the UNF had withdrawn from it (Reddy 2008d). After the so-called 'Vitharana draft', a devolution proposal submitted by the APRC in January 2007, was rejected by the SLFP and its coalition partners for being too progressive – and after the counterproposal by the SLFP was, in turn, rejected by most parties in the APRC in May 2007 – a new agreement was reached. The parties agreed on a relatively progressive proposal envisaging power devolution at the provincial level (ibid.; ICG 2007b: 24). However, Rajapaksa blocked the elaboration of this proposal and induced the APRC to limit its activities to the elaboration of an interim report entitled 'Action to be taken by the President to fully implement relevant provisions of the present Constitution as a prelude to the APRC proposals' (ibid.: 25). As suggested by its title, this document merely reiterated existing constitutional provisions. Correspondingly, it deceived the hopes of moderate Tamils.

The Provincial Council elections carried out in the Eastern province in May

---

14 Ironically, the Sri Lankan government did not ban the LTTE until January 2009, and therefore carried out a war against a formally legal organization.

15 The 13th Amendment made Tamil an official language and provided for the establishment of a provincial council system in most of the country. However, these councils had never been established in the north and east, the areas they were originally conceived for, due to opposition by both the LTTE and the radical Sinhala JVP (ICG 2008e: 7).

16 In October 2006 the SLFP had signed a MoU with the UNF, which could have represented a unique chance to reach a negotiated solution to the ethnic conflict. However, political tensions between the two rival parties emerged soon, and the MoU was torn to tatters in January 2007.

2008, which took place without major incidents, allowed Rajapaksa to demonstrate the government's willingness to promote democracy and devolution. Moreover, the elections were interpreted by the government as a confirmation of the popular acceptance of the de-merger of the Eastern and Northern provinces (Reddy 2008a).

In the military field, the year 2008 was marked by a steady advance of the Sri Lankan army in the north, after the ousting of the Tigers from the east, and by an impressive shrinking of the areas under LTTE control. While in 2006, when the hostilities broke out, the LTTE controlled parts of the Eastern province, the whole districts of Kilinochchi and Mullaithivu, and some parts of Mannar and Vavuniya in the Northern province, by the end of 2008 it was confined to parts of Kilinochchi and Mullaithivu in the Wanni region.[17] When the Sri Lankan military crossed the border of the Kilinochchi district, the displacement of a huge number of civilians – estimated to be as high as 200,000 – began (Fuller 2009). Trapped between the advancing Sri Lankan armed forces and the retreating LTTE rebels, the civilians were used by the LTTE as human shields in order to prevent the Sri Lankan armed forces from using heavy weapons and, thereby, from advancing too fast.

On 2 January 2009, the LTTE's administrative capital Kilinochchi fell into the hands of the government forces (Mayilvaganan 2009). Shortly thereafter, the Sri Lankan military managed to regain control over the entire A9 highway, which cuts the island from north to south, thereby reconnecting Jaffna with the rest of the country. On 17 January, the Sri Lankan army chief, Lt.-Gen. Sarath Fonseka, declared that the LTTE had been confined to a small jungle area in the Mullaithivu district. In the course of the following months, the situation dramatically escalated. The territory on which the Tigers were confined shrank further, with huge numbers of civilians trapped in it without access to adequate medical facilities and with a shortage of medicines, food, and other essential goods. In April 2009, as their situation was becoming desperate, the Tigers called twice for a truce, but the Sri Lankan government rejected it, declaring that it would fight until the LTTE's surrender. Also the international community – among others, the United Nations, Great Britain, France, and Sweden – tried to induce Rajapaksa to allow for a pause in the fighting and to permit humanitarian missions to access the conflict zone, but did not manage to change the government's approach. According to Human Rights Watch,

> [i]n violation of the laws of war, the LTTE has refused to allow civilians to flee the fighting, repeatedly fired on those trying to reach government-held territory, and deployed forces near densely populated areas. The civilians who remain under LTTE control, including children, are subject to forced recruitment into LTTE forces and hazardous forced labor on the battlefield.
> (HRW 2009: 1)[18]

---

17 The Wanni is the territory covered by jungle, which the LTTE controlled in the north-east.
18 For an assessment of war crimes committed by both conflict parties, see ICG (2010).

After government forces managed to break through a fortification built by the LTTE, a huge exodus of civilians began from the battle zone. As many as 115,000 people managed to flee the conflict area. On 16 May 2009 the Sri Lankan military took control of the entire coastline for the first time since the beginning of the civil war. The remaining LTTE combatants were therefore caught in a minuscule pocket of territory. On the same day, President Rajapaksa declared that the LTTE had been defeated militarily (GOSL 2009c), even though heavy fighting continued in the remaining territory held by the Tigers, where the top LTTE leaders were hidden. Finally, on 18 May 2009 the Sri Lankan government claimed to have killed Prabhakaran along with other LTTE leaders as they were trying to flee the combat zone (Bosleigh 2009). On 19 May, in a speech in the Sri Lankan parliament, Rajapaksa officially declared the war as terminated and celebrated his government's 'proud victory [...] achieved today by defeating the world's most ruthless terrorist organization' (GOSL 2009a).

The military campaign of the Sri Lankan government raised strong criticism in the international community. First, the Sri Lankan government put the national media under strict control and ordered all independent journalists to leave the conflict area. Because of the restricted access to the war-affected zones, most of the information available was disseminated by the conflicting parties, thereby leading to a high degree of uncertainty concerning the real status of events. Similarly, the Sri Lankan government asked aid agencies to vacate the Wanni, provoking protests by sections of the international community. Among others, the UN Secretary General expressed his 'deep concern over the increased hostilities in northern Sri Lanka, and the grave humanitarian consequences for civilians', underlining the importance of allowing humanitarian organizations to access the conflict zone (UN 2008a). In the final phase of the conflict, the international pressure on Colombo continued to grow. In several countries, especially in Great Britain, Canada, Australia, the US and Norway, Tamil diaspora communities held demonstrations to induce the governments to put more pressure on President Rajapaksa. Besides the atrocities committed by both parties on the battlefield, the issue of the Internally Displaced Persons (IDPs) was also of concern for the international community. Moreover, hundreds of thousands of Tamil civilians were held for months in military controlled refugee camps to which international aid agencies were given only partial access.

While some Western countries put pressure on the Sri Lankan government, other countries – among them China, Japan, Russia, and Vietnam – impeded the discussion of atrocities in Sri Lanka in the UN Security Council (Nessman 2009). And India too, as will be discussed below, pursued an ambivalent policy.

India's Foreign Policy Strategies Towards Sri Lanka

Against the background of the events leading to the outburst of Eelam War IV in the years 2003–6 and of the dramatic escalation of violence in the years 2006–9, we will now proceed to analyse India's foreign policy strategies in dealing with the conflict in Sri Lanka. The analytical framework developed in Chapter Two will guide the analysis. Therefore, the identification of India's foreign policy strategies in dealing with Sri Lanka is based on four main factors: goals, means, reactions, and perceptions. For the sake of clarity and readability, the analysis starts with the means employed by New Delhi – that is, with India's foreign policy behaviour – and moves on to the Sri Lankan government's reactions and perceptions, as well as to the commonalities or divergences in the goals pursued by both countries.

From Non-Involvement to Tacit Support: India's Foreign Policy Means

As mentioned above, the failure of the IPKF mission and the assassination of Rajiv Gandhi forced India to follow a 'hands-off policy' towards Sri Lanka. Therefore, India did not interfere with the Norwegian mediation efforts, thereby distancing itself from its traditional approach of not allowing external actors to get involved in South Asian affairs. The Norwegian diplomats, on their part, regularly updated India on the progress of negotiations.[19] During the peace talks leading to the ceasefire agreement of 2002, India found itself in the paradoxical position of formally supporting the efforts for a negotiated political settlement of the crisis, while one of the actors involved was banned in India and its leader was persecuted for murder by an Indian court. The Indian attitude in those years can be defined as 'conscious neglect': while India clearly refused to play an active role in the neighbouring country, at the same time it constantly observed the situation in Sri Lanka. The main tools India employed to keep its leverage on Sri Lanka during the years preceding the outbreak of Eelam War IV (2003–6) were economic and developmental incentives as well as soft persuasion – typical tools of an intermediate and soft hegemonic strategy.

Generally speaking, the Indo–Sri Lankan relationship was good during this first phase, especially under the presidency of Chandrika Kumaratunga. With President Rajapaksa, India had a somehow more difficult relationship right from the beginning,[20] but overall relations were positive. In the field of economy and trade, bilateral ties had become closer with the signing of a bilateral free trade agreement (FTA) in 1998, which had positive repercussions on the Sri Lankan economy (Kelegama/Mukherji 2007: 5–20). In June 2002, a further step towards an intensification of economic relations was taken with the agreement to work towards a Comprehensive Economic Partnership Agreement (CEPA) covering not only trade in goods, but also in services and foreign direct investment (FDI).[21]

Moreover, Sri Lanka was one of the main recipient countries of Indian foreign aid (Price 2004: 13); it obtained support by New Delhi after the 2004 Tsunami

---

19 Interview with government official, New Delhi, 20 November 2008.
20 India's uneasiness with the new government was reflected, for example, in the abandonment of the project of a defence agreement with Sri Lanka.
21 Ultimately, because of reservations on the part of Sri Lankan companies and leftist parties, the CEPA was not finalized during the 2008 SAARC summit as originally planned.

(Price 2005: 15); and it took advantage of a moratorium on its debt announced by India in 2005.[22]

It is not clear to what extent these forms of support to Sri Lanka were perceived by the Indian government as tools to gain better leverage on events on the island or to influence developments related to the ethnic conflict. While the development projects and loans offered by India were not explicitly bound to any conditionalities,[23] we can infer from them India's intention to expand its influence on Sri Lanka.[24] Beyond this, at least in the case of the tsunami, the Indian effort clearly had strategic reasons related to New Delhi's fear of the presence of external actors in its sphere of influence: As a reaction to the US sending 1,500 marines and an amphibious ship to Sri Lanka, India deployed as many as 1,000 military personnel, five Navy vessels, a field hospital, and six helicopters to help the population hit by the natural disaster (LankaNewspapers 2005).

While economic concessions and bilateral aid are factors which India possibly used to increase Sri Lanka's dependence on it and, as a consequence, to increase its chances to influence Colombo, these relations can also be seen the other way round. In fact, as will be outlined later in more detail, the growing economic interdependence with India represented a useful tool for President Rajapaksa to increase India's stakes in the stability of Sri Lanka and induce it to support the government's fight against the LTTE.

At the level of the verbal foreign policy means employed by India, these displayed a high degree of continuity until 2006, with India trying to persuade the Sri Lankan government to seek a peaceful solution to the crisis. These persuasion efforts were expressed in very moderate tones and were accompanied by expressions of commitment on the part of India. A typical example is the following passage from a press briefing from 2003:

> As far as we are concerned we are supportive of the peace process and we are committed to the unity, sovereignty and territorial integrity of Sri Lanka and to the restoration of peace through a peaceful, negotiated settlement which takes care of the aspirations of all elements of Sri Lankan society.
>
> (Lok Sabha 2003)

The degree of intensity of the statements issued during this period shows that these were very moderate efforts to persuade the Sri Lankan government to follow the approach favoured by New Delhi. India, therefore, resorted to soft persuasion (expressions of hope, belief),[25] to expressions of support and commitment (e.g.,

---

22 See also MEA (2009a, 2005r).

23 On the aid policies of the so-called 'emerging donors', see Woods (2008).

24 According to Price (2005: 18), India 'perceives its assistance strategy largely in terms of self-interest, primarily since that is how it perceives other donors to have treated India'.

25 See, for example, MEA (2004b): 'The Prime Minister has said that *we very much hope* that a peaceful and negotiated solution will be found which will maintain the unity, territorial integrity and sovereignty of Sri Lanka and satisfy all sections of the people of Sri Lanka [emphasis added]'.

MEA 2003a), but also, although to a lesser extent, to diplomatic pressure, empha-sizing the need to adopt certain measures (e.g., MEA 2005lc).

After the election of Rajapaksa as Sri Lanka's president in 2005, India did not change its approach in any significant manner, paying attention to keep its position of non-involvement in the conflict, as emerges quite clearly from the joint statement issued after Rajapaksa's first visit to Delhi: 'The two sides agreed that an enduring solution can emerge *only through internal political processes* that promote consensus and reconciliation [emphasis added]' (MEA 2005h).

As the security situation started deteriorating in 2005, however, India's state-ments changed in tone, conveying an increasing sense of urgency. India resorted to hard persuasion (expressions of concern, e.g., MEA 2005k) and to diplomatic pressure (condemnation, urgency).[26] However, the growing concern voiced by Indian foreign policy makers did not represent anything like an actual threat, since in none of the official statements issued in these years did India outline the consequences Sri Lanka would face if not complying with India's wishes. Overall, therefore, in the years 2003–6 India resorted to a mix of incentives and persuasion efforts to induce the Sri Lankan government to pursue a peaceful solution of the ethnic conflict.

This kind of approach changed, however, during the second phase analysed – that is, 2006–9. In those years, a striking divergence became observable between the non-verbal and the verbal means employed by India, leading to an inconsistent and reactive policy. While at the level of verbal behaviour, India started employing hard persuasion and pressure as well as vague threats to induce Colombo to act with greater restraint in dealing with the Tamil minority, at the non-verbal level New Delhi began providing significant support to the Sri Lankan government in its fight against the LTTE.

Because of the ethnic and historical affinity between Tamils on both sides of the Palk Straits, supporting the Sri Lankan government militarily had always been politi-cally impossible for India. A number of political parties in Tamil Nadu openly backed the LTTE, for example the Pattali Makkal Katchi (PMK), the Viduthalai Siruthaigal (the Dalit Panthers of India, DPI), and the Marumalarchi Dravida Munnetra Kazhagam (MDMK).[27] Similarly, sections of the ruling party in Tamil Nadu, the Dravida Munnetra Kazhagam (DMK), which was an important coalition partner of the Congress in the UPA central government, had been expressing their sympathy for the LTTE. As a consequence of the widespread support for LTTE activities in Tamil Nadu, Rajapaksa's proposal to India of jointly patrolling the Palk Straits to weaken the LTTE provoked strong opposition by the government of Tamil Nadu (*The Hindu*

---

26 See, for example, MEA (2006b): 'India condemns all violence especially that which involves loss of civilian lives including that of children'.

27 Vaiko, the leader of the MDMK, which was part of the United Progressive Alliance until March 2007, openly supported the LTTE and the notion of Tamil Eelam. For this reason, he was arrested under the Prevention of Terrorism Act in 2002 and for sedition in 2008.

2008a). However, after the discovery of an extensive LTTE network in Southern India in 2007 (Hariharan 2007; Jayanth 2007), the Tamil Nadu state police increased its activities aimed at weakening the LTTE, and New Delhi agreed to improve coastal security by, among other measures, training the Tamil Nadu Coastal Security Group for patrolling the Palk Straits (*India Defence* 2007). Moreover, between 2006–9, the Indian and the Sri Lankan navies cooperated in several operations against the Sea Tigers (Gokhale 2009: 125). In particular, provision of intelligence by the Indian Navy allowed the Sri Lankan Navy to destroy several 'floating warehouses' of the LTTE (ibid.; Suryanarayan 2010: 172).

When it comes to the topic of military assistance, a significant change in India's approach took place between the first and the second phases analysed. While Sri Lanka had earlier been on India's negative list for arms exports, it was removed from the list after the signing of the 2002 CFA (Sambandan 2003). During a meeting between Prime Ministers Wickemasinghe and Vajpayee in October 2003, Colombo showed its interest in Indian non-offensive military supplies and in an increase in the pre-existing cooperation in training. Moreover, discussions were held about a possible defence cooperation agreement desired by Colombo (MEA 2003c). A formal agreement on defence cooperation was ultimately not finalized, but the interactions in matters of defence and security between the Indian and the Sri Lankan government intensified nonetheless. In fact, in 2007 India changed its approach to the conflict and started supporting more explicitly – albeit covertly in order to avoid excessive criticism from Tamil Nadu – the military campaign of the Sri Lankan government. Although the arms exports were limited to so-called 'non-offensive' weapons, overall the military assistance provided by India to Sri Lanka was 'significant' (ICG 2008e: 20). In fact, India not only provided life-saving equipment like flak jackets to the Sri Lankan government, but also an offshore patrol vessel in 2007 (SIPRI 2011a). Moreover, the Sri Lankan air force allegedly received five helicopters as a gift by India in 2006 (Gokhale 2009: 121), while two air surveillance radars were openly provided to Sri Lanka in 2006 and 2007 respectively.

While the provision of weapons and military equipment by India was relatively limited, India massively supported the Sri Lankan military in terms of training, and even increased the number of Sri Lankan soldiers to be trained in 2008.[28] This encompassed not only weapons training, but also courses at the National Defence College in New Delhi (Cherian 2003).[29] The naval cooperation between India and Sri Lanka was reportedly very good (Gohkale 2009: 124–7). Apart from that, high level meetings reportedly took place regularly between political representatives of India and Sri Lanka between 2007–9 (ibid.: 122–3).

At this point the question emerges of how to interpret India's military support for the Sri Lankan government. It seems difficult to characterize it as an Indian

---

28 MEA (2009a); interview with Sri Lankan diplomat, New Delhi, 24 November 2008.
29 According to DeVotta (2010: 52), approximately 800 Sri Lankan officers are trained in India every year.

incentive to induce Colombo to adopt India's declared preferences – peace and devolution of powers. On the contrary, behind India's decision to provide weapons to Colombo there seems to have been a more immediate concern: India wanted to limit Sri Lankan weapon procurements from other countries and, as a consequence, preferred to step in itself to address Sri Lanka's needs. For example, India managed to dissuade Sri Lanka from buying a 3D radar system from China, and persuaded Colombo to acquire it, instead, from India (Reddy 2007a). However, China clearly turned out to be the main provider of weapons for Sri Lanka in 2008, accounting for over 80 per cent of total supplies (SIPRI 2011a). Besides China, Pakistan too played a major role in supporting the Sri Lankan government: Pakistan had been one of Sri Lanka's weapons suppliers for years, the two countries drafted a defence pact in 2008, Pakistan reportedly advised the Sri Lankan government for its military operations, and Pakistani pilots allegedly flew jet fighters for the Sri Lankan air force (DeVotta 2010: 49–50).

Therefore, if we consider the provision of military equipment to Sri Lanka as an incentive to follow the approach preferred by New Delhi, this incentive is related to the goal of limiting the influence of external powers in the region. This assessment is confirmed by a remarkable episode that took place in 2007. On 31 May, National Security Adviser M.K. Narayanan explicitly stated that India did not approve of the Sri Lankan government's arms purchases from countries like China and Pakistan and made public India's readiness to respond to Sri Lanka's 'defensive requirements':

> We are the big power in this region. Let us make it very clear. We strongly believe that whatever requirements the Sri Lankan government has, they should come to us. And we will give them what we think is necessary. We do not favour their going to China or Pakistan or any other country. [...] We will not provide the Sri Lankan government with offensive capability. That is the standard position... radar is seen as a defensive capability. If a country wants us to help them with defensive capabilities, we will provide them. That is our position.
>
> (*The Hindu* 2007)

The beginning of the statement with the reminder of India's size (and power) constitutes one of the rare cases in the past years in which a high government official explicitly underlined India's position as the regional power in a tone reminiscent of Indira Gandhi's in the 1980s. Although 'technically' this declaration does not represent a threat since India did not announce the consequences Sri Lanka would face if not complying with New Delhi's wishes, it definitely constitutes a verbal coercive declaration and, therefore, an indicator of a hard hegemonic approach on the part of India. The indignant reactions this statement produced in Sri Lanka (see below) confirm this assessment.

While India started supporting the military operations of the Sri Lankan government in 2007, at the level of verbal foreign policy means it still emphasized the need for a political solution – and it did so in an increasingly imperative tone.

The intensification of the conflict and the suffering of the Tamil civilian population in Sri Lanka induced New Delhi – most probably under pressure from the DMK and other parties in Tamil Nadu – to put, at least at the rhetorical level, a considerable degree of political pressure on the government of Sri Lanka. Consequently, the Indian national security advisor summoned the Sri Lankan deputy high commissioner on 6 October 2008 to protest about the way in which Sri Lanka was carrying out its military operations (MEA 2008h). This exertion of diplomatic pressure by India's most senior official in charge of security issues amounted to a much harder approach towards Sri Lanka on the part of New Delhi in comparison to previous years. Some days before, India had expressed its discontent with the Sri Lankan government and the way it was handling the conflict, when Prime Minister Manmohan Singh had refused to meet the Sri Lankan president Rajapaksa on the sidelines of the UN General Assembly in New York. On 16 October 2008, India finally resorted to what could be defined as a (non-specific) threat: the external affairs minister declared that New Delhi would 'do all in its power' to improve the humanitarian situation in Sri Lanka (MEA 2008j). In a telephone conversation with President Rajapaksa, Prime Minister Manmohan Singh further increased the pressure on Sri Lanka emphasizing that 'the safety of civilians must be safeguarded at all costs' (MEA 2008i). In a remarkable spate of statements in the following days, the Indian government continued to emphasize that in India's view there was 'no military solution to the ethnic conflict' and that a 'political process for a peacefully negotiated settlement' was needed (MEA 2008k, 2008f). Despite Colombo's reassurances to India, however, no significant changes took place in the military course adopted by Rajapaksa. New Delhi, on its part, made no move to intensify its threats. Possible forms of threat could have constituted India's request that Sri Lanka sign a ceasefire agreement with the LTTE, underscored by the imposition of a blockade on the island, economic sanctions, or even the threat of military intervention. However, nothing of this kind took place. On the contrary, after October 2008, Indian statements were still hard in their tone,[30] but no longer included threats. Even though the situation in Sri Lanka reached a previously unthinkable apex in human suffering and killings of Sri Lankan Tamil civilians, the Indian government, at that time involved in the campaign for the May 2009 general elections, did not take any measures to further pressurize Colombo.

Beyond India's implicit support for the military campaign of the Sri Lankan government, a more radical shift could be observed in New Delhi's approach to the Rajapaksa regime – a shift that regarded sensitive issues like the terms of a potential political settlement as well as human rights violations by the Sri Lankan government. For example, India reacted to the interim report issued by the All Parties Representatives Committee (APRC), which Rajapaksa created to formulate

---

30 For example MEA (2009d): 'We are very unhappy at the continued killing of innocent Tamil civilians in Sri Lanka. These killings must stop. The Sri Lankan Government has a responsibility to protect its own citizens. And the LTTE must stop its barbaric attempt to hold civilians hostage'.

suggestions about power sharing, by defining it as a 'welcome first step' towards a settlement acceptable to all communities of Sri Lanka (MEA 2008c).

On 18 May 2009, when the end of military hostilities and the death of Prabhakaran were announced by the Sri Lankan government, the Indian ministry of external affairs issued a statement neutral in tone. While it avoided congratulating the Sri Lankan government for its victory, it also refrained from condemning the conduct of the military campaign and pledged, instead, to cooperate with Colombo in providing relief to displaced people (MEA 2009f). After the end of the war, moreover, India backed the Sri Lankan government in international forums like the United Nations Human Rights Council (UNHRC), where it contributed to prevent an investigation of the government's (and the LTTE's) war crimes. Together with countries like China, Pakistan, and Russia, India voted against a motion proposed by Western countries at a special session of the UNHRC held on 28 May 2009. Instead, India supported a motion of the Rajapaksa administration, which depicted the result of the war as a 'liberation' of Sri Lankan Tamils from the LTTE, but ignored the atrocities committed against civilians during the last months of the war (BBC News 2009; *The Hindustan Times* 2009). This episode reveals the rather limited concerns of the central government in New Delhi about Sri Lankan Tamils; moreover, it highlights the substantial rapprochement that took place between New Delhi and Colombo.

Overall, therefore, during the second phase analysed (2006–9), India resorted to a peculiar mix of incentives in the form of support for the military campaign of the Sri Lankan government while, at the same time, employing hard verbal tools and threats on the issue of protecting the Tamil civilian population.

Engaging India: Sri Lanka's Approach

Having assessed the foreign policy means adopted by New Delhi, we will now proceed to a brief analysis of the Sri Lankan government's reactions and perceptions in dealing with India. For a better legibility and in order to avoid repetitions, reactions and perceptions will be dealt with together even though, analytically, the two elements are separated.

The assessment of Indian–Sri Lankan relations as provided by a Sri Lankan diplomat interviewed in New Delhi constitutes a good first overview of Sri Lanka's official position towards India under the Rajapaksa administration. By way of an introduction, the interviewee outlined the ambiguity of New Delhi's position and India's need for influence over Sri Lanka:

'The Indians grapple with two issues: first, they think that as the dominant power in the region, the neighbours should understand India's sensitivities. And, second, they do recognize that [to induce] their neighbours to be receptive to their concerns they have to be very skilful, attentive.'[31]

31 Interview with Sri Lankan diplomat, New Delhi, 19 November 2008.

In particular, the diplomat conveyed the position that Sri Lanka would have wished a greater involvement on the part of India both during the peace process and later, during Eelam War IV. During the whole period analysed, in fact, the Sri Lankan government displayed a clear interest in getting support from New Delhi in its fight against the LTTE. At the same time, however, all the other actors involved in the Sri Lankan conflict also wanted India's support for their cause, as illustrated by Reddy (2006b): 'It is as if every interested party wants New Delhi to become a partner in its own pursuits. In other words, no one is ready to concede an unfettered role to India'. President Rajapaksa invoked a greater military involvement on the part of India in order to get support in his government's fight against the LTTE. The intensification of economic relations with India was an important tool in this regard. As the Sri Lankan diplomat interviewed in New Delhi put it quite bluntly, the strengthening of bilateral economic relations between India and Sri Lanka was the result of Sri Lanka's desire to induce New Delhi to have an interest in the island's stability and, correspondingly, a stake in a military defeat of the LTTE.[32]

The Sri Lankan government also tried to foster India's engagement in the conflict. Under Prime Minister Wickremasinghe, Sri Lanka almost managed to sign a defence cooperation agreement with India. The issue was discussed during several high level bilateral visits after 2003 (MEA 2004e; 2004c; 2005g). However, ultimately the deal was not finalized and India rejected the renewed offer of a defence pact made by President Rajapaksa during his first official visit in December 2005. In the following years, the Sri Lankan government kept on trying to convince New Delhi about the importance of maritime security, especially since the LTTE formed its 'navy', the Sea Tigers. As a consequence, Sri Lanka requested that India patrol the seas jointly with the Indian Navy. Moreover, Colombo tried to gain military support from India by diversifying its arms supplies, that is, by pursuing a policy of balancing with other countries, well knowing that India would react to it. According to the International Crisis Group (2008e: 20), 'the Sri Lankan government has skilfully used its overtures to those countries to entice India to increase both economic and military support over the past year'. To summarize, the Sri Lankan government's foreign policy towards India was characterized by efforts to keep India engaged, particularly in the years 2003–6.[33]

However, as New Delhi started exercising pressure on the Sri Lankan government in 2006, this attitude was met with growing resistance by Rajapaksa. The same applied for the criticism coming from foreign countries and international organizations on the Sri Lankan government's handling of human rights, and on the expulsion of aid workers and journalists from the conflict zones.[34]

---

32 Ibid.
33 Similarly, the LTTE and other Tamil parties and groups also tried to gain India's support (Reddy 2006b), and the different pressures on New Delhi, combined with domestic constraints in India, contribute to explain India's indecisive approach to Sri Lanka in the years 2003–6.
34 For example, the Sri Lankan defence secretary, Gotabhaya Rajapaksa, in May 2007 reportedly summoned the British high commissioner for having visited a Sri Lankan journalist who had received a death threat from Gotabhaya Rajapaksa himself (BBC Sinhala 2007).

In this context, the reactions to the statement on weapons purchases made by the Indian national security advisor in 2007 deserve particular consideration. Even though the government of Sri Lanka did not react officially to Narayanan's statement, the blunt assertion of India's power position in South Asia and the implicit threat to Sri Lanka not to purchase weapons from countries like Pakistan and China provoked a wave of critique and indignation in the Sri Lankan media.[35] The discussion – where it was conducted in a relatively objective way – revolved mainly around the issues of Sri Lanka's sovereignty and India's attitude as a regional bully (Parthasarathy 2007). The 'traditional' perception of being threatened by an overwhelmingly larger neighbour, which had characterized the Indira Gandhi era and the period of the IPKF operations, came to the fore again. In an article in the newspaper *The Island*, the Sri Lankan retired diplomat K. Godage (2007), for example, compared Narayanan's statement to India's policies of the 1980s, when 'Indian hegemonists sought to use the stupid mismanagement of our foreign relations […] to "Bhutanise" this country and transform us into a vassal state'.

Similar reactions came from some Sri Lankan political parties. The ultra-nationalist JVP, for example, issued an open letter to the Indian high commissioner titled 'India Should Not Return to Bad Neighbour Policy' and blamed India for having prevented Sri Lanka from acquiring the above-mentioned 3-D radar system from China (Reddy 2007c).

The negative perceptions about India as a regional bully, a big brother, and a bad neighbour imposing its will on smaller countries were reflected, at the level of foreign policy behaviour, in an attitude of resistance towards India on the part of the Sri Lankan government. Rajapaksa, in fact, continued to pursue his fight against the LTTE despite India's (and the international community's) demands for a political solution. A statement issued in October 2008 by Sri Lankan Foreign Minister Rohita Bogollagama reveals very well the discourse dominating in Sri Lanka and hints at an alleged manipulation of India by the LTTE:

> While our security forces are engaged in their present humanitarian operation to free our people from the fascist and dictatorial control of the LTTE terrorists, […] critics of Sri Lanka and sympathisers of the LTTE are attempting to portray a misleading and totally false notion that the government is opting for a military solution to address the problems of the minorities. It is unfortunate that some of our friends too have been influenced by this malicious propaganda.
>
> (GOSL 2008)

While perceptions about India became increasingly negative, the Sri Lankan government nevertheless tried not to compromise relations with India while

---

35 In an editorial of the Sri Lankan newspaper *The Island* (2007), for example, India was defined as a 'sadist' and its attitude compared to that of Nazi Germany.

consistently following its path of militarily defeating the LTTE. The result of this approach was a policy of appeasement towards India based on compliance on minor issues, such as the radar purchase from China, and on a continued reassurance about the intention to take care of the 'safety and wellbeing of the Tamil community' (MEA 2008i, 2008f). As part of these concessions, a session of the APRC was summoned on 11 October 2008 (Reddy 2008b) and the Sri Lankan government accepted the distribution of relief material for IDPs on the part of India (Reddy 2008c). Similarly, during the final months of the war, Rajapaksa reassured highly-placed Indian government representatives that his government would implement the 13th Amendment to the constitution (MEA 2009h, 2009c). In the meantime, however, the military campaign continued unabated, and no provisions were taken to protect civilians. Overall, therefore, Sri Lanka pursued a policy of appeasement without compliance, since no concrete measures were taken to satisfy India's demands. Ultimately, India's pressurizing tactics concerning the fate of Sri Lankan Tamils caught in the crossfire did not yield any results.

India and Sri Lanka: Diverging Goals

As a further indicator of the strategies pursued by the Indian government in its interactions with Sri Lanka, we need to take into consideration both countries' goals and the degree to which they were compatible. While a commonality of goals would be an indicator of a leader-follower relationship, diverging goals can help us identify hegemonic or imperial strategies. As we will see, in the case of Sri Lanka we have a high degree of divergence on some fundamental goals and, particularly since 2007, a convergence towards the goals promoted by Sri Lanka. In the following analysis, we will distinguish between core goals, on the one hand, and secondary and instrumental goals on the other. The latter are more specific objectives related to single issue areas.

The two core security-related goals pursued by India in the context of the war in Sri Lanka were a) stability; and b) the limitation of external actors' activities on the island.

The goal of stability basically corresponded to the desire to put an end to the ethnic conflict and was therefore mainly expressed by the Indian government in terms of 'peace'. In almost all declarations referring to Sri Lanka in the years 2003–9 (and earlier), India expressed its desire for a peaceful settlement of the crisis. During the negotiations facilitated by Norway, India expressed its hope for a 'lasting peace' (MEA 2002b); when the negotiations collapsed, Indian government officials expressed the desire for an 'early resumption of the peace process' (MEA 2004e); later, the MEA declared itself 'deeply concerned at the recent escalation of violence in Sri Lanka and the repeated violations of the ceasefire' (MEA 2005k); and even despite the intensification of military operations in August 2008, India did not give up its stated goal of peace in Sri Lanka (MEA 2009b). However, while we can assume that the goal of peace, that is, the reaching of a settlement capable of guaranteeing stability to Sri Lanka, was genuinely pursued by New Delhi since it corresponds to India's broader goals for South Asia (see Chapter Three), we need to distinguish this goal from India's preferences about the concrete way to achieve peace.

While Indian foreign policy makers had repeated the importance of a 'negotiated political settlement' of the crisis,[36] India's attitude towards the Rajapaksa regime raises some doubts – particularly, when it seems that New Delhi at a certain point started espousing Rajapaksa's belief in the need for a military solution of the long-standing conflict. As one of the interviewees put it in 2008, 'somewhere along the line, in the last one year or two, somebody in the Indian government seems to have decided clearly that now it is trying to help the [Sri Lankan] government, and without making too much noise about it'.[37] The turning point in the policymakers' approach is difficult to determine, but the crackdown on the LTTE network in 2007 can be taken as a good indicator for the changed mood in New Delhi. Despite continuing to affirm that '[o]ur policy towards Sri Lanka is based on the conviction that there is no military solution to the conflict' (Rajya Sabha 2008), New Delhi started supporting the Sri Lankan government's military efforts in a much more direct way. Given the ban on the LTTE and the arrest warrant issued for Prabhakaran, Indian policymakers started embracing the view that 'destroying the LTTE [was] a legitimate activity'.[38] Or, as a former Indian diplomat put it,

'We are basically supporting the Sri Lankan counterterrorism.'[39]

Besides the provision of non-offensive weapons and other forms of military support, another element qualifying India's stated goal of a political settlement of the conflict is represented by what India did *not* do. This is particularly relevant for the second phase analysed (2006–9). Had New Delhi been really committed to a peaceful solution, it could have at least declared itself to be in favour of a ceasefire. This would have been compatible with the constraints deriving from Tamil Nadu politics and with India's approach of non-involvement in Sri Lanka. However, this did not happen for a long time. Only in February 2009, when the war had already turned into a huge humanitarian crisis, did the Indian external affairs minister invite – in a relatively mild tone – the Sri Lankan government to accept the LTTE's offer for a ceasefire in order to guarantee safe passage to the civilians caught in the crossfire (MEA 2009g). This late and indecisive turn, together with External Affairs Minister Mukherjee's statement in January 2009 that '[...] military victories offer a political opportunity to restore life to normalcy

---

36 This expression has been used throughout the period analysed.
37 Interview with expert, New Delhi, 19 November 2008. The goal to put an end to the armed conflict by defeating the LTTE was also related to India's desire to put an end to the negative spill-over effects related to the war: smuggling of weapons, refugee inflows, killings of Indian fishermen by the Sri Lankan navy and the Sea Tigers, etc. (ICG 2008e: 20). Between January 2006 and the end of October 2008 more than 22,900 Sri Lankan Tamil refugees arrived in India, 16,631 of whom arrived during the year 2006 (MEA 2009a).
38 Interview with government official, New Delhi, 20 November 2008.
39 Interview with expert, New Delhi, 7 November 2008.

in the Northern province and throughout Sri Lanka, after [...] years of conflict' (MEA 2009e), confirms New Delhi's tacit support for Colombo's way of dealing with the LTTE. One of the experts interviewed even expressed the allegation that the Indian support for the Sri Lankan military effort might have gone far beyond the provision of defensive weapons, and might well have included the covert participation of Indian forces in military operations or, at least, the supply of a broader range of weapons.[40] While the issue of India's support for the Sri Lankan government forces has been the object of a heated political debate between political parties in Tamil Nadu and the central government in New Delhi, there are no elements to confirm the allegation of an active military involvement on the part of India in the campaign against the LTTE. The consequences of India's tacit support for Colombo's decision to eliminate the LTTE were therefore, according to the sources available, limited to New Delhi's 'silence' on certain issues, to the provision of defensive equipment and training, and to the low degree of pressure exercised on the Sri Lankan government.

Given this contradiction between the stated goal of peace and, starting from 2007, the support given to the Sri Lankan government, we can assume that New Delhi's core goal for Sri Lanka was represented by *stability* rather than peace – that is, by the desire for a return to normalcy, even if this implied a quick and deadly military campaign.[41] India was heavily affected by negative spill-over effects related to the war like the smuggling of weapons, refugee inflows, killings of Indian fishermen by the Sri Lankan navy and the Sea Tigers, etc. (ICG 2008e: 20). In this context, when it became clear that the war could not be stopped, India espoused the Sri Lankan government's view that peace could only be achieved through war. In the short term, therefore, the goal of peace was put aside and replaced by the objective of quickly and effectively defeating the LTTE.

The second core goal pursued by India with regard to the conflict in Sri Lanka was the limitation of external actors' activities on the island. This goal was not often explicitly stated by the Indian government. In fact, New Delhi formally welcomed the Norwegian facilitation efforts in the neighbouring country – in which India could not act as a mediator anymore because of the proscription of the LTTE as a terrorist organization. Similarly, the Indian government expressed its support for the SLLM and, in 2006, its appreciation for the Sri Lankan government's willingness to resume the peace talks mediated by Norway (MEA 2006i). However, one of the government officials interviewed alluded to the reason why the Norwegian facilitation was not perceived as a threat to India's predominance in the region: the government of India had always known that the Norwegians lacked the leverage and the knowledge of the local situation necessary to achieve any settlement. In his words, 'the Sri Lankans decided to go to the Norwegians.

---

40 Interview with expert, New Delhi, 19 November 2008.
41 The Indian correspondent Gokhale (2009: 124) even goes so far as to argue that New Delhi put some pressure on Colombo to terminate the war before the Indian general elections of May 2009.

But it was clear that they [the Norwegians] would not succeed!'.[42] Therefore, we could conclude that New Delhi was comfortable with the Norwegian presence in Sri Lanka mainly because it was sure that Norway's efforts would not alter the equilibrium.

A further differentiation is also needed concerning the 'external actors' involved. While Norway, as a small and remote country with no apparent specific interests in South Asia, did not represent an actual problem for New Delhi, the presence of other states, which were enemies or competitors for India, did.[43] The May 2007 statement by National Security Advisor Narayanan, with the explicit affirmation of India's self-perception as the dominant power in South Asia, clearly reflects India's attitude.

Besides the core goals of stability, and of limiting the influence of external actors in India's sphere of influence, New Delhi had several secondary and instrumental goals. These concerned the resolution of the ethnic conflict, the future political settlement in Sri Lanka, and the fate of the civilians involved in the war.

As far as the settlement of the Sri Lankan crisis is concerned, India repeatedly stated that the negotiations about the solution of the ethnic conflict should provide for the respect of the 'unity, sovereignty and integrity' of Sri Lanka.[44] India has therefore consistently supported the principle of the indivisibility of the Sri Lankan state. New Delhi's decades-old fear of secessionist spill-over effects to single Indian states, most notably to Tamil Nadu, helps explain India's interest in the territorial unity and integrity of Sri Lanka.

Together with the notion of territorial integrity, however, India also consistently acknowledged the need for forms of power devolution that met – according to a standard formulation – 'the aspirations of all communities' (e.g., MEA 2004g). However, in the time span analysed, India was eager to avoid giving the impression that it was interfering in the internal affairs of Sri Lanka, and therefore generally refrained from suggesting concrete institutional solutions for devolution. In the statements issued between April 2003 and May 2009 a more concrete reference to the kind of arrangement favoured by India emerged only once: 'the unity of Sri Lanka in a federal system' (MEA 2004a).[45] Otherwise, India highlighted that the kind of political settlement for Sri Lanka was an internal political issue of the neighbouring country, in which New Delhi did not want to interfere (e.g., MEA 2003b).

Despite this caution, in January 2008 the Indian ministry of external affairs defined the proposal elaborated by the APRC, which reduced devolution of powers

---

42 Interview with government official, New Delhi, 17 November 2008.
43 One of the experts interviewed stated, referring to Sri Lanka, Nepal, and Bangladesh: 'And what India would want is [...] that Pakistan and China are less influential in the three countries [sic]. Regrettably both Pakistan and China are influential there'. Interview with expert, New Delhi, 25 November 2008. He also emphasized that India 'pays attention' to the activities of external countries in South Asia and attaches importance to keeping relations with neighbouring countries at the bilateral level: 'For example at the donors conference on Sri Lanka India was present as an observer but it would not join a multilateral agreement in its own region!'.
44 This formulation was reiterated throughout the years 2003–9 with small variations.
45 Moreover, India offered to share its 'constitutional experience' with Sri Lanka (MEA 2006j).

merely to what was already included in the 13th Amendment to the Sri Lankan constitution, as a 'welcome first step' (MEA 2008c). This approach represented – in terms of how far-reaching Sri Lanka's devolution of powers should have been in India's view – a setback in comparison to the preceding statement related to federalism. Also later, in October 2008, the Indian government kept on calling for the implementation of the 13th Amendment to the constitution as a solution for the devolution of powers (MEA 2008f), even though this amendment had been criticized by representatives of Sri Lankan Tamils as insufficient.[46] Therefore, on this issue too, like on the issue of the conduct of the military campaign, a convergence between Sri Lanka's and India's goals seems to have taken place. What is particularly interesting about this is the 'direction' of this convergence, since it was New Delhi that came to follow the approach pursued by Rajapaksa.

Starting from October 2008, when the LTTE remained confined to a small strip of land in the Mullaitivu district and tens of thousands of civilians came to be caught in the crossfire, the issue of the safety of those civilians took centre stage for the Indian government. India started expressing its preoccupation about civilian casualties, human suffering, and the problem of refugees (e.g., Rajya Sabha 2006d; Lok Sabha 2007b; MEA 2008d). New Delhi's statements in this regard became increasingly pressurizing, with the threats formulated by the government in its interactions with Colombo in October 2008 (MEA 2008j, 2008f) confirming the importance of this goal. In April 2009, the external affairs minister stated:

> We are very unhappy at the continued killing of innocent Tamil civilians in Sri Lanka. These killings must stop. The Sri Lankan Government has a responsibility to protect its own citizens. And the LTTE must stop its barbaric attempt to hold civilians hostage. There is no military solution to this ongoing humanitarian crisis, and all concerned should recognise this fact. The only lasting solution will come from political efforts to address the real concerns of the Tamil people, giving them lives of dignity within the Sri Lankan mainstream.
>
> (MEA 2009d)

New Delhi's sensitivity to the problems of Sri Lanka was boosted, as illustrated above, by the state government of Tamil Nadu, which exerted considerable pressure on the central government to pay greater attention to human rights issues and to the suffering of the Tamil population in Sri Lanka. As one of the interviewees put it,

> [...] it's also again a sort of responsibility-to-protect relation [...]. There is a bottom line in terms of [...] civilian casualties, in terms of human rights violations, in terms of migration to India.[47]

---

46 This is related, among other things, to the fact that, with the re-merger of the Eastern and Northern provinces, one of the fundamental features of the 13th Amendment, was revoked (*Sunday Observer* 2008).

47 Interview with expert, New Delhi, 7 November 2008.

It was, in fact, the critical situation of Tamil civilians and IDPs that induced the DMK to repeatedly threaten New Delhi to pull out of the central government (Murari 2009). Given the importance of the DMK in the governing coalition, this threat made the goal of protecting the civilians caught in the conflict particularly relevant for the UPA government in New Delhi. However, the political parties in Tamil Nadu were ultimately not able to effectively oppose the tacit support India provided to the Sri Lankan government in its military campaign.[48] Overall, therefore, the goal of protecting Tamil civilians may have been an objective of the Indian government, but the core goal of stability seems to have ended up prevailing.

Having determined the main goals pursued by New Delhi, we now need to assess to what extent these goals corresponded to those of the Sri Lankan government as an important step for the identification of India's foreign policy strategies. According to the Sri Lankan diplomat interviewed in New Delhi in November 2008, Sri Lanka's main foreign policy goals were the 'protection of national security and integrity' and economic growth.[49] The central goal of maintaining the territorial integrity of Sri Lanka clearly corresponds to India's interest in avoiding setting a precedent of secessionism in its vicinity.

As far as India's goal of stability is concerned, it was broadly shared by Sri Lanka, even though stability was framed in terms of national security and economic growth. When it comes to the goal of peace and of how to put an end to the armed conflict, however, divergences emerge. While the governments of Sri Lanka had expressed their commitment to peace throughout the period analysed (e.g., GOSL 2004, 2005), with Rajpaksa's accession to power, the previous commitment to peace was broken and the temporal horizon of the goal of peace (still stated at the rhetorical level) was shifted. The objective of long-term peace, in fact, was used to justify the military offensive against the LTTE, as revealed by this speech by Rajapaksa:

> In the Presidential election held in 2005 you brought me to the leadership of our land. It was to battle against this misfortune of fate; to defeat it and to bring victory to the nation over it. It was to defeat the foundations of a cowardly peace based on the victory of separatist terror, and instead establish a genuine and dignified peace for our land.
>
> (GOSL 2009b)

As Uyangoda (2009) puts it, 'what was new in the Rajapaksa administration's approach was the goal of defeating, as opposed to weakening, the LTTE militarily and then making the LTTE irrelevant to any political solution to the ethnic conflict'. Starting from 2007, therefore, a military defeat of the LTTE or,

---

48 This can be explained with coalition politics in Tamil Nadu itself, where the DMK had to rely on the Congress for support for its minority government.
49 Interview with Sri Lankan diplomat, New Delhi, 19 November 2008.

in Rajapaksa's terminology, of the 'cowardly forces of terror' (GOSL 2009b), became the main goal of the Sri Lankan government – and the precondition for some kind of political settlement of the ethnic conflict. Sri Lanka's refusal, in March–May 2009, to give in to international actors pressurizing the government to agree to a humanitarian ceasefire is a further sign of Colombo's determination to defeat the LTTE, and its unwillingness to negotiate an agreement with the Tigers (Fuller 2009).

Therefore, a remarkable development in both India's and Sri Lanka's goals took place over the years. While, until 2006, both countries had a clear preference for a negotiated political settlement, from 2006 onwards the Rajapaksa administration increasingly believed in a military solution of the ethnic conflict through the defeat of the LTTE. India's support for this military campaign, which started around 2007, seems to reflect a shift in New Delhi's goals. This shift – and this was the most remarkable development in bilateral relations – represented an adaptation on the part of India to the objectives of Rajapaksa's government. When, in January 2009, the Indian minister of external affairs stated that a military victory represented a precondition for a return to normalcy, India had definitively abandoned its goal of a negotiated settlement and had conformed to Colombo's approach. That is, confronted with the foreseeable victory of the Sri Lankan military and with its own inability to influence events, India adapted its goals to the changed circumstances. Therefore, the convergence of goals between India and Sri Lanka did not take place because India managed to convince Sri Lanka of the correctness of its stand – which would have been a sign of a socialization process and for a successful leading or soft hegemonic strategy on the part of India. The process took place the other way round, with the impulse for change in the Indian attitude coming from the Sri Lankan side. As suggested above, it is difficult to determine what factors were crucial in leading to the change in India's approach. Most probably, a combination of factors – above all the desire to keep other countries out of the region and the realization that there was no return in Rajapaksa's approach – induced the Indian elite to change its mind.

When it comes to the issue of devolution and power sharing between Sinhalese and Tamils in Sri Lanka, Rajapaksa's commitment to a true devolution of powers was not convincing during the period analysed – nor was it later, since no forms of power devolution were implemented at the time of writing, one and a half years after the end of the war. The very fact that Rajapaksa's SLFP was allied with radical Sinhala parties like the JVP and the JHU did not represent a good precondition for a true devolution of powers (ICG 2007b: 20).

In his nationalist electoral manifesto, the so-called 'Mahinda Chintana' (Mahinda Vision), Rajapaksa explicitly stated his goal of preserving: '[...] the sovereignty of Sri Lanka, the territorial integrity, the *unitary structure of the State*, the identities of the different communities, the need to ensure peaceful co-existence amongst such communities [emphasis added]' (GOSL 2009d). Rajapaksa's reluctance to devolve power to Tamils became evident when it came to the de-merger of the Northern and Eastern provinces. When the Supreme Court issued its verdict about the de-merger, President Rajapaksa could have stepped in to neutralize the impact of the verdict, which was based only on procedural irregularities. But, as outlined above, he did not.

The fact that the so-called All-Party Representative Committee, which de facto included only the governing parties, was put in charge of the elaboration of a solution for devolution on the island is another sign indicating Rajapaksa's unwillingness to seriously find a solution with the participation of Tamil representatives. India reportedly pressurized the Sri Lankan government in 2006 and set the deadline of 15 December 2006 for the elaboration of devolution proposals by the APRC. The Sri Lankan government gave in to the Indian pressure, but, in the long run, Rajapaksa managed to procrastinate the APRC's final decision (ICG 2007b: 24). The final achievements of the APRC – the compilation of an interim report reiterating what was already written in the constitution – account for the limited readiness of the Sri Lankan government to allow for a wide-ranging devolution of powers.

Also on the issue of the safety of civilians during the last months of the war there was a divergence in goals between India and Sri Lanka. In fact, during the final phase of the conflict, the Sri Lankan military reportedly used heavy weapons inside the so-called 'no fire zone', in which thousands of civilians were caught (ICG 2010).[50] Moreover, Tamil refugees from the north were interned in camps, to which international aid organizations and journalists were denied access. Therefore, the fear of an ethnic cleansing on the part of the Sri Lankan government spread not only among the Tamil diaspora all over the world, but also among foreign observers.[51]

The most unequivocal divergence in goals between Sri Lanka and India is represented, however, by the issue of external involvement. In fact, it was the purchase of weapons from Pakistan and China that led to one of the most serious confrontations between India and Sri Lanka in 2007. These diverging goals, and particularly the clear clash on India's core goal of limiting the presence of external actors in Sri Lanka, confirm the lack of the requirements needed to assess a leadership strategy on the part of India. If we consider leadership as related to the socialization of the followers by the leader on the basis of a commonality of core goals, then India would have been able to induce the Sri Lankan government to stop fighting; to reach a negotiated settlement; and to take into consideration the aspirations of the Tamils. On the contrary, we can affirm that it was Sri Lanka that managed to induce a change in India's policy on the conflict.

---

50 According to a UN Report released in March 2011, as many as 40,000 civilians may have been killed in the final phase of the war (United Nations 2011: 41). Most of these civilian casualties were the result of government shelling (ibid.: ii).

51 For example, the Indian author Arundhati Roy in an article published in *The Times of India* accused the government of Sri Lanka of carrying out a genocide of Tamils, and equated the refugee camps with concentration camps. Colombo dismissed her suspicions as 'false and damaging assertions' (Ministry of Foreign Affairs – Sri Lanka 2009).

Overview: Unsuccessful Hegemonic Strategy

Table 4.1 provides an overview of the core and secondary goals of both India and Sri Lanka, of the foreign policy means employed by both countries, and of Sri Lankan perceptions about India.

Table 4.1   India–Sri Lanka: goals, means, and perceptions

		India	Sri Lanka
GOALS Core goals	*Issue Area* Conflict resolution: long term	Stability	Stability
	External actors	• Non-involvement of unfriendly or competing powers • Non-involvement of India	• Supply of weapons: involvement of other countries. • Keeping India engaged = Involvement of India • 2008–9: non-enmeshment of the international community on human rights issues, etc.
Secondary and instrumental goals	Conflict resolution: short term	• 2003–7: negotiated political settlement • 2007–9: military defeat of LTTE (undeclared goal)	• 2003–5: negotiated political settlement • 2006–9: military defeat of LTTE
	Future political settlement	• Unity	• Unity
		Devolution: • Federalism • From January 2008: 13th Amendment	Devolution (stated goal): • Under Rajapaksa: limited devolution (13th Amendment 'minus').
	Fate of civilians	2008–9: safety of civilians	2008–9: fight to the finish

MEANS
(actions/ reactions)
		2003–6:
		• Moderate persuasion
		• From 2005: requests and exhortations
		• 2006: dissuasion on issue of Chinese radar
		• Incentives (mainly to keep external powers out):
		  – Development assistance
		  – Economic cooperation
			2003–6:
			• No change in government's attitude: resistance
			• From 2006: increasingly confrontational attitude
			• 2006: compliance on issue of Chinese radar
			• Engaging India
			• No limitation in relations with other countries

	India	*Sri Lanka*
	2007–9: • Unspecified threat (Narayanan's statement) • Pressure • Indirect support: weakening LTTE network in Tamil Nadu • Tacit support: military equipment, training, patrolling • 2009: diplomatic support	2007–9: • Confrontation / resistance • Limited compliance, reassuring India
PERCEP-TIONS		2003–6: India as a potential military partner 2007–9: • India as bad neighbour and regional bully • India influenced by LTTE propaganda

Source: Author's compilation.

To sum up the results of the analysis carried out above, India's foreign policy towards Sri Lanka in the years between 2003–9 was characterized by

• a multiplicity of goals
• inconsistencies among goals
• multiple inconsistencies between goals and means.

As a result, New Delhi pursued a foreign policy characterized by many elements of contradiction and a high degree of ambiguity. While in the first years analysed this was not the case, with the changed approach to the conflict in the year 2007, India's foreign policy became more and more contradictory. While, on the one hand, India expressed its concerns about the military escalation of the conflict, on the other hand it contributed – albeit indirectly – to the escalation of the conflict through the provision of military assistance to Colombo. Moreover, India did not stop its economic and development cooperation with the Sri Lankan government despite its (stated) dissatisfaction with the way Rajapaksa was handling the crisis. Especially on the issue of Tamil civilians involved in the conflict, India adopted, at the rhetorical level, an increasingly sharp tone and even resorted to threats. But these threats were never implemented, no actions followed, and no sanctions were imposed.

This inconsistent approach on the part of India was related, to a great extent, to the diverging interests of the different actors involved. As in a typical two-level game, the Indian government had to cope, on the one hand, with the pressures coming from its coalition partners and civil society in Tamil Nadu and, on the other hand, with the international environment. Moreover, the government in New Delhi had its own score to settle with the LTTE. While the Tamil Nadu government induced India to highlight the goal of the safety of civilians, it was India's desire in particular to avoid an excessive involvement of external powers, especially China and Pakistan, in its sphere of influence that induced it to support a government towards which it otherwise did not feel much sympathy.

How can we define the strategy – or, better, the mix of strategies – pursued by India in its relations with Sri Lanka? A leadership strategy can be excluded because of the divergence in goals between the Indian and the Sri Lankan governments on important issues like the involvement of external actors or the role of India in the conflict with the LTTE. Moreover, if we consider India's moderate persuasion efforts between 2003–5 as attempts to socialize the government of Sri Lanka and induce it to follow the approach preferred by India, these efforts clearly failed – and not only because the nationalist SLFP came to power. India, therefore, did not manage to make its own goals the common goals of both countries.

Also an imperial strategy on the part of India has to be excluded for the whole period analysed since New Delhi never threatened to intervene militarily in Sri Lanka. The negative experience of the IPKF operation made this option taboo for New Delhi.

Since India pursued its own goals, adopting a variety of foreign policy means reaching from persuasion, to incentives, to threats, we can conclude that the Indian government adopted a hegemonic strategy. This is confirmed by Sri Lanka's negative perceptions of India's approach, as well as by Sri Lanka's reactions, which ranged from compliance paired with critique to resistance.

Going more into detail, this strategy can be considered as a set of different hegemonic strategies pursued, at times, simultaneously. From 2003–5, India's strategy can be defined as soft hegemonic since it was based on persuasion efforts paired with incentives. Starting from 2005, however, India's tone became harsher and its requests and exhortations met an increasing degree of resistance on the part of Sri Lanka. At the same time, economic and development-related incentives continued to be employed as instruments to gain leverage on Sri Lanka. These are indicators of an intermediate hegemonic strategy on the part of India.

In 2007, India adopted a hard hegemonic strategy towards Sri Lanka, with Narayanan's threat. This kind of approach was followed until the end of the period analysed, when India increased its diplomatic pressure on Colombo on issues related to the fate of civilians. The 'hard' character of this hegemonic strategy is confirmed by the perception in Sri Lanka of India as a bad neighbour and a regional hegemon, and by the refusal of Sri Lanka to comply with India's wishes (resistance). Interestingly, parallel to this hard hegemonic strategy, India continued to pursue an intermediate hegemonic strategy based on the provision of incentives (military training, defensive weapons, patrolling, etc.) to the Sri Lankan government with the aims of limiting the influence of external actors on it and of keeping some leverage on Sri Lanka.

When it comes to the issue of leverage, the question emerges about how successful India's strategies were. In the context of a goals-means analysis, the best way to assess the success or failure of certain policies is to take the actors' goals as a benchmark. If we do so, we see that India's approach to Sri Lanka was mainly unsuccessful. As one of the experts interviewed said, '[s]upporting is one thing, influencing is another thing. [...] You should have, in times of crisis like this, a certain leverage'.[52] India did not manage to persuade the Sri Lankan government of the value of a negotiated settlement to the crisis, it was not able to prevent it from buying weapons and entertaining economic relations with external countries, and it could not stop the indiscriminate killing of civilians during the last days of the war. On single issues, the Sri Lankan government complied with India's wishes, but only on matters of limited relevance like the acquisition of a radar system from China. On other topics, like devolution, Colombo temporarily gave in to India (as in the case of the APRC preliminary deliberations), but in the long run it followed its own approach.

Rather than being able to influence the Sri Lankan government, it seems that India itself has been influenced by Colombo. India's tacit support for the elimination of the LTTE and its overt support for Sri Lanka's motion at the United Nations Human Rights Council confirm this assessment. Moreover, India even expressed its approval of Rajapaksa's intention to devolve powers to the extent envisaged in the 13th Amendment – while it had previously supported a federal solution. Therefore, in the end, the Sri Lankan government turns out to be the more successful actor, which was able to reach its goals of defeating the LTTE and of inducing India (and other countries) to conform to its approach.

52   Interview with expert, New Delhi, 25 November 2008.

5 Nepal's Peace Process and India's Partially Successful Hegemonic Strategy

In the years 2002–8 momentous historical changes took place in Nepal. Starting from 1996, the country had been affected by a bloody civil war fought by the Communist Party of Nepal (Maoist) (CPN-M) with the goal of subverting the traditional feudal order based on the Hindu monarchy and establishing a secular republic. This conflict, with its total death toll of 13,000, posed a serious security concern for neighbouring India. Moreover, the domestic political situation in Nepal became extremely volatile after the Nepalese king Gyanendra dissolved parliament in 2002 and carried out a coup d'état in 2005. This chapter aims to assess India's policies towards Nepal between the start of the erosion of democracy in 2002 and the termination of the civil war through a power-sharing agreement, the abolition of monarchy through a popular movement, the re-establishment of democratic institutions, and the creation of an entirely new political system. The final point of the analysis is represented by the election of the Maoist leader Prachanda as the first prime minister of the Republic of Nepal in August 2008. As Mehta (2010: 130) puts it, '[a]n extreme Left-wing guerrilla force had earned the right to head the government through democratic means, fulfilling the mandate of the ten-year-long people's war to write a new constitution and declare Nepal a republic, dismantling the 240-year-old monarchy'.

After outlining the historical background and the reasons for the 'special character' of Indo–Nepalese relations, this chapter proceeds to detail the main events taking place in 2002–8. The subsequent analysis of India's approach to the peace process and the re-establishment of democratic institutions in Nepal reveals that India pursued, in 2002–5, a predominantly intermediate hegemonic strategy based on attempts to induce the Nepalese king to restore democracy. Between 2005 and 2006, New Delhi increased its pressure on the king whilst, at the same time, exercising a significant informal leadership role by promoting a dialogue between the Nepalese political parties and the Maoist rebels which ultimately put an end to the civil war. Finally, between 2006 and 2008, India pursued a soft hegemonic strategy and supported the implementation of the peace process in Nepal. Overall, India's predominantly hegemonic strategy can be considered to have been partially successful since New Delhi managed to keep its leverage on Nepal and contribute to the solution of the political crisis in the country, albeit in a reactive way.

Indo–Nepalese Relations: Historical Background

A look at the history of India–Nepal bilateral relations provides several insights useful for analysis. In fact, many issues that are presently contentious have their origins in the past, and historical events continue to deeply influence mutual perceptions in the two countries.

The first significant aspect that influences the relationship between India and Nepal, and in particular Nepalese self-consciousness, up to the present day is the fact that Nepal was never colonized by the British. At the same time, the country always had to cope with its geopolitical position as a small landlocked state placed between two great powers – China and India. Nepal, which emerged as a modern state from the expansion of the kingdom of Gorkha under Prithvi Narayan Shah in 1768, managed to keep its independent status, even though it had to accept the stationing of a British resident in Kathmandu in 1801 (Whelpton 2005: 41) and, in the second half of the 19th century, the subordination of its foreign relations to British control (Singh 1988: 86). When India was under British colonial domination, Nepal had to struggle to safeguard its – at least formal – independence from the two great Asian powers of that time: China, which had a supervisory role in Tibet, and British India. As Prithvi Narayan himself put it, as early as in the eighteenth century, his kingdom was comparable to 'a yam between two rocks' (Whelpton 2005: 37).

Nepal's position between India and China contributed to independent India's early efforts to include Nepal in its sphere of influence. In fact, given the immediate threat posed to the newly-established Indian state by the formation of the People's Republic of China in 1949 and their subsequent occupation of Tibet in 1950, India tried to formalize its close relationship with the strategically important Nepal through a Treaty of Peace and Friendship,[1] which is still in force. The treaty provided for an obligation of mutual consultation in case of tensions with neighbouring countries, while the letters of exchange accompanying the treaty stipulated the development of 'effective countermeasures' in case of security threats by third countries (Rose 1971: 186).[2] Because of these provisions, the 1950 treaty has been widely criticized by different political actors in Nepal as 'unequal' and its abrogation has been repeatedly demanded (Upreti 2004: 8). At the same time, the 'special character' of Indo–Nepalese relations was established by articles 6 and 7 of the treaty, which provided for the extension of reciprocal rights to citizens of both countries in matters of residence, trade, ownership of property, etc. This implies that the Indo–Nepalese border is entirely open, 'a border that, in many of

---

1 For the integral text of the treaty, see Gopal (1995: 8–11).
2 Moreover, India and Nepal concluded an Arms Assistance Agreement in 1965 under which India pledged to supply weapons, ammunition, and equipment for the entire Nepalese army while Nepal would import arms 'from and through the territory of India', thereby excluding a direct import from China. Even though Nepal receded from the agreement in 1966, India still considered it valid in later years, which led to the de facto blockade of 1989 mentioned below (Subedi 1997: 229–30).

the modern understandings of the term, is not a border' (Hachhethu/Gellner 2010: 136–7).

Besides the issue of Indian–Chinese competition, and India's efforts to limit the Chinese influence on this country, the second main factor consistently affecting bilateral relations between India and Nepal over the past decades has been India's influence on domestic political developments in Nepal. The main feature of India's repeated interferences with Nepal's internal affairs is a tug-of-war between the principles of democracy and stability, with India displaying a clear preference for stability in this strategically important neighbouring country. In 1951, for example, India mediated a compromise between the feudal Rana regime[3] and the Nepali Congress, a democratic party that had been founded on the model of the Indian National Congress, with which it had close relations. Even though India's mediation put an end to the Rana rule, it did not provide for the establishment of a genuinely democratic system in Nepal, which would have implied a radical uprooting and a major destabilization of the country (Rose 1971: 194; Singh 1988: 104). Similarly, when in 1960 the Nepalese king Mahendra established the *Panchayat* system, an undemocratic, partyless form of decentralization,[4] India despite not being satisfied with this development did not interfere with it. This policy was adopted by India in order not to alienate its smaller neighbour, whose strategic importance as a buffer had grown enormously since the Chinese attack and subsequent war with India in 1962 (Wagner 2005b: 168–70; Nayar/Paul 2004: 149–52). King Mahendra, on his part, made it clear that he wanted to follow a policy of 'diversification' of Nepal's international relations to reduce its dependence on India and that he was interested in cultivating relations with *both* India and China (Singh 1988: 153; Rose 1971: 209–13). Therefore, in 1961 the Nepalese king reached an agreement with China for the construction of a road from Kathmandu to the Nepal–Tibet border, which was immediately perceived by India as a security threat (ibid.: 239–242). As a reaction, India hardened its attitude towards the Nepalese government by loosening restrictions on the anti-monarchic Nepalese rebels operating from Indian territory (Singh 1988: 204; Whelpton 2005: 99). To counter China's influence, India also started a policy of massive economic aid to Nepal (Singh 1988: 200).

The third episode in which India played an important role in Nepal's democratic development, albeit in an indirect way, was the abolition of the *Panchayat* system in Nepal through a strong pro-democracy movement in 1990. The triggering factor for the 1990 upheaval was a trade and transit conflict with India, which led to the establishment of a de facto blockade by India in 1989. While the official reason

---

3 The Ranas were a dynasty of prime ministers established in 1846, who governed Nepal until 1951 (Whelpton 2005: 46–7).

4 The *panchayat* (assembly) system provided for different levels of decentralization, from the village up to the state level. However, only the representatives at the village level were elected directly by the people. Political parties were excluded from the political process and executive power remained, to a large extent, in the hands of the king (ICG 2005: 3–4).

for it was Nepal's refusal to sign a unified trade and transit treaty, the underlying reason was a renewed attempt by Nepal to balance against India. In fact, Nepal had bought weapons from China in 1988 without informing India, and this move was interpreted by New Delhi as a violation of the letter and the spirit of the 1950 treaty (Whelpton 2005: 113). To aggravate matters further, Nepal had introduced restrictive measures against Indian citizens, imposing restrictions on among others work permits and immigration, which were not envisaged in the 1950 treaty. The establishment of a blockade on the part of India was a clear signal to Kathmandu that New Delhi was not willing to tolerate Nepal's efforts to emancipate itself from India's control. According to Parajulee (2000: 191), 'the trade and transit dispute […] was the culmination point of a growing uneasiness with the structure of the bilateral relationship, characterized by Nepal's desire for "independence" and India's desire for "control"'.

As a consequence of the de facto blockade and of the hardship it caused, the Nepalese population started protesting against the government. This is how the people's movement (*Jan Andolan*) began, which ultimately led to the abolition of the *Panchayat* regime.[5] The ban on political parties was lifted and a new, democratic constitution was promulgated in November 1990, transforming Nepal from an absolute into a constitutional monarchy (Whelpton 2005: 113–21). The king, however, retained broad powers: the right to appoint and to dismiss the government, to limit fundamental freedoms, and to directly command the army. These were the provisions of the 1990 constitution that not only contributed to Nepal's chronic instability but were ultimately misused by King Gyanendra when he seized power between 2002–5. To summarize, India played an indirect, 'triggering' role in Nepal's transition to democracy in 1990. More than the introduction of democratic principles and practices, New Delhi was interested in keeping Nepal within its sphere of influence, if necessary by punishing it for any violation of this principle.

The most significant development in Nepal in the 1990s was the launch, in 1996, of the 'People's War' by the Communist Party of Nepal (Maoist). The roots of Maoism in Nepal can be traced back to the period of the anti-Rana struggle (1950–51), when a Nepalese communist movement was formed in India.[6] In the early 1970s, some extremist groups influenced by the Chinese Cultural Revolution and by the spread of Naxalism in India came into being.[7] Among them, the CPN-Maoist under the leadership of Pushpa Kamal Dahal, alias Prachanda, and Baburam Bhattarai, two 'young, well-educated and ideologically motivated leaders' (Muni 2003: 3), declared its People's War against the Nepalese state in February 1996 (Upreti 2008: 20–2).

---

5 For an account of the 'people's movement', see Raeper/Hoftun (1992).
6 For a detailed account of the formation and evolution of the Maoist movement in Nepal and its numerous splits, see Muni (2003: 1–10, 79–81).
7 The Indian Maoists came to be called Naxalites from the name of the village in West Bengal, Naxalbari, where they started their operations.

The ideology followed by the CPN-M was a mixture of Marxism, Leninism, and Maoism, with a stronger focus on the latter and an emphasis on the need to adapt Maoist ideology to the local conditions of Nepal (ibid.: 54–5).[8] In the context of the formal launch of their movement in February 1996, the Maoists formulated a charter with 40 demands to the government.[9] These included 'demands related to nationalism', which mainly referred to Nepal's relations with India and focused on the abolition of the 1950 treaty and of the Mahakali Treaty,[10] perceived as unequal and unfavourable to Nepal; 'demands related to the people's living', which focused on social justice, the provision of medical services and education, and the fight against corruption; and 'demands related to public welfare'. The latter addressed areas related to domestic governance. The Maoists specifically requested the drafting of a new constitution by elected representatives, the abolition of all special privileges of the king and the royal family, and the transformation of Nepal into a secular state. Moreover, they called for the abolition of the untouchable status of *Dalits* (Muni 2003: 12), for the end of caste discrimination, for gender equality, as well as for decentralization to minority communities. In the course of time, the Maoists focused especially on the goals related to the future of the Nepalese state as a 'new democracy', most notably the abolition of monarchy and the corresponding transformation of Nepal into a republican state, the establishment of an interim government, the election of a constituent assembly, and the drafting of a new constitution (ibid.: 19–24). As we will see, these demands turned into reality in the period analysed.

To achieve their goals, the Maoists had formed a People's Liberation Army (PLA). Their struggle was guided by Mao's principle of encircling the cities, starting from the rural areas, and their main support base was in the Western part of the country, where the living conditions were particularly poor; but it quickly expanded to other areas. The Maoists got support from indigenous people (*Janajatis*) and *Dalits*, who constitute 35 per cent of the Nepalese population (ibid.: 12). Their opposition to gender discrimination also allowed them to gain supporters among women, with large numbers of female cadres joining the PLA. However, the CPN-M also managed to gain sympathizers and supporters among the lower-middle class, particularly among teachers and students, who greatly contributed to the diffusion of their ideology.

In the first years of the People's War, the PLA carried out attacks against the Nepalese armed police as well as against activists of the Nepali Congress and the Communist Party of Nepal – Unified Marxist Leninist (CPN-UML) and government officials. However, they refrained from attacking the Royal Nepalese Army (RNA), which owed its allegiance to the king. In fact, the CPN-M had a

8 Later, this Nepalese version of Maoism was called *Prachanda Path*.
9 See '40-Point Demand of the Maoists', cited in Muni (2003: 82–7).
10 The treaty, signed in January 1996, regulated the use of the Mahakali River providing for an hydro-electric and irrigation project at Pancheshwor and for a redistribution of water shares from Tanakpur dam (Whelpton 2005: 189, 195).

'tactical understanding and tacit co-operation' with King Birendra, who was interested in weakening the democratic political parties, and therefore prevented the government from using the RNA to fight the Maoists (ibid.: 29–30).

However, after the death of Birendra and the coronation of his brother Gyanendra in 2001, an important change took place in the Maoist strategy: the carrying out of attacks against the army, and a transformation of the conflict into a full-fledged civil war. On 1 June 2001 crown prince Dipendra had shot his father and almost the entire royal family dead before taking his own life (Whelpton 2005: 211–16). This – still unsolved – 'palace massacre' deeply shocked the Nepalese nation. Gyanendra, the brother of the late king, succeeded to the throne. However, the Nepalese population suspected him of having been involved in the palace massacre and therefore never truly accepted him as the legitimate monarch. The Maoists immediately accused Gyanendra of the assassination and voiced the suspicion that the CIA and the Indian secret service Research and Analysis Wing (RAW) had been involved in the events. To a certain extent, therefore, the Maoists used the national trauma provoked by the royal massacre to radicalize their fight. In fact, they had managed in the meantime to strengthen their army by collecting weapons through raids on the police, and had created a financial base for their fight through bank robberies and extortion, as well as through funds donated by sympathizers in India (ibid.: 206). In this way, they had extended their influence to all of Nepal's 75 districts (Mishra 2004: 627) and had established 'people's governments' in many areas, replacing the institutions of the Nepalese state (Whelpton 2005: 209; Upreti 2008: 113). After some attempts to hold peace talks under a ceasefire agreement in the period between August and November 2001, the Maoists broke the ceasefire and started attacking, for the first time, the Royal Nepalese Army (Mishra 2004: 637; *The New York Times* 2001). As a reaction, the government declared a state of emergency and started deploying the RNA to fight the rebels. However, even though the RNA was heavily supported by external forces, notably India and the USA, it had difficulties in asserting itself against the Maoists.

Nepal's Peace Process

As outlined above, the analysis of India's strategies in dealing with the peace process in Nepal covers the years 2002–8. This time span can be divided into three main phases. The first phase is characterized by the gradual erosion of democratic principles starting with the dissolution of parliament by King Gyanendra on 4 October 2002 and ending in his coup d'état on 1 February 2005. The second phase covers the period of Gyanendra's autocratic rule up to 24 April 2006, when a popular movement forced the king to reinstate democracy. Finally, the third phase is represented by the period of democratic transition until the establishment of a democratically elected government under Maoist leadership on 18 August 2008.

2002–5: The Erosion of Democracy

In 2002, with the justification of fighting the Maoist rebellion more efficiently, King Gyanendra gradually curtailed democratic liberties and focused on increasing the concentration of power in his own hands. On 4 October 2002, Gyanendra announced the dismissal of Prime Minister Deuba (Nepali Congress) and his cabinet, dissolved the parliament and nominated Lokendra Bahadur Chand of the royalist Rashtriya Prajatantra Party (RPP) as prime minister. This appointment took place without any consultation with the political parties (Ghosh 2003).

The subsequent years were marked by a consolidation of the king's power and, at the same time, by the growing tensions amongst the three main political forces that had emerged in Nepal: the king, the Maoists, and the political parties. The monarchy had entered into active politics and was trying to retain its position of power despite growing criticism. The king's main goal was the defeat of the Maoists – and to achieve this goal he gained the support of international actors like the USA, India, and the UK, which feared a further spread of Maoist violence in Nepal and, ultimately, the 'loss' of Nepal to China's influence. The political parties, on their part, wanted to re-establish a democratically elected government and were, overall, favourable to the principle of constitutional monarchy. The Maoists, on the contrary, were fighting for the abolition of monarchy and for the transformation of Nepal into a republic. Hence, there were huge divergences between the political parties and the Maoists in terms of their goals. However, both the political parties and the Maoists were interested in limiting the influence of the RNA as a political actor, and emphasized the need of bringing it under political control.

The tensions between the political forces in Nepal were exacerbated in January 2003, when the Maoists negotiated a ceasefire with the RNA (Baral 2004: 75); the political parties were, however, excluded from these negotiations.[11] After having agreed to the ceasefire, the Maoists adopted more moderate tones, emphasizing their willingness to hold peace talks and even their readiness to accept a constitutional monarchy, if this was what the people wanted. The democratic parties particularly feared the formation of a coalition between the monarchy and the Maoists, and suspected that the CPN-M would end up supporting Gyanendra's regime.

Dissatisfied with the situation, and particularly with the government installed by the king, the parties started organizing strikes, protests and road blockades. In May 2003, after weeks of protests, they managed to force the prime minister installed by the king to resign. However, no significant change took place, as on 4 June King

---

11   As a precondition for the ceasefire, the Maoists had requested the government to declassify their organization as a terrorist group (Nepalnews 2003a). The Maoists' decision to agree on a ceasefire might have been related to the growing strength of the RNA, which after the attacks of 9/11 had been supported much more extensively than before by external countries, especially by the USA. In the context of the war on terrorism, the USA had listed the CPN-M as a terrorist organization and had added a military component to their aid programme to Nepal (Manchanda 2003b, 2003a ; Muni 2008b: 181).

Gyanendra replaced him with another royalist from the RPP, Surya Bahadur Thapa (Nepalnews 2003b). This happened despite protests by the democratic political parties, which continued to agitate against the appointment of a candidate who did not enjoy democratic support (ICG 2003: 1).

In the meantime, the peace negotiations between the Maoists and the government stalled, violence spread again and, ultimately, the ceasefire collapsed in August 2003. By 2004, the Maoists controlled almost 80 per cent of Nepal's territory and, with a weeklong blockade of Kathmandu in September 2004, it became clear that they were succeeding in their efforts to move from the rural areas towards the cities (Manchanda 2004b).

2005–6: From Gyanendra's Coup to Jan Andolan II

The erosion of democratic principles reached its apex when King Gyanendra, supported by the RNA, carried out a coup d'état by dismissing the government and enforcing direct royal rule on 1 February 2005. Moreover, citing the constitution of 1990, Gyanendra declared a state of emergency. The fundamental freedoms were restricted, several newspapers, and television and broadcasting channels were banned, demonstrations were prohibited, and all the leaders of Nepal's democratic parties were placed under house arrest. Gyanendra arbitrarily appointed a 10-member council of ministers of which he assumed chairmanship (Hutt 2006: 120). The king justified his intervention with the necessity of fighting the Maoist rebellion more effectively. However, Gyanendra's takeover hardly improved the security situation in Nepal and did not lead to any significant success in the fight against the Maoists (Upreti 2008: 146–7).

Nevertheless, Gyanendra's coup d'état led to what can probably be defined as the most turbulent phase in Nepal's history (Baral 2008: 32). The political parties, united in a loose coalition called Seven Party Alliance (SPA),[12] intensified their agitation and became increasingly averse to monarchy. Gyanendra's coup, therefore, opened a new dialogue between the democratic parties and the Maoists. After the coup, Maoist leader Prachanda seized the opportunity to incite the SPA to join the Maoists in their opposition to the king (Alam 2005). In the end, the king's seizure of power made a rapprochement between the other political forces in Nepal possible, thereby laying the foundation for the peace process and, as a consequence, for the end of the civil war in Nepal (Mehta 2008: 135).

Besides the Maoists and the democratic parties, civil society assumed a decisive role in opposing the king in April 2006. Two months earlier, the king had called for municipal elections, which were widely perceived as a farce (Gellner 2007: 82). The democratic parties boycotted the elections and called for a general strike on 6

---

12 The following parties formed the SPA: Nepali Congress (NC), Communist Party of Nepal (Unified Marxist Leninist, UML), Nepal Sadbhavana Party (Anandidevi, NSP (A)), Nepali Congress (Democratic, NC(D)), Janamorcha Nepal, Nepal Workers and Peasant Party (NWPP), and United Left Front (ULF). See ICG (2007a: 1).

April (Chandrasekharan 2006), and from this strike, which was protracted beyond the originally planned three days, a popular movement emerged. With reference to the movement of 1990, this new rebellion was called *Jan Andolan II*. Very soon it became the largest mass protest to ever have taken place in Nepal. 'What happened on 24 April 2006 was incredible – a collection of one to two million people out on the streets of Kathmandu breached the red lines around the Royal Palace. It seemed all of Kathmandu, including a few Royalists, were out there on the streets' (Mehta 2008: 135). The protest was not limited to Kathmandu, where the largest numbers of protesters gathered, but it spread to at least 65 out of 75 districts of Nepal (Cherian 2006b). The crowds violated the curfew imposed by the king and continued their protest despite the security forces' readiness to use violence against them – ultimately, 21 people died and over 4,000 were injured in *Jan Andolan II* (Gellner 2007: 83; Amnesty International 2007).[13] The SPA requested the king to solve the crisis by adopting a roadmap based on the following steps: reinstating parliament, forming an all-party government, commencing talks with the Maoists, and carrying out elections for a constituent assembly.

Given the ongoing protests, on 21 April 2006, the king declared that he was ready to return to the status quo that preceded his coup and invited the parties to nominate a new prime minister (ICG 2006b: 10). However, this did not include a restoration of parliament, which had been dissolved in 2002. Moreover, guaranteeing the nomination of a new prime minister did not imply that the king would not dismiss him as he did with Sher Bahadur Deuba on 1 February 2005 (ibid.: 11). Since the demonstrators on the streets were not willing to give in to such a compromise, the protests intensified. Finally on 24 April, confronted with a situation that became almost impossible to control, King Gyanendra was forced to put an end to his absolute rule by announcing the reinstatement of the lower house of parliament (UNMIN 2006a).

2006–8: Democratic Transition

Gyanendra's declaration put an end to *Jan Andolan II* and paved the way for the signing of a Comprehensive Peace Agreement (CPA) with the Maoists, and for a period of democratic transition and state restructuring. On 27 April, the Maoists declared a ceasefire. On 28 April, the Parliament held its first session since 2002, and two days later an SPA-government headed by Girija Prasad Koirala of the Nepali Congress was formed. In its historic session of 18 May 2006, the parliament affirmed its own sovereignty, leaving only a representative function to the king (Gellner 2007: 83). It was also decided that subsequent Nepalese governments would take the denomination *Government of Nepal* instead of *His Majesty's Government*. Similarly, the *Royal Nepalese Army* was to be renamed as *Nepal Army* and was to be put under the control of the government (*The Kathmandu Post*

---

13 The Maoists supported the protest movement, for example by forcing villagers to join the uprisings in the cities (Gellner 2007: 83).

2006). Moreover, Nepal was transformed into a secular state with the removal of the adjective 'Hindu' from its official denomination (ibid.).

At the same time, the government started negotiating with the Maoists, who had been declassified as a terrorist organization. The former conflict parties reached a power-sharing agreement providing for the creation of a new interim government with the participation of the Maoists. Moreover, the government agreed to the Maoists' request to dissolve the current parliament, in which the rebels were not represented (Jha 2006),[14] and to form a new interim parliament, in which 73 out of 330 representatives would be Maoists. A constituent assembly would be elected by June 2007 with the aim of writing a new constitution (Gellner 2007: 85). The rebels, on their part, agreed to dismantle their parallel institutions and to renounce the use of violence. In order to avoid a deadlock in negotiations, the conflict parties left the final decision on the contentious issue of the fate of the monarchy to the constituent assembly. These provisions were included in the Comprehensive Peace Agreement of 21 November 2006, which officially put an end to the Nepalese civil war, after more than a decade (UNMIN 2006b). The CPA also provided for the management of arms and armies under the supervision of the United Nations. It was decided that the Maoist combatants would be confined to cantonments and their weapons would be put under the supervision of the United Nations; similarly, the Nepal Army would be confined to its barracks and would store the same number of arms as those stored by the Maoists. In January 2007, the United Nations Security Council (2007) resolved to establish a political mission in Nepal (United Nations Mission in Nepal, UNMIN) to monitor the management of arms and armed personnel, to assist in the monitoring of the ceasefire agreement, and to support the planning, preparation, and conduct of the constituent assembly elections.

In January 2007, an interim constitution came into effect, the old parliament was dissolved and the planned interim constituent assembly with Maoist participation started working. On 1 April 2007, the new government containing five Maoist ministers was sworn in (eKantipur 2007; *International Herald Tribune* 2007).

The inclusion of Maoist representatives in the interim government represented a major step forward in the integration of Maoists in Nepal's democratic institutions and, overall, in the peace process. The Maoists, however, also made use of their position of strength to exercise some pressure on the government for their own goals: the CPN-M ministers pulled out of the government in September 2007, over the dispute about the role of monarchy and the future form of state in Nepal (Whelpton 2008: 189) and Prachanda even resorted to an ultimatum to obtain the deposition of the king, threatening Koirala's government with a new armed rebellion (NZZOnline 2007).

Finally, the government gave in and on 23 December 2007 the Maoists and the SPA signed a 23-point Agreement (UNMIN 2007), in which the following issues

---

14 Moreover, the parliament reinstated by the king had no political legitimacy since its mandate had expired in May 2004 (Krämer 2006).

were settled: the Maoists would rejoin the government; in return, the SPA declared its readiness to abolish monarchy. Therefore, the interim constitution had to be amended to include, among other things, the following provision: with the first session of the constituent assembly, Nepal would become a federal democratic republic.

Elections for the new parliament, which was also Nepal's constituent assembly, finally took place after two postponements on 10 April 2008. The elections were the first to take place across the whole country since 1999. Before the elections, some violent incidents occurred that were carried out mainly by members of the Young Communist League (YCL), the youth organization of the CPN-M. Several Maoist activists were also killed during the pre-election period. However, despite intimidations, threats and electoral frauds by the youth wings of most of the political parties, international observers mainly judged the elections as sufficiently fair and free and, overall, as successful (ICG 2008b: 9–12). Even though they were not able to reach an absolute majority, with 202 seats out of 575,[15] the Maoists achieved a 'stunning victory [...] which surprised the world' (Mehta 2010: 125).[16]

The new constituent assembly held its first session on 28 May 2008, during which it almost unanimously proclaimed the Republic (560 votes out of 564) (eKantipur 2008a). With that, the House brought an end to the 240-year-old Shah dynasty. King Gyanendra was requested to leave his palace within fifteen days.

After this first session of the parliament, it was quite a long time before a new president was elected and a new government was formed. The Maoists, who initially were in favour of a presidential system but had not been able to get their way, wanted to have their leader Prachanda elected both as president and as prime minister. However, since the Nepali Congress and the CPN-UML claimed at least one of these functions for themselves, Prachanda later focused his attention on the more influential position, that of prime minister. Finally, at the end of July, the two parties reached an agreement. The parliament elected Ram Baran Yadav, the secretary general of the Nepali Congress, as president with a scant majority of 308 votes out of 590, and the former rebel leader Prachanda as the new prime minister with 464 votes out of 594 (eKantipur 2008b). On 18 August 2008, Prachanda finally took charge of office as the first prime minister of the Federal Democratic Republic of Nepal (eKantipur 2008c).

India's Foreign Policy Strategies Towards Nepal

Having illustrated the main events of 2002–8, India's foreign policy strategies towards Nepal will be analysed with specific reference to this country's internal political crisis and to the peace and democratization process. As in the previous chapter, the analysis will proceed by identifying the foreign policy means employed by India, the reactions and perceptions of Nepal, as well as the two

---

15   A further 26 seats were allotted by the cabinet (ICG 2008b: 23).
16   For an analysis of election results, see ICG (2008b).

countries' goals and the degree of their compatibility. Since different actors were involved to varying degrees in Nepalese politics during the period analysed, the 'counterpart' of the Indian government will vary in the course of the analysis. During the first phase the king and his government will be the actors under scrutiny since they were clearly recognisable as the executive. With the progressive delegit-imization of the king in the second phase, the counterpart of the Indian government becomes more difficult to identify. The Maoists and the SPA also need to be taken into account as important actors with whom India interacted.

Incentives, Pressure, and Informal Mediation: India's Foreign Policy Means

In the years 2002–5, which were characterized by the gradual erosion of democracy in Nepal brought about by King Gyanendra, India's approach towards this country was marked by the recourse to incentives of different kinds as well as to persuasion.

India's 'traditional' position on the domestic political settlement in Nepal was the so-called 'twin-pillar' (or 'two pillar') approach: New Delhi was in favour of a coexistence of the two principles of constitutional monarchy and multiparty democracy as it had been in place until 2002 (Mishra 2004: 639). However, after King Gyanendra dissolved the parliament and dismissed the cabinet on 4 October 2002, India's approach towards Nepal was characterized, at the verbal level, by very moderate protests, neutral reaffirmations of India's position as well as by the recourse to soft persuasion efforts and expressions of commitment.[17] On the day after King Gyanendra dissolved the parliament, the Indian position was conveyed in a MEA press briefing:

> India [...] hopes that the present crisis will be resolved soon within the framework of constitutional processes, paving the way for elections at the earliest and installation of a democratically elected Government in the interest of peace, stability and development in Nepal. Any interim arrangement should be based on consultation and consensus.
>
> (MEA 2002c)

In the same context, India reiterated its traditional twin-pillar approach to Nepal, which was repeated throughout the first phase analysed. The idea that 'a national consensus needs to be evolved based on the principles of multiparty democracy and constitutional monarchy' was related to the belief that such a consensus would be the best guarantee for a successful fight against the Maoist insurgency (MEA 2003e). At the same time, India consistently emphasized that this twin-pillar approach corresponded to the popular will of the Nepalese citizens, thereby trying to avoid charges that it was attempting to hegemonically shape events in

---

17 See, for example, MEA (2003e): 'India would, as always, continue to extend its support to Nepal in the spirit of the longstanding and traditional friendship between our two countries'.

Nepal. The following statement by External Affairs Minister Sinha in a television interview highlights the extent to which India was worried about appearing to interfere in Nepal's internal affairs:

> I would very humbly plead, I would plead with all the humility at my command, that the statements issued by India should not be taken as interference in the internal affairs of Nepal because we have no such intention at all. We have scrupulously kept away from any interference in the internal affairs of Nepal. I am aware of the fact that there are elements which often bring this up as a sign of India's interference. We have not done so. We give our advice only when we are asked for this advice.
>
> (MEA 2003d)

India's main concern during the first phase analysed was the spread of the Maoist insurgency in Nepal and the Nepalese state's difficulties in coping with it. In September 2004, the Indian and Nepalese prime ministers defined the Maoist insurgency as 'a common threat to the security of both [...] countries' (MEA 2004d). In fact, India itself had (and still has) to cope with Maoist rebels, the so-called Naxalites, who are active in a growing number of Indian states.[18] The open border between India and Nepal reportedly allowed for contacts between Nepalese Maoists and Naxalites (Lakshman 2002) and India feared that a seizure of power by Maoists in Nepal would boost the Naxalite insurgency (Ramana 2002).[19]

It was against this background that India supported the Nepalese government's fight against the Maoists by providing assistance and weapons to the RNA and the Nepalese police. As illustrated in Table 5.1, India was Nepal's main supplier of weapons.[20]

While this significant share of Nepal's total arms imports covered by India was primarily related to the common goal of defeating Maoism, India also used weapons supplies as an incentive to induce Nepal to comply with its requests. For example, India reportedly made the provision of further military help dependent upon the agreement on the part of the Deuba government on a new extradition treaty. India wanted this in order to cope with cross border crime and with the

---

18 On Naxalism in India, see, for example, Ramana (2008), Singh (2006, on international linkages chapter 7.2). In 2005, Prime Minister Manmohan Singh reported to parliament that 170 Indian districts were controlled by Naxalites (Kaushik 2006: 267) and defined left-wing extremism as 'the single-biggest internal security challenge ever faced by our country' (Muni 2008a: 17).

19 On the problems of border security on the open Indo-Nepalese border, see Mehta (2001).

20 According to SIPRI data and estimates, in 2002 India delivered at least three (but possibly up to 31) ex-Indian armoured personal carriers (APCs) of the type Casspir; between 2003 and 2004, it delivered 10 light helicopters to Nepal's police to be used to fight against Maoist rebels as well as two further helicopters; moreover, in 2004 about 100 multi-purpose APCs were delivered as aid to Nepal (with Nepal covering 33 per cent of the costs). Finally, in 2005 one more helicopter was donated to Nepal. See SIPRI (2011a).

Table 5.1 Esimated values* of arms imports to Nepal, 2002–8 (in millions of constant 1990 US$)

	2002	2003	2004	2005	2006	2007	2008	Total
Belarus		5						5
China				1				
Czech Republic							1	1
India	0**	4	22	4				29
Poland	3		3					6
Russia			7					7
UK			1					1
Ukraine	5							5
Total	8	9	32	5			1	55

* Trend indicator values.

** A 0 indicates that the value of deliveries is less than US$ 0.5m.

Source: SIPRI (2011a).

suspected activities of the Pakistani secret service Inter-Services Intelligence (ISI) in Nepal (Manchanda 2004b).[21]

Besides military assistance, India continued to provide development aid to Nepal as it had done in the previous decades.[22] After Bhutan, Nepal remained the second largest South Asian recipient of non-plan grants and loans from the Indian MEA (Price 2004: 13).[23] Even though a sharp decline in India's aid to Nepal from Rs. 1,090 million to 590 million took place from 2001/02 to 2004/05, this can be traced back to the redistribution of MEA grants and loans towards Africa, which in the same time span saw an increase of aid from Rs. 50 million to 1,050 million (ibid.).

Between 2002 and 2005, therefore, India's overall relations with Nepal continued to be good despite the erosion of democratic principles promoted by the king. Albeit disapproving of the king's moves curtailing democracy in Nepal, India employed mainly soft and intermediate hegemonic means and continued to support the king's fight against the Maoists.

21 In the following years, however, the signing of a new extradition treaty was repeatedly postponed.
22 India had been providing aid to Nepal since the 1950s and had been the country's largest donor between the mid–1960s and the 1970s. A large part of India's aid was directed at infrastructure projects with a strategic dimension aimed at balancing against China (Khadka 1997: 1047–8).
23 According to an Indian government official dealing with Nepal, a large part of India's assistance to Nepal taking place at the level of capacity building, technical cooperation, advice, for example in the judiciary sector, etc. is not even quantified. Interview with government official, New Delhi, 1 December 2008.

Things changed slightly, however, during the second phase under scrutiny. King Gyanendra's coup d'état on 1 February 2005 provoked a policy change on the part of New Delhi. In fact, India – together with the US, UK, and EU – reacted to the coup by putting diplomatic pressure (denunciations and criticism) on Gyanendra, defining the king's action as 'a cause of grave concern to India' (MEA 2005p). Besides diplomatic pressure, at the level of verbal statements, New Delhi resorted to typical tools of hard persuasion (exhortations and requests, e.g. Rajya Sabha 2005b) combined with soft persuasion efforts (mainly expressions of India's wishes and preferences, e.g. MEA 2005q) and expressions of India's commitment 'to supporting all efforts aimed at restoring political stability and economic prosperity in Nepal' (ibid.). New Delhi particularly requested the king to restore the freedom of the media, to release political leaders, journalists, and human rights activists, and to reinstate multiparty democracy (e.g., MEA 2005n).

At the diplomatic level, New Delhi underlined its pressure by refusing to take part in the thirteenth SAARC summit, which was set to take place in Dhaka at the beginning of February 2005 citing 'recent developments in our neighbourhood, which have caused us grave concern' but not explicitly mentioning Nepal (MEA 2005m). While this move was initially perceived as a critique of Gyanendra, it later became clear that this was also related to the political situation in Bangladesh (Stachoske 2005: 133).[24] In any case, King Gyanendra was not impressed by India's announcement to boycott the summit (ibid.) and did not undertake any measures to satisfy India's demands for a restoration of democracy.

At the level of foreign policy actions, India reinforced its verbal efforts by placing sanctions on Gyanendra's regime. Immediately after the coup, New Delhi, together with Great Britain, imposed an embargo on weapons supplies to Nepal (MEA 2005j; Rajya Sabha 2005c). However, even though King Gyanendra did not display any intention to restore democracy, India continued to provide training to Nepalese troops, and in April 2005 New Delhi took into consideration a resumption of arms supplies after the king lifted emergency regulations (Varadarajan 2005a; MEA 2005d; Suryanarayana 2005). India's unchanged support for the king was further confirmed by its support for Nepal at the United Nations Commission on Human Rights: Together with the US and the UK, India managed to block a resolution aimed at reprimanding Nepal and appointing a Special Rapporteur on the human rights situation (Bidwai 2005).

New Delhi's cooperation with Gyanendra's regime can be explained by India's belief in monarchy as the best guarantor of stability in Nepal (Muni 2008b: 186). Moreover, as Muni (ibid.) points out, external actors – among them India – were interested in the survival of the monarchy in order 'to have one more political player on the Nepalese political chessboard so as to be helpful in pursuance of their respective vital national interests and also for manipulating situations that are seen to be politically uncomfortable'.

One more factor determining the Indian government's interest in resuming arms

24 See Chapter Six.

supplies and in continuing to provide training to the RNA can be considered to have been India's traditional desire to limit China's (and Pakistan's) influence in Nepal. India especially feared that the weapons embargo would lead Gyanendra to procure arms from China, as had already happened in 1988.[25] This fear was further reinforced by an intensification of diplomatic interactions between Nepal and both China and Pakistan in the aftermath of Gyanendra's coup (Bidwai 2005).

The half-hearted nature of India's pressure on the king was further confirmed, in April 2006, by India's ambiguous dealing with the increasingly tense situation during *Jan Andolan II*. The huge support that the movement found among the Nepalese population made it clear to Indian policy-makers that the situation was getting out of control and that they needed to undertake something to avoid a dramatic escalation of violence. Therefore, the Indian government increased its pressure on the king, requesting Gyanendra to release the political leaders, professionals, and students who had been arrested.[26] India mixed its exertion of pressure with hard and soft persuasion efforts (expressions of concern, exhortations, as well as expressions of hope, advice).[27]

On 21 April 2006, India made its last high-level attempt to persuade the king to undo his move by sending a special envoy to Kathmandu. The Indian prime minister chose Karan Singh – the son of the last maharaja of Kashmir and a relative of the Nepalese monarchs – as an envoy. He had served as a diplomat, a minister, and an MP for the Congress Party. Despite Karan Singh's affinity to the Nepalese royal family, he did not manage to persuade Gyanendra to make substantial concessions.[28] However, the compromise solution proposed by Gyanendra on 21 April, which envisaged the transfer of executive power to an SPA-government, was welcomed by New Delhi (MEA 2006n). In fact, this solution corresponded to India's traditionally preferred twin-pillar approach. Similarly, other countries like the US, the UK, China, and also the EU welcomed the king's announcement (ICG 2006b: 10–11). As a consequence of this action, however, India and the rest of the international community lost their credibility in the eyes of the Nepalese population (ibid.: i) and of the SPA, who were not satisfied by the king's limited concessions. As we will see in the section devoted to Nepal's perceptions, the

---

25 Interview with journalist, New Delhi, 10 December 2008.
26 For example MEA (2006e): 'The situation is an evolving one. [...] we are concerned over the arrests and detention, once again, of several political leaders, professionals and students which we *strongly deplore*. These actions by the government in Nepal are counter-productive. [...] We *urge* the *immediate* release of those arrested and a return to the path of dialogue and reconciliation [emphasis added]'.
27 For an example of hard persuasion, see MEA (2006o); for soft persuasion, see, for example, MEA (2006f): 'We hope that in view of the seriousness of the situation, a genuine effort will be made by His Majesty's Government of Nepal to initiate a dialogue with the political parties at the earliest'.
28 Instead, Karan Singh pressurized the parties to let the king leave in a dignified manner. Interview with expert, New Delhi, 28 November 2008.

Nepalese population interpreted India's choice of Karan Singh as an envoy as a clear political statement and a signal of New Delhi's support for monarchy. [29]

The dramatic unfolding of events on Nepal's streets ultimately made it impossible for India to continue with its ambiguous policy of support for the monarchy, which clearly contrasted with the popular will in Nepal. The protests were growing, and New Delhi apparently understood that the king could not be supported politically anymore. As an interviewee put it, 'the king had become unpopular, there was a great unrest among the population. And in Nepal we cannot say "It's your business!" because of the open border'.[30]

Therefore, a sudden turn-about in India's approach to Nepal took place: on 22 April 2006 Indian Foreign Secretary Shyam Saran officially put an end to the twin-pillar approach and adopted a policy of appeasement and persuasion targeted at the Nepalese population:

> We have supported the restoration of democracy in Nepal. When we have been saying the twin pillars of constitutional monarchy and multiparty democracy, we have been reflecting only what the people of Nepal and the political parties in Nepal have wanted. If today or tomorrow the people of Nepal wish to see a different future for themselves, different kind of political arrangements for themselves, that is for the people of Nepal to decide, not for India to decide.
>
> (MEA 2006k)

On the one hand, India pursued the path cited above, trying to induce the king to reinstate democracy but, at the same time, supporting him until the situation threatened to run out of control; on the other hand, at a more informal level, India greatly contributed to the peace and democratization process in Nepal. In fact, during the highest phase of the popular uprising in April 2006, India reportedly played a constructive role in avoiding a violent quelling of the mass movement by influencing the Royal Nepal Army (Cherian 2006a). Even more importantly, India informally mediated between the Maoists and the SPA between 2004–5, allowing for a dialogue that ultimately led to the signing of the CPA and to the fall of the king. In February 2004, a secret meeting reportedly took place in Lucknow between Madhav Nepal of the CPN-UML and CNP-M members (Manchanda 2004a). Further rounds of talks ultimately led to the signing of the so-called 'New Delhi Agreement' (Mehta 2008: 135) in November 2005. In this document, both the SPA and the Maoists agreed on the central issues that were later included in the CPA (UNMIN 2005). While the exact procedures of India's 'backing' (Gellner 2007: 81) of the dialogue between the Maoists and the Nepalese parties are not known, the experts interviewed agreed that it was an informal process based on personal contacts between Indian and Nepalese political leaders. The Indian government, in any case, allowed the leaders of the CPN-M, which had been

---

29   Interview with expert, New Delhi, 7 November 2008.
30   Interview with government official, New Delhi, 27 November 2008.

labelled as a terrorist organization in 2001 (Mishra 2004: 637), to travel to India.[31] Beyond this, the Indian interviewees emphasized that New Delhi's role was limited to the provision of a neutral discussion forum – basically, to the provision of good offices – but that no actual mediation efforts or micro-management was carried out by India.[32] Some Nepalese sources, however, argue that India's involvement must have been more extensive and that the peace process was, in fact, 'micro-managed' by New Delhi (Jha 2008).

To summarize, if we look at the foreign policy means employed by New Delhi in the second phase under scrutiny (2005–6), a contradictory pattern emerges: on the one hand, New Delhi increased its diplomatic pressure on King Gyanendra and even resorted to a hard tool like an embargo to underscore its dissatisfaction with the royal coup; on the other hand, India did not give up its twin-pillar approach until the escalation of *Jan Andolan II* and continued to support the king by training the RNA for the fight against the Maoists. Simultaneously, and even more paradoxically, India promoted informal talks between the Maoist rebels and the Nepalese parties which ultimately led to a peaceful solution to the war, but which also made the formation of an anti-monarchic coalition possible in the first place.

With King Gyanendra's reinstatement of democracy on 24 April 2006, a new phase of India's involvement in Nepal's process of peace and democratization began. This phase was characterized by India's clear support for the peace process, particularly for the successful implementation of the provisions of the CPA and the 'restructuring' of the Nepalese state (Baral 2008). Besides the recourse to verbal tools of soft persuasion and diplomatic praise, India also supported the 2008 elections and facilitated further negotiations between the CPN-M and the other political parties, and in 2007, between the Madhesis of the Tarai and the interim government.

The process of the facilitation of talks between the Maoists and the political parties promoted by India continued during the third phase analysed. The announcement of the ceasefire by the CPN-M on 27 April 2006, in particular, was followed by further negotiations. India's involvement became more and more official, and even the Maoists gradually renounced their anti-India rhetoric and actively sought India's support (FES 2006: 4). The composition of the Indian government favoured this rapprochement. In fact, the Congress-led United Progressive Alliance (UPA) central government was supported on this matter by the Left Front. Some members of this coalition of leftist parties, among them Sitaram Yechuri of the Communist Party of India (Marxist) (CPI(M)), had close personal contacts to the CPN-M and played a central role in convincing the Maoists to fully join the peace process (ibid.). Later, India continued to keep a watchful eye on the implementation of the peace process. New Delhi was particularly interested

---

31 Interview with journalist, New Delhi, 10 December 2008.
32 Ibid.; Interview with expert, New Delhi, 7 November 2008; Interview with government officials, New Delhi, 20 and 27 November 2008.

in avoiding excessive delays in the elections,[33] and again played a constructive role by getting involved in a mediation between the interim government and the representatives of the Madhesis (Pattanaik 2008b: 224). The inhabitants of the Tarai, the southern strip of plain territory bordering India, had long been discriminated against by the Nepalese monarchy because of their affinity to Indians, from whom they are 'indistinguishable culturally' (Hachhethu/Gellner 2010: 137). During the Maoist 'People's War', however, Madhesis developed a new consciousness and started calling for political participation in the 'new' Nepal.[34]

In early 2008, the United Democratic Madhes Front (UDMF), a coalition of small Madhesi parties, called for an extensive autonomy of the Tarai and launched its own popular movement at the beginning of February 2008 to underscore its claims. On 27 February, after the entire Tarai was paralyzed for 16 days, the government agreed on some of the Madhesis' requests.[35] The issue of the creation of an autonomous Madhes province was, however, very controversial. Therefore, it was decided that the matter would be left to the constituent assembly to resolve.

India played an important role in these negotiations and managed to convince the UDMF to reach an agreement with the government, thereby facilitating the execution of elections on 10 April 2008. India's interest in the Madhesi cause can mainly be explained with New Delhi's desire to stabilize the Tarai plain as far as possible. In fact, the security situation during 2007 in the Nepalese areas bordering India had deteriorated with armed gangs and criminal organizations being active there; reports had been spreading in India about the activities of Islamist groups, the opening of several *madrasas*, and a possible role of the Pakistani secret service ISI in the Tarai.[36] Moreover, given the close connections between the Indian and the Nepalese population across the border, India was interested in avoiding the potential diffusion of a secessionist movement across the Tarai and, from there, to India. Therefore, we can assume that the main factor inducing India to get involved in the Madhesi issue was the fear of spill-over effects from the neighbouring country across the open border. Additionally, there are reports about, and alleged interest on the part of India in, the strengthening of Madhesi parties in order to split the Maoist electorate, and thereby weakening the CPN-M (Jha 2007).

When it came to the constituent assembly elections, on 10 April 2008, India actively supported their execution. The Indian and the Nepalese election commissions had close relations, and India shared its experience by training Nepalese

---

33 See MEA (2007k).

34 For a detailed account of events, see Whelpton (2008:185–7). Interestingly, the Maoists themselves had tried to politically split the Madhesis, perceived as supporters of India. Interview with journalist, New Delhi, 26 November 2008.

35 The government agreed, among other things, to admit Madhesis, members of ethnic minorities, and *Dalits* into the armed forces, to define the victims of the Tarai movement as martyrs, and to indemnify their families. See Nepalbiznews (2008).

36 Interview with expert, New Delhi, 25 November 2008; Interview with journalist, New Delhi, 26 November 2008.

election observers. Moreover, New Delhi provided voting machines, computers, and vehicles to the government of Nepal to support the elections.[37]

Despite its intensive commitment to a facilitation of the peace process, New Delhi however, took care to follow a low-key approach towards Nepal (Pattanaik 2008b: 224) in order to avoid fomenting the latent anti-Indianism of the Nepalese population. At the diplomatic level, the degree of pressure on the part of India was considerably reduced – which, of course, was also related to the good prospects of the ongoing peace process. The content analysis of New Delhi's official documents and statements belonging to this third phase reveals that India resorted more extensively to diplomatic praise (appreciation, congratulations, e.g. MEA 2006g, 2006a), soft persuasion (hope, expressions of confidence, e.g. MEA 2007j, 2007e), and expressions of commitment (readiness to help, support, e.g. MEA 2006g, 2007e).

During the peace process, moreover, India was forced to make far-reaching compromises on its goal of limiting the influence of external actors on Nepal. In fact, the international community had started displaying a sudden interest in the country's internal situation when the images from the *Jan Andolan II* reached the world. Up to this moment only the US had shown an interest in the Himalayan kingdom in the context of its war on terrorism after 9/11, and had been massively supporting the RNA with military aid (Manchanda 2003b). During *Jan Andolan II*, India and the US had been coordinating their Nepal policy – despite their divergences on several issues. The US were, in fact, suspicious of the integration of the Maoists in the political process, and only hesitantly expressed their support for the 12-point agreement between CPN-M and SPA brokered by India.

In spring 2007, tensions between India and the US emerged again when it came to the formation of an interim government. In fact, while the US considered the complete disarmament of the Maoists as an essential precondition for their participation in the interim government, India displayed a certain degree of flexibility on this issue. India managed ultimately to allow for a participation of the CPN-M in the interim government even though all the phases of the decommissioning process had not yet been completed (Muni 2008b: 180–5).

To some extent, the presence of the United Nations in Nepal was also a problem for India. As early as in April 2006, the Maoists had been pushing for mediation by a neutral international organization, preferably the UN. While the UN itself, along with the US and other Western countries, endorsed this proposal, India, which had always been opposed to an involvement of the UN (Upreti 2004: 9), clearly rejected it.[38] New Delhi was interested in limiting the influence of external actors in Nepal and in avoiding the creation of a precedent for the UN's interference in

---

37 See Embassy of India – Kathmandu (2009); Interview with government official, New Delhi, 17 November 2008.

38 See the interview with Baburam Bhattarai, in which he stated: 'I understand that India is reluctant to see the U.N. get involved but I want to stress that at this stage of the road map, we need India's cooperation' (Varadarajan 2006).

intra-state conflicts in South Asia. However, with Prime Minister Koirala, who visited Delhi in June 2006, admitting to his government's inability to disarm the Maoists alone, India was ultimately forced to accept the UN mission. It was also clear at the same time that neither was the Nepal Army the right actor to perform this task, since its own arms needed to be registered, nor would India be accepted in such a role by the Maoists (Muni 2008b: 181). Therefore, no other actor except the UN came under consideration.

After the elections, India expressed its satisfaction with the application of democratic procedures in the neighbouring country through diplomatic praise (congratulations, e.g. MEA 2008g) and soft persuasion (cajoling, expressions of hope, and expressions of commitment and support).[39] However, it must be taken into consideration that the result of the elections – the sweeping victory of the CPN-M – was unexpected for the Indian political elite, and that 'New Delhi had great difficulty digesting [them]' (ICG 2008c: 13). While the most important Indian leftist party, the CPI(Marxist), welcomed the Maoist victory (ibid.), most other political actors in India feared that the Maoists would assert their declared goal of establishing a one-party system and, once in power, would turn away from India and return to 'traditional' anti-Indianism. This fear seemed to find a foundation when Prachanda, who had been elected prime minister by the parliament on 14 August 2008, broke with the tradition of Nepalese prime ministers paying their first state visit to India to acknowledge the two countries' special relationship (Whelpton 2009: 56). Instead, Prachanda made his first visit abroad to China, meeting President Hu Jintao and Prime Minister Wen Jiabao on the occasion of the closing ceremony of the Olympic games (Mehta 2010: 132). However, on 14 September 2008, Prachanda finally visited New Delhi and conveyed a surprisingly positive impression on the Indian elite. He also allayed India's fears by under-lining his desire to maintain Nepal's traditional close relations with India, and by announcing an increase in Nepal's production of hydroelectric power and his willingness to export power to India (Bansal 2008; MEA 2008a).[40]

To summarize, in the years between *Jan Andolan II* and the election of Prachanda as the prime minister of Nepal, India employed exclusively 'soft' foreign policy means. At the same time, it played a constructive role in the negotiation process between the political parties and the Maoists, as well as between the Nepalese

---

39 See, for example, MEA (2008g): 'You are India-open – open to an India that is economically dynamic, a vast and growing market and a source of skills and technology that is not always so easy to access. Yet, you have an open border with India. You have free access to our market. Please make use of it, and we could establish a very mutually rewarding economic partnership between our two countries'. See, among the numerous expressions of support, MEA (2008b): 'He [the Indian vice president] expressed India's continued support and assistance in the transition to a democratic, inclusive, stable and prosperous Nepal and looked forward to working closely with his counterpart in further strengthening the bonds of friendship between the two countries'.

40 Interview with expert, New Delhi, 28 November 2008.

government and the Madhesis, thereby substantially contributing to the peace process.

Between Engagement, Resistance, and Compliance: Nepal's Approach

If we shift our focus from India to Nepal, we need to take into account the perspective of the different actors in Nepal involved in relations with India. These include, as mentioned above, the king, the democratic parties, and the Maoists. Moreover, the perceptions of the broader Nepalese population will also be discussed. The assessment of perceptions and reactions on the part of the different actors in Nepal allows us to provide better insights into the complex internal political situation in that country and into the equally complex relationship of Nepal with its powerful southern neighbour.

As far as perceptions about India are concerned, a high degree of suspicion and fear of the overwhelmingly larger neighbour have always characterized Nepal's approach to India. Two main factors have contributed to the diffusion of anti-Indian sentiments in Nepal. The first factor is represented by the geo-political situation of Nepal, which leads to a high degree of dependence and vulnerability towards India. As Chadda (2000: 117) puts it, '[a] cooperative India can open vast markets and provide substantial capital for investment in the Nepali economy. An unfriendly India, however, can devastate Nepal's fragile economy', as was demonstrated by the 1989 blockade.

The second main factor contributing to the widespread suspicion about India was New Delhi's history of enmeshment in Nepal's domestic affairs and its 'active and effective presence at every landmark event in Nepal's contemporary history' (Menon 2001). As Upreti (2004: 9) puts it, 'Indian influence is experienced even in changing government, selecting prime minister, ministers and filling other powerful positions'. The historical precedents of India's interventions in all of Nepal's main political transitions since the 1950s even induced some authors (e.g., Shah 2004) to suspect an Indian involvement in the promotion of the Maoist rebellion.

The Maoists, for their part, had traditionally adopted a strong anti-India rhetoric based on the notion that India's influence on Nepal was disproportionate and detrimental to the development of the country. The 1950 Treaty of Peace and Friendship with India was particularly perceived as 'unequal' and its abolition constituted one of the core Maoist demands (Mishra 2004: 634).

At the same time, the Nepalese monarchy was also suspicious of India and, according to Muni (2003: 62), '[t]he contribution of monarchy in shaping Nepalese nationalism along anti-Indian lines has been the single largest', dating back to King Mahendra's vigorous efforts to escape India's sphere of influence by cultivating relations with China. Overall, therefore, 'powerful vested interests have injected an anti-Indian ethos into Nepalese nationalism' (Menon 2001) and political leaders have been 'overtly appealing to the public's anti-Indian sentiment, while covertly trying to keep India happy' (Mishra 2004: 644).

This ambiguity of the Nepalese political actors towards India was reflected in Nepal's official reactions to India's foreign policy strategies in the years 2002–8.

During the first phase analysed, King Gyanendra pursued a twofold approach towards New Delhi. On the one hand, he was able to manipulate India's anxiety about a Maoist takeover in Nepal in order to get New Delhi's military and political support in the fight against the Maoists. According to observers, King Gyanendra was well aware of India's identification of monarchy with an element of stability and therefore knew that New Delhi considered him as indispensable to avoid 'losing' Nepal to the Maoists and potentially, from an Indian perspective, to the Chinese (Manchanda 2004c). At the same time, the king was equally able 'to exploit India's determination to be the top player' for his own purposes, inducing New Delhi to continue to provide weapons and military assistance out of the fear of being replaced by China (ibid.) – a move resembling Rajapaksa's efforts to keep India engaged in Sri Lanka.

On the other hand, however, while trying to engage India, Gyanendra at the same time simply ignored New Delhi's repeated efforts to try to induce him to return to the twin-pillar approach. Therefore, we can talk about a policy of resistance on the part of Nepal since Gyanendra did not comply with India's wishes.

After his coup on 1 February 2005 and the subsequent freezing of weapons supplies by India, Gyanendra continued to resist New Delhi's pressures. More than this, to balance against India, the king 'played the China card' more vigorously than before. In February 2005, Gyanendra highlighted the importance of an agreement reached three months earlier, on a bus service between Kathmandu and Lhasa (Mohan 2005), thereby sending a clear signal to India that he was seeking China's support.[41] Moreover, shortly after Gyanendra's coup, the Chinese foreign minister visited Nepal, while Pakistan offered the king an aid package of US\$ 5 million (Bidwai 2005). The king's strategy was effective to a certain extent, since the Indian government took into consideration a resumption of weapons supplies and did not stop the training of Nepalese soldiers.

Later, during *Jan Andolan II,* the king resisted India's persuasion efforts and even its diplomatic pressure. So, Gyanendra's decision to reinstate democracy should ultimately be considered more a result of the escalation of protests in Kathmandu and in the whole country than of India's persuasion efforts. At most, Karan Singh's efforts to guarantee a dignified and safe exit for the king from the political scene might have contributed to induce the king not to insist further on his position.[42]

The other political actors in Nepal were highly critical of India's continued (and fruitless) support for the monarchy during the first and second phase analysed. The

---

41 After his coup, King Gyanendra also sought to gain international legitimacy, among others at the 2005 SAARC summit in Dhaka, emphasizing that his takeover had yielded positive results for the security situation in Nepal (*Indian Express* 2005).

42 Interview with expert, New Delhi, 28 November 2008.

most telling example was the reaction in Nepal to the sending of Karan Singh as a special envoy of the Indian prime minister. This visit, in fact, disappointed the Nepalese protesters, who interpreted Karan Singh's mission as a signal of New Delhi's support for monarchy.[43] Moreover, India's support for Gyanendra's 21 April offer was rejected by the people on the streets. As Muni (2008b: 172) puts it, '[t]he popular mood in Kathmandu started questioning India's credentials and there was a real threat of the popular anger turning against India for its partiality in favour of the King'.

At the same time, however, it must be kept in mind that India's informal facilitation efforts between the Maoists and the SPA were highly successful thanks to the close personal ties between political actors in Nepal and in India.

During the phase of democratic transition between the end of *Jan Andolan II* and the establishment of an elected government under Maoist leadership, India's engagement for early elections and for the solution of the crisis in the Tarai were equally successful. This depended on the compliance of the different actors involved, from the interim government to the Madhesi representatives, and even the CPN-M. Putting aside their traditional anti-India attitude, the Maoists even started looking for India's support. For example, in June 2006 Baburam Bhattarai met the Indian ambassador with the aim of gaining India's support in the institutionalization of the peace and democratization process (FES 2006: 4). Conversely, the Maoists' call for an international monitoring of the ceasefire and supervision of elections, preferably by the UN, can be explained, as outlined above, by the impossibility of other actors to get involved. Prachanda's cooperative attitude towards New Delhi during his first state visit as Nepal's prime minister ultimately underlines the 'traditional' importance of India as a point of reference for Nepal.

At the same time, however, we need to acknowledge the fact that New Delhi's huge involvement in the democratic transition in Nepal raised old fears of domination by India and of the loss of sovereignty amongst the Nepalese people. For example, the consultation of Indian experts in the drafting of the new constitution was widely perceived in Nepal as if the constitution was being 'written in Delhi'.[44] Subsequent policies pursued by New Delhi in the years after 2008, when sections of the Indian establishment sought to marginalize the Maoists, and reportedly even to manipulate the election of a new prime minister, have contributed towards reinforcing these negative perceptions about India (Varadarajan 2010).

43 Interview with expert, New Delhi, 7 November 2008.
44 Informal conversation with a Nepalese expert, New Delhi, 6 November 2008. Also an Indian government official acknowledged the existence of this feeling among the Nepalese population. Interview with government official, New Delhi, 17 November 2008.

India and Nepal: From Diverging to Partially Converging Goals

Having assessed the foreign policy means employed by India and the reactions and perceptions in Nepal, we will now proceed to the analysis of India's main goals in the years 2002–8, and of their compatibility with those of Nepal. As with Sri Lanka, the goals will be grouped into core and secondary or instrumental goals, with the latter being more specific objectives related to the domestic situation in Nepal and to the peace process.

The two fundamental goals pursued by India throughout the time span analysed were stability – conceived of as domestic political stability in Nepal, as well as a limitation of destabilizing spill-over effects to India – and keeping Nepal in India's sphere of influence, that is, limiting the activities of external actors in this country.

The content analysis of India's official documents reveals that the goal of stability was explicitly expressed all over the period analysed in formulations like the following: '[a]s a close and friendly neighbour of Nepal, India wishes to see an early return to peace, stability and development in Nepal' (MEA 2006m). The importance of this goal finds a confirmation in India's broader goals for the whole region (see Chapter Three) and in the history of India's relations with Nepal, in which stability has always constituted a primary objective for New Delhi.

Although, at the rhetorical level, the Indian government representatives associated stability with the establishment of a democratic political settlement,[45] a look at India's actual policies reveals the clear predominance of the goal of stability over democracy.[46] As discussed above, the Indian government was ready to compromise on the principle of democracy and preferred, instead, to support King Gyanendra until April 2006, when the protests threatened to run out of control.

During the third phase analysed, the goal of democracy became compatible ultimately with that of stability, thereby explaining India's efforts for early elections and a peaceful settlement of the Madhesis' grievances. At the same time, these efforts were related to India's desire to avoid spill-over effects across the open border. As outlined by one of the government officials interviewed, the poverty of the Indian states of Bihar and Uttar Pradesh bordering Nepal made them particularly vulnerable to destabilizing factors like the Madhesi agitation and the spread of crime and violence in 2007.[47]

Coming to India's second core goal for Nepal – keeping the country in its own sphere of influence – this corresponds to one of the long-standing fundamental goals in India's regional policy. In Nepal, as in the case of Sri Lanka, the external actors were of two kinds. On the one hand, India was interested in avoiding the presence of competing powers like China and Pakistan in Nepal. With regard to

---

45 '[...] democracy in Nepal is the best guarantee of [...] stability' (MEA 2004k).
46 The predominance of the goal of stability over democracy was confirmed by a high government official at the MEA. Interview with government official, New Delhi, 27 November 2008.
47 Interview with government official, New Delhi, 17 November 2008.

China, Nepal has always been a 'buffer' for India, and China's activities in Nepal have always been a source of concern for New Delhi.[48] As far as Pakistan's activities are concerned, they were allegedly concentrated in the Tarai and were largely related to the establishment of *madrasas* in this area because of the presence of a large Muslim population. Moreover, India feared an infiltration of Nepal by the Pakistani secret service ISI.

In April 2005, when India came to know about planned weapons exports from Pakistan and China to Nepal, government officials expressed their concern about the situation and threatened to 'take steps as appropriate' (Rajya Sabha 2005d). Most probably, and similar to the case of Sri Lanka in 2007, it was the risk of being substituted by China or Pakistan as Nepal's major weapons supplier that prompted the debate about a resumption of arms supplies by New Delhi in April 2005 (Varadarajan 2005a).

Besides the competing powers China and Pakistan, other external actors also had a growing influence on Nepal in the period analysed. As discussed above, the US had displayed a high degree of interest in the internal developments in Nepal after 9/11, and had become increasingly active in supporting King Gyanendra in his struggle against Maoist 'terrorism'. Correspondingly, India showed a growing 'uneasiness at the expansion of the military profile of the U.S. in Nepal' (Manchanda 2003a).[49] Even though the US ultimately acknowledged India's traditional position of influence in Nepal and agreed to follow India's policies also on 'uncomfortable' issues like the inclusion of the CPN-M in the political process, some divergences still remained (Muni 2008b: 180). Moreover, India also displayed a certain uneasiness about the presence of a United Nations mission in its neighbouring country. Eventually, however, it had to concede that no other actor or institution was suitable enough to carry out this task (Jha 2006) and, therefore, accepted the UNMIN. To summarize, as in the case of Sri Lanka, a distinction between external actors needs to be made: while India was ready to compromise on the presence of extra-regional actors like the UN and the US, which did not impinge upon its status as the most influential country in Nepal, it was more intransigent on the activities of direct competitors in its own sphere of influence, namely China and Pakistan.

Besides the core goals of stability and of maintaining its influence on Nepal, India pursued several secondary goals related to its own security vis-à-vis this country, especially the limitation of negative security externalities from Nepal, border security, and the protection of Indian citizens and businesses in Nepal. The goal of limiting negative security externalities was openly expressed by the Indian government in statements like the following: 'India is concerned that a

---

48 According to one of the interviewees, starting from the 1970s India drew some 'red lines' on China's activities in Nepal, with the requirement that China should not be allowed to operate in the Tarai. Interview with expert, New Delhi, 25 November 2008.

49 See also Mishra (2004: 639).

further deterioration of the situation in Nepal will result in spill-over effects across the open border, particularly in the neighbouring States. We have taken steps to strengthen security in border areas' (MEA 2005q). The problem of border security was not only related to a general criminalization of the border areas due to the spread of smuggling and criminal activities, but also to the fear of infiltrations by terrorist groups into India. To increase border security, India and Nepal created a Joint Working Group on Border Management in 2003, and decided to hold home secretary level talks on the issue of peace, security, and crime prevention in border areas (Rajya Sabha 2003d). The goal of security also found expression in India's objective of avoiding the use of Nepal's territory for activities detrimental to India, which was repeatedly raised with Kathmandu (e.g., Rajya Sabha 2006c). Similarly, when the Maoists were still active and carrying out attacks against Indian companies operating in Nepal, the protection of Indian nationals, property, and businesses in Nepal became an important objective for New Delhi.[50]

Coming to New Delhi's preferences about the settlement of the crisis in Nepal, an evolution of India's goals could be observed across the three phases analysed. During the first phase, India's main preoccupation was with a Maoist takeover in the neighbouring country. Even though India at the level of official statements emphasized that it did not consider 'a purely military solution' as a possible way of dealing with the crisis (MEA 2004d), its continued support of the king's military efforts in terms of arms supplies and training for the RNA seems to confirm that a consistent part of the Indian establishment believed in the correctness of a military approach. Moreover, in the 'triangular' (king, parties, Maoists) politics of Nepal, the twin-pillar approach implied that India wished for a cooperation (a 'national consensus') between the monarchy and the democratic parties *against* the CPN-M:

> India has consistently held the view that the problems confronting Nepal including the Maoist insurgency can be addressed effectively only on the basis of a national consensus between the two constitutional forces, namely multiparty democracy and constitutional monarchy.
>
> (Rajya Sabha 2005e)

During the second phase analysed, however, a section of the foreign policy-making Indian elite realized that the integration of the Maoists into the political mainstream was the most viable solution for a durable peace in the neighbouring country. India therefore started calling for the Maoists to abandon violence (MEA 2005e), while informally, New Delhi actively supported, through its mediation, the integration of the CPN-M into the political process. Moreover, Indian policy makers hoped that the integration of the Maoists into the political mainstream

---

50 See MEA (2004f). In 2003, there were 265 approved Indian joint ventures in Nepal, 100 of which were operational, active in sectors like tourism, infrastructure, and consumer durables and non-durables (Shrestha 2003: 55–6).

would have an exemplary function of inducing the Naxalites operating in India to abandon their armed struggle and to join politics as a political party.[51]

Finally, during the third phase analysed, after the signing of the Comprehensive Peace Agreement in November 2006, the Indian government emphasized the need for fair and free elections and New Delhi played a considerable role in supporting the democratic transition. Moreover, when the Madhesi agitation spread in the Tarai, New Delhi took the need for inclusiveness in the 'new' Nepali state seriously. This was demonstrated by its mediation efforts in the Madhesi issue. Interestingly, however, Indian policy makers linked the principle of inclusive democracy, again, to the issue of political stability:

> A plural democracy like India has learnt to celebrate its diversity and counts this as one of the pillars of its democracy. It is my hope that Nepal will do so, too, because only a more inclusive, a more accommodative approach is required for a stable and enduring democracy.
>
> (MEA 2008g)

In order to assess the degree of commonality or divergence in India's and Nepal's goals, we will focus again, not only on the actors vested with executive power in the various phases analysed, but also on the SPA and the Maoists as the other main political players in Nepal. While India's core goal of having a stable neighbour in the north was, in principle, shared by the Nepalese government throughout the time span analysed, a high degree of divergence was noticeable on the objective of keeping Nepal in India's sphere of influence in all the three phases. During the first and second phases, Gyanendra's opposition to this goal was self-evident: the weapons purchases from China and Pakistan (and also, to a certain extent, the massive military support obtained from the US) were clear attempts to escape from India's all-encompassing influence. Preserving the country's sovereignty and autonomy from India's influence had always been one of Nepal's primary foreign policy goals. And as outlined above, the tension between autonomy and dependence had always been the primary feature in Nepal's relations with India. In addition to this, it was also observed during the third phase analysed that India's goal of avoiding the presence of external actors was opposed by Nepal. Both the Maoists and the political parties were in fact interested in the involvement of a neutral international agency, preferably the UN, in the peace process. India ultimately aligned itself with this position, recognizing the fact that the UN was the actor best suited to monitor the ceasefire and the management of weapons as well as to supervise the elections.

While India's goals concerning security and the limitation of spill-over effects did not encounter significant opposition from the main political actors in Nepal, its objectives related to the settlement of the crisis and the implementation of the peace process were opposed by single actors on the Nepalese side. During

---

51   Interview with expert, New Delhi, 7 November 2008.

the first phase analysed, when New Delhi primarily pursued the objectives of avoiding a Maoist takeover and of supporting the fight against the Maoists, these goals corresponded to those of the king as well as of the democratic parties. However, we can hardly affirm that this basic convergence in goals was the result of a successfully implemented leadership strategy on the part of India since the king and the Nepalese parties had a genuine interest in coping with the civil war in the country. A divergence in goals between the Indian government and King Gyanendra emerged as sections of the establishment in New Delhi realized that the integration of the Maoists into the political mainstream was an essential step in the peace process.[52] This goal was shared, however, by the SPA and by the CPN-M itself, which both agreed to take part in India's facilitation efforts and to overcome their mutual suspicions. Therefore, a convergence of goals between India and the 'new' political forces of Nepal took place during the second phase analysed, and India played a substantial role in channelling these common goals towards a negotiated settlement of the civil war. Finally, during the third phase, India's goal of achieving an inclusive democracy taking into account the interests of groups like the Madhesis came to be broadly shared by the Nepalese interim government. In fact, Kathmandu reacted to the growing violence in the Tarai by agreeing to several constitutional amendments to allow for the inclusion of previously marginalized groups into Nepal's political life (Hachhethu/Gellner 2010: 140).

Overview: Partially Successful Hegemonic Strategy

Summarized in Table 5.2 are the main goals pursued by India and their compatibility with Nepal's goals, the foreign policy means of both the countries, and Nepal's predominant perceptions. This overview highlights the degree to which India's involvement in the turbulent peace and democratization process was complex. India variously interacted with different actors and adapted its preferences and foreign policy means to the changing situation in the neighbouring country.

The most significant feature of India's involvement in Nepal's domestic affairs between 2002 and 2008 was represented by the coexistence and contemporary pursuance of different goals on the part of India. This implied the recourse to contrasting foreign policy means at the same time. On the one hand, during the first phase analysed, New Delhi displayed its dissatisfaction with the erosion of democratic principles by King Gyanendra, but simultaneously entertained good relations with him and provided military and economic assistance to Nepal. On the other hand, during the second phase following Gyanendra's seizure of power in February 2005, New Delhi's stated goal of re-establishing democracy and the hard hegemonic measures employed to force the king to put an end to his autocratic rule contrasted with India's continued support for the twin-pillar approach. Moreover – and even more strikingly – while the Indian government continued to train

---

52   Interview with journalist, New Delhi, 10 December 2008.

Table 5.2   India–Nepal: goals, means, and perceptions

		India	*Nepal*
GOALS	*Issue Area*		
Core goals		Stability	(Stability)
		Keeping Nepal in India's sphere of influence = limitation of the activities of external actors.	• 2002–5 and 2005–6: counter-balancing India by cultivating relations with China and Pakistan (+ military support from the USA) • 2006–8: Maoists and SPA: involvement of UN.
Secondary goals		Security: • Avoiding spill-over effects; • Border security; • Protection of Indian nationals, property, and businesses in Nepal	(Security) (2002–5: border security: establishment of Joint Working Group in 2003)
	Settlement of the crisis	2002–5: Avoid Maoist takeover (military defeat of the CPN-M); twin-pillar approach	2002–5: King Gyanendra: Avoid Maoist takeover (military defeat of the CPN-M)
		2005–6: Integration of CPN-M into the political mainstream	2005–6: King Gyanendra: non-involvement of Maoists in political life SPA: Integration of CPN-M into the political mainstream Maoists (majority): Integration into political mainstream
		2006–8: Inclusive democracy	Interim government: inclusive democracy
MEANS *(actions/reactions)*		2002–5: • Soft persuasion • Incentives and support	
		2005–6 • Hard persuasion (+ soft persuasion and expressions of commitment) • Sanction: embargo on arms supplies Facilitation of SPA-Maoist • Tacit support (military training) talks. During Jan Andolan II: Half-hearted pressure From 22 April 2006: persuasion and appeasement of population	2002–6: Resistance (playing the China card; ignoring pressure)
		2006–8: • Diplomatic praise • Soft persuasion • Expressions of commitment • Incentives for the successful establishment of democracy • Mediation	2006–8: Compliance
PERCEPTIONS			2002–5: India as a threat 2005–6: India as pro-monarchic (population, parties) 2006–8: India as supportive actor/India still intrusive (constitution 'written in Delhi')

Source: Author's composition.

Nepalese troops for the fight against the CPN-M, it simultaneously allowed the wanted Maoist leaders to travel to India, and also mediated talks with the Nepalese democratic parties. The turning point towards a more consistent approach on the part of India was represented by the abandonment of the twin-pillar approach on 22 April 2006. In fact, starting from this moment, India also formally supported the process of democratic transition, aiming at an early execution of elections and at the establishment of a possibly inclusive system capable of addressing the griev-ances of previously marginalized groups in Nepal's population.

At this point, the question emerges of how to interpret India's foreign policy in the time span analysed. Despite a certain degree of convergence on the goal of stability between the Indian and the Nepalese governments, it seems difficult to talk about a leadership strategy, especially during the first two phases analysed. In fact, a clear divergence in goals existed on the issue of the involvement of external actors in Nepal's affairs, most notably in the provision of military assistance to the RNA. King Gyanendra's reactions to India's attempts to induce him to reinstate democracy, consisting of a complete disregard for India's persuasion efforts (first phase) as well as for its sanctions and pressure (second phase), confirm this assessment.

Therefore, we can talk about a predominantly intermediate hegemonic strategy employed by India during 2002–5, paired with elements of soft hegemony (persuasion efforts). If we consider New Delhi's primary goal to have been the defeat of the Maoists and the stabilization of Nepal, India's strategy was far from being successful since the CPN-M was still extremely powerful in 2004 (Manchanda 2004b).

The analysis of the second phase covering 2005–6 is equally complex. The recourse to sanctions and hard persuasion tools is an indicator of a hard hegemonic strategy employed by India. This finds a confirmation in Gyanendra's sudden intensification of relations with Pakistan and China after India's weapons embargo. Given the failure of this hard hegemonic approach and the risk of losing its leverage on this neighbour, India continued, however, to provide training to Nepalese troops and supported the monarchy until 22 April 2006. However, in this case too, India's approach did not yield any positive results since the king did not alter the course of his policy. The dramatic intensification of the popular movement in April 2006 finally forced India to change its own policy and to abandon its tradi-tional twin-pillar approach.

The first two phases were therefore characterized by the unsuccessful resort to an intermediate and a hard hegemonic strategy, respectively.

However, during the second phase, India's facilitation efforts in the talks between CPN-M and SPA constituted a parallel strategy pursued by New Delhi. This two-pronged approach is highlighted in grey in Table 5.2. According to the sources available and to the assessments provided by the experts interviewed, India's informal mediation in negotiations between the Nepalese political parties and the Maoists can be considered to be a successfully implemented informal leadership strategy. In fact, we can assume that India was able to produce a convergence of the CPN-M's and the SPA's goals with its own objective of reaching a settlement of the crisis and stabilizing the country. The fact that the Maoists and the democratic parties voluntarily turned to India for support confirms the assessment of a leadership approach. According to one of the experts interviewed, the pursuing of parallel strategies was determined, in the first place, by a lack of coordination between the different Indian ministries having different objectives.[53] As a consequence, for the second phase analysed, we can talk about a predominantly hard hegemonic strategy pursued by India towards the Nepalese government, with parallel elements of informal leadership in India's interactions with the other Nepalese political actors.

Coming to the third phase analysed, the prevalence of diplomatic praise, soft persuasion, and expressions of commitment is an indicator of a soft hegemonic strategy on the part of India. Given the compliance of the interim government and of the other actors involved, India's strategy, in this case, can be considered to have been successful. India's strong interest in avoiding a destabilization of the Tarai and in limiting the spill-over of secessionist tendencies by the Madhesis as well as New Delhi's alleged interest in weakening the Maoists' support base before the election by supporting the demands of the Madhesis would confirm the primarily 'egoistic' character of India's approach. This allegation seems to find a confirmation in New Delhi's dismay over the Maoists' electoral victory in 2008 (ICG 2008c: 12–13) and its unexpressed fears about 'losing' Nepal to China after Prachanda became prime minister. The suspicions about India writing Nepal's new constitution also reflect the coexistence of both compliance and residual elements of resignation and criticism on the part of the political actors in Nepal.

To summarize, we can consider the strategy pursued by India in the period analysed to have been a partially successful hegemonic strategy with parallel elements of informal leadership.

Overall, India's strategy can be considered successful for three reasons. Firstly, because India managed to remain the most influential actor in Nepal – that is, it managed to continue keeping Nepal in its sphere of influence. The facilitation of talks between CPN-M and SPA reveals the continued importance of New Delhi as a point of reference for all political actors in Nepal, even for those traditionally opposed to India. At the same time, India's informal leadership allowed New Delhi to keep its leverage on those political actors, who were emerging as the most important players in the future of Nepal. As Varadarajan (2010) puts it, New Delhi 'had the ability to work behind the scenes with a wide cross-section of players in order to produce a political outcome that broadly benefited both Nepal and itself'. Secondly, India's strategy can be defined as successful because New Delhi was able to influence events in order to avoid a bloodbath and a descent of Nepal into complete anarchy. In fact, the rapprochement informally promoted by India between the SPA and the Maoists was essential to lay the foundation for the peace process and the country's democratic transition. Thirdly, India's strategy can be

53 Interview with journalist, New Delhi, 10 December 2008.

defined as successful because major negative spill-over effects were avoided in the case of the insurgency in the Tarai. In fact, by inducing the government to address the Madhesis' and other groups' grievances, New Delhi managed to stabilize the situation in the areas bordering India.

However, there are some factors qualifying India's success in dealing with Nepal, which lead us to define New Delhi's strategy as *partially* successful. In fact, New Delhi was unable to achieve its core goal of limiting the influence of external actors on Nepal. While this was particularly evident during the first and the second phase, the involvement of the UN during the third phase was also accepted by New Delhi only as a necessary evil, since no other actor could neutrally monitor the ceasefire agreement and the management of armies and weapons. Moreover, India's strategies were often extremely reactive or, as an expert put it, 'India was overrun by events'.[54] This was particularly true during *Jan Andolan II*, when New Delhi was forced to abandon its twin-pillar approach by the escalation of the protest movement.

---

54 Interview with expert, New Delhi, 28 November 2008.

6 Security Threats from Bangladesh and India's Failed Hegemonic Strategy

Bangladesh is one of the most problematic neighbours of India. It is the most 'difficult and worrisome' (Mehta 2004: 147) neighbour after Pakistan, in India's perception. The tensions in bilateral relations are determined principally by two factors: by geographical conditions and by threat perceptions, with the former influencing the latter. Bangladesh and India share a border that is over 4,000 km long, extremely porous and almost unmanageable. The geographic location of Bangladesh makes it 'India-locked' in the west, north, and east, while its opening to the sea is not only affected by the jurisdiction of India, but also by those of Myanmar/Burma, Thailand, and Indonesia. This physical encirclement by the overwhelmingly larger neighbour – what a Bangladeshi diplomat has termed a 'bear hug' (ur Rashid 2008) – has been influencing Bangladesh's perceptions about India, leading to a permanent fear of losing independence and of being manipulated by India. Moreover, the linguistic and cultural affinity between the population of the Indian state of West Bengal and that of Bangladesh has led to a widespread need in Bangladesh to construct and affirm an identity independent from that of India. Islam soon emerged as a factor that was able to produce this distinct sense of identity, leading to what Dixit (1999: 269) has called the 'Islamisation of Bangladesh'.

The analysis of Indo–Bangladesh relations, and particularly of India's strategies towards Bangladesh, will cover the years between 2001–8. It will focus on the problem of Islamic fundamentalism, which represented India's primary security concern in the period analysed, and also on a series of other security issues variously related to it; particularly the problem of insurgents from the north-eastern states of India finding safe haven in Bangladesh and the issue of 'illegal' migration to India. These problems constituted the second and third most pressing issues for the Indian government during the time span analysed (Dutta 2008a: 215)[1] and were related, in turn, to the topics of border management and of alleged Pakistani activities in Bangladesh.

The starting point of the analysis is the electoral victory of the four-party alliance led by the Bangladesh Nationalist Party (BNP) on 1 October 2001, which

---

1 This assessment was confirmed by one of the government officials interviewed. Interview with government official, New Delhi, 20 November 2008.

led to the participation of Islamist parties in the government of Bangladesh. The final point of the period analysed, marred by rampant corruption, political instability, and finally by the temporary rule of a military-backed caretaker government (CTG), is the elections of 29 December 2008, which not only implied a return to democracy but also a clear electoral defeat of Islamist parties.

As in the preceding cases, this chapter provides, first, a brief overview of the history of Bangladesh's bilateral relations with India, and outlines the most significant domestic developments in Bangladesh until the beginning of the time span analysed. A basic understanding of Bangladesh's history allows us to trace the origins of the political culture of polarization, repeated outbreaks of violence, and frequent interventions by the military, all of which strongly affected Indo–Bangladesh relations and contributed towards shaping India's perception of Bangladesh as an 'ungovernable' country and a 'bad case'.[2] Even more importantly, historical animosities having their roots in the liberation war of 1971 determined Bangladesh's hostility towards India to a large extent. As one interviewee put it, 'you have to take a look at the political history of the subcontinent to understand why some of the things that happen are not rational'.[3]

In the subsequent sections, the main events taking place in the period analysed will be outlined and the analytical framework for the assessment of regional power strategies will be applied to the study of Indo–Bangladesh relations. The focus will be on India's main security concerns: Islamic fundamentalism and the related problems of insurgent activities, migration, and border management. As we will see, India pursued hard and intermediate hegemonic strategies, but was entirely unable to induce Bangladesh to accommodate its security interests. Therefore, India's hegemonic approach between 2001–8 has to be considered as a total failure.

Indo–Bangladesh Relations: Historical Background

India played a decisive role in the formation of Bangladesh as an independent state in 1971. With West Pakistan's population being composed of Punjabis, Paktuns, Sindhis, and Baluchis and East Pakistan having a highly homogeneous population made up of 98 per cent Bengalis, the two wings of Pakistan, separated by 1,600 km of Indian territory, had almost nothing in common apart from Islam. The more populous Eastern wing was heavily discriminated against by the West: it was underrepresented in the Pakistani parliament (Baxter 1997: 69), the central administration, and the military (ibid.: 64–5). Moreover, it was economically discriminated against (dos Santos 2007: 25; Baxter 1997: 67–8), leading to an almost 'colonial' pattern of economic relations between the two wings (Dixit 1999: 12).

In 1952, when the central government tried to enforce Urdu as the state language for the whole of Pakistan, East Pakistani grievances grew further (Baxter

2 Interviews with experts, New Delhi, 14 November and 25 November 2008.
3 Interview with expert, New Delhi, 7 November 2008.

1997: 62–3). The movement for increased autonomy of East Pakistan turned into a struggle for independence after elections in 1970, when West Pakistani leader Zulfikar Ali Bhutto of the Pakistan People's Party (PPP) refused to accept the victory of the Bengali nationalist party Awami League (AL) and of its leader Sheikh Mujibur Rahman (Mujib). The central government reacted to the protests in East Pakistan by starting a 'preventive war' in March 1971 (dos Santos 2007: 29). The brutal operations of the Pakistan military led to a hardening of East Pakistani resistance with the formation of a Bengali liberation army called *Mukhti Fauj* (later *Mukhti Bahini*) composed of students, Awami League activists, policemen, and the East Pakistani Rifles (ibid.: 32).

Although India did not publicly support the break-up of Pakistan and the independence of Bangladesh in the initial stage (Sisson/Rose 1990: 142–3), it allowed the formation of an exile government of the self-proclaimed independent Bangladesh on Indian territory in a location that came to be called 'Mujibnagar'. By October 1971, it considerably increased its support for the Bangladeshi freedom fighters (ibid.: 211). As a reaction, Pakistan carried out air strikes against Indian air bases on 3 December 1971, leading to the outbreak of the third India–Pakistan war following those of 1948 and 1965.

Despite Pakistan's attacks on two fronts against India, the military campaign was short and successful for the Indian and Bangladeshi forces. After a few days, on 16 December 1971, Pakistan signed the instruments of surrender and Bangladesh officially became an independent state (Dixit 1999: 106–9).

After Bangladesh's independence, India significantly supported the young state – paying attention, however, not to appear excessively dominating. On 19 March 1972, the two countries signed a Treaty of Peace, Friendship and Cooperation, and the new constitution of Bangladesh taking effect in December 1972 echoed the Indian constitution, enshrining the principles of nationalism, socialism, secularism, and democracy.

Despite the initially excellent relations, however, Mujib soon started to try reducing his country's dependence on India by approaching the US, UK, China, and other countries. Moreover, despite the principle of secularism enshrined in the constitution, by 1973 Mujib discovered Islam as an essential element of nationalism able to differentiate Bangladesh from India. Therefore, Bangladesh sought to become a member in the Organisation of The Islamic Conference, and Mujib started a rapprochement with Pakistan (ibid. 183–4).

Initially enjoying enormous popularity as the 'father of the nation', Mujib very soon started displaying paternalistic and authoritarian traits. The virtual absence of a parliamentarian opposition, given the Awami League's overwhelming electoral victory in March 1973, contributed to a marginalization of the parliament and made the power of the executive almost unchallenged (ibid.: 168). In January 1975, the Bangladeshi constitution was amended to transform the country into a presidential system with full executive powers for Mujib and to allow for the formation of a single party (Baxter 1997: 92). As the law and order situation in the country was deteriorating, Mujib's popularity continued to decrease. Ultimately, on 15 August 1975, Mujib and almost his entire family, together with other senior leaders of the liberation movement, were assassinated in a military coup staged by a group of officers. Only Mujib's two daughters, among them the later leader of the Awami League and Prime Minister Sheikh Hasina Wajid, were spared since they were abroad.

Sheikh Mujibur Rahman's assassination paved the way for a long period of domestic instability and a series of military takeovers in Bangladesh. In 1975 the chief of staff of the army, Ziaur Rahman (Zia), emerged as Bangladesh's new leader, starting a 16-year period of military or quasi-military rule (Mukharji 2008b). During this period, the principle of secularism was weakened and growing ties emerged between Zia and the religious forces that had supported the Pakistani army in 1971, among others the Jamaat-e-Islami (Ganguly 2006: 4). As a result, Zia repealed the ban on religious parties that had been put in place by Mujib. At the same time, in 1978 he created the Nationalist Front, led by the Jatiyo Ganotantrik Dal (JAGODAL, National Democratic Party) (Baxter 1997: 98). This party was later named Bangladesh Nationalist Party (BNP), and became one of the main political forces in Bangladesh under the leadership of Zia's widow.

Under Zia, Indo–Bangladesh relations were marked by what Dixit (1999: 243) calls a 'tenuous normalcy': Zia tried to resist Indian influence without overtly challenging New Delhi, but relations were marred by both countries' claims on the New Moor Islands in the Bay of Bengal, and by Dhaka's suspicions about Indian support for the insurgency in the Chittagong Hill Tracts. When President Ziaur Rahman proposed the establishment of the South Asian Association for Regional Cooperation (SAARC) in 1980–1981, the Indian government led by Indira Gandhi initially reacted with reservation, fearing that SAARC would be used by small South Asian countries to balance against India, but ultimately had no alternative but to join the organization (ibid.: 242).

The assassination of Zia in May 1981 was followed by a series of coups d'état, and Bangladeshi politics in the 1980s continued to be dominated by the military. In March 1982, Chief of Staff Major General Ershad staged a coup and later suspended the constitution, and assumed full powers under martial law. In June 1988, Ershad promoted a constitutional amendment that made Islam the country's state religion (Baxter 1997: 114).

Ershad's authoritarian regime was opposed by the two main political parties, the Awami League led by Sheikh Hasina Wajid, Sheikh Mujibur Rahman's daughter, and the BNP led by Khaleda Zia, Ziaur Rahman's widow. Both demanded the reinstatement of democracy, the release of political prisoners, and an end of martial law and press censorship (ibid.: 110). In December 1990, the democratic opposition's violent demonstrations ultimately forced Ershad to resign, putting an end to a period marked by rampant corruption, economic crisis, and political oppression (Dixit 1999: 247–8). A neutral caretaker government led by Chief Justice Shahabuddin was created with the aim of holding free and fair parliamentary elections – a practice that would be repeated in the following years and would even be enshrined in Bangladesh's constitution.

Elections were ultimately held on 27 February 1991 and Khaleda Zia's BNP, which won 140 seats out of 300, formed a government in alliance with the Islamist party Jamaat-e-Islami (ICG 2006a: 3). Despite this return to democracy after 16 years of military rule, Indo–Bangladesh relations remained characterized by a high degree of suspicion and hostility. The controversial bilateral issues remained the same as they had been during the first years of Mujib's government and as they would continue to be, affecting the bilateral relations in the following years – and also during the time span analysed in this study. Among them were the delineation of the maritime boundary; the jurisdiction over the New Moor Islands in the Bay of Bengal; the problem of 'illegal' migration to India, whose existence Khaleda Zia explicitly denied; the issue of alleged Bangladeshi support for the United Liberation Front of Assam (ULFA) and other separatist rebel groups allegedly operating from sanctuaries on Bangladesh's territory with the help of Bangladesh intelligence authorities and the Pakistani secret service ISI; and the dispute over the sharing of the waters of the Ganges.

Some improvements in Indo–Bangladesh relations took place with the electoral victory of the Awami League and the appointment of Sheikh Hasina as prime minister in June 1996. The elections were preceded by a period of severe political instability and heated political debate. The Awami League boycotted elections in February while demonstrators on the streets demanded the introduction of a constitutional amendment providing for the holding of elections under a neutral caretaker government (CTG) as it was done in 1991 (Baxter 1997: 125–6). A CTG system was ultimately introduced by constitutional amendment. Since this issue became contentious in the following years, it must be noted that the amendment stipulates that the last retired Chief Justice of the Supreme Court become the chief of the caretaker government and assist the election commission in holding free and fair elections (Mukharji 2008a: 62).[4] The Awami League's victory in 1996 was, in principle, a good premise for constructive relations with India, since because of its history of cooperation with India in the liberation war, together with its more secular approach, it had always been the party closest to India. Therefore, Sheikh Hasina displayed a certain degree of readiness to cooperate with India, assuring New Delhi that her country would not give support to Indian separatist groups, and deciding to join bilateral and sub-regional economic cooperation agreements with India. Moreover, in 1996, the two countries signed an agreement on the sharing of the Ganges waters (Dixit 1999: 261). At the same time, however, domestic compulsions and the desire to assert Bangladesh's distinct identity induced Sheikh Hasina to keep a certain distance from India as her father had done.

Overall, therefore, despite India's fundamental role in the independence of Bangladesh, bilateral relations became problematic shortly after independence, and a whole range of contentious issues could not be solved in the following decades. Given the tense political climate in Bangladesh, even the traditionally India-friendly AL paid attention not to make too extensive concessions to New Delhi. This historical background contributes to explain the difficult bilateral relations between the two countries in the time span analysed. The starting point

---

4 See Supreme Court of Bangladesh (2011).

of analysis is represented by the formation of a BNP-led coalition government formed after the elections held in October 2001.

Political Instability in Bangladesh: From the BNP to the Caretaker Government

The years between 2001–8 were characterized by a high degree of political instability in Bangladesh. While most of the contentious issues in Indo–Bangladesh relations remained in place, the participation of Islamist parties in the governing coalition of Bangladesh and the increasingly violent atmosphere in that country raised new concerns in New Delhi. The first phase analysed covers the years of the BNP-led government (2001–6). In the second phase analysed (2007–8), a military-backed caretaker government (CTG) took over power in Bangladesh, contributing to a partial normalization of relations with India. Following the pattern of the previous chapters, the analysis of India's foreign policy strategies is preceded by a brief assessment of the main developments in Bangladesh in the period analysed.

2001–6: The BNP-led Government

The five years of BNP-led government under the leadership of Khaleda Zia were marked by two main trends. First, corruption weakened the state institutions and the economy (ICG 2008d: 5), while the bitter political rivalry between BNP and AL contributed to destabilize the country. Second, an increase in Islamist terrorist activities took place in Bangladesh, which was initially met with indifference by the government, but was ultimately addressed with a relatively successful crackdown on extremist groups.

The BNP, founded by General Zia and led by his widow Khaleda Zia after his assassination, has traditionally been nationalistic and close to the military. Generally, the BNP has had an anti-Indian attitude and has favoured, instead, close relations with Muslim countries, particularly with Pakistan. The emphasis on traditional values and the desire to affirm a 'Bangladeshi' identity separate from the cultural-linguistic 'Bengali' one induced the BNP to forge alliances with religious parties.

The four-party governing coalition coming to power in 2001 was formed by the BNP, the Jatiya Party-N (a splinter group of a party founded by General Ershad), and by two Islamist parties, the Jamaat-e-Islami (Jamaat) and the Islami Oikya Jote (IOJ, Islamic Unity Front). Founded in 1941, the Jamaat was opposed to the independence of Bangladesh and supported Pakistan during the 1971 war against Mujib's liberation movement (Ganguly 2006: 4). The party's declared goal has been to transform Bangladesh into an Islamic state by operating within the framework of the parliamentary system. Considered to be 'well organised and politically sophisticated' (ICG 2006a: 15), the Jamaat was able to present itself as the 'clean' alternative to the corrupt mainstream political parties in the 2001 elections. Despite its securing of only 17 seats in the parliament, it was awarded two important ministries (agriculture and social welfare) in the BNP-led government under Khaleda Zia. The IOJ, on the contrary, won only two seats in the 2001 elections. With a mainly rural support base and a 'less reasonable and sophisticated' image (ibid.: 16), the IOJ had the goal of quickly establishing an Islamic state, drew political support through *madrasas,* allegedly supported the Taliban and al-Qaeda, and had close connections to the Harkat-ul-Jihad-al-Islami (HuJI, Movement of Islamic Holy War), Bangladesh's main Islamist terrorist group (ibid.).

Besides the HuJI, a large number of other militant Islamist groups have been operating in Bangladesh since the 1990s. Among them, are the Jamaat ul Mujahideen Bangladesh (JMB) and the Jagrata Muslim Janata Bangladesh (JMJB). The Islami Chhatra Shibir (ICS), the youth wing of the Jamaat, has also been allegedly involved in several bomb attacks and targeted assassinations (Lintner 2003).[5]

After the BNP-led coalition came to power in October 2001, extremist Islamist groups became 'more blatant in their attacks on the country's minorities and secular forces' (ibid.), feeling that they had the backing or at least the protection of the government. The number of terrorist attacks grew and related '[f]atalities increased from zero to an average of 34 per year between 2001 and 2006' (Alamgir 2009: 45). In the weeks immediately following the October 2001 elections, a series of attacks against minority groups, especially against the Hindu community, took place in Bangladesh, with 30 people killed and 1,000 injured in the time span of a week (SAHRDC 2001). Between October 2001 and April 2006 as many as 15,000 cases of killings, rapes, torture, and arson attacks, as well as land-grab and damage to property, were carried out against minorities in Bangladesh (*The Daily Star* 2006d).[6] Even though the attacks were often carried out by village gangs and ordinary people, who tried to grab land by forcing Hindus to migrate to India – that is, not by extremist Islamist groups – a general trend towards a religious radicalization and, consequently, the creation of a fertile ground for Islamist groups emerged from 2001 onwards.

In 2002, against the backdrop of the 'war against terrorism', when the international press started reporting on Islamist terrorism in Bangladesh, the BNP government openly denied the existence of Islamist militancy in the country (Ganguly 2006: 1). However, a wave of religiously and politically motivated assassinations in 2004–5, raised international attention on the issue once again. In May 2004, a bomb attack injured the British high commissioner (Perry 2006); in August 2004, opposition leader Sheikh Hasina survived a grenade attack carried out against her; during the same year as many as 24 AL politicians were killed in terrorist attacks (Anam 2005; Manik 2008); and in January 2005 the former AL finance minister and UN under-secretary General Shah A.M.S. Kibria was assassinated. These events provoked a wave of reactions at the international level and

---

5 On these groups, see Lintner (2003) and ICG (2006a: 16).
6 For a discussion of the links between violence, forced migration of Hindus from Bangladesh to India, and land-grab, see Mohaiemen (2009) and SAHRDC (2001).

considerably increased the pressure by international donors (Perry 2005) on the government of Bangladesh to fight extremists. As a consequence, the JMB and the JMJB, whose existence had been denied until some months before by the Bangladeshi government, were banned in February 2005 and several militants were arrested shortly thereafter (ICG 2006a: 16; Ganguly 2006: 7).

Despite these measures, however, Islamist terrorist activities in Bangladesh continued in the second half of 2005. On 17 August, as many as 459 coordinated minor bomb blasts took place at government institutions and public places in a time span of an hour in 63 of the 64 districts of the country (Behuria 2007: 155; *The New York Times* 2005). The JMB claimed responsibility for the attacks. In the following months '[b]omb threats and bombing became almost common-place' (Gupta 2006: 2). In October and November 2005, serial blasts and attacks were carried out on court buildings in different parts of the country, and on 27 November, several diplomatic missions were reportedly threatened by a regional wing of al-Qaeda (ibid.; Hussain 2005).

The BNP-led government ultimately started a more efficient crackdown on Islamist terrorist groups. The Rapid Action Battalion (RAB), a paramilitary force created to fight organized crime and notorious for its extrajudicial killings (Alamgir 2009: 46; ICG 2006a: 10), was deployed to deal with Islamist terrorists. In a few months, huge amounts of weapons and ammunition were seized and the RAB carried out a series of high profile arrests.[7]

The efficiency with which the government managed to tackle the Islamist challenge when put under pressure aroused suspicions about the previous unwill-ingness of the BNP and its allies to deal with the problem. This was, in turn, related to the alleged relations between the governing Islamist parties and underground groups, even though 'links [were] hard to establish' (ibid.: 18). The fact that the JMJB had attacked leftist groups for example, led to the assumption that this group had been 'quite openly cultivated' by the conservative BNP government (ibid.). As Ganguly (2006: 6) puts it, '[t]here is little doubt that the Bangladeshi state in general, and the Khaleda Zia coalition regime in particular, has tacitly permitted these groups to pursue their activities without much hindrance'.

The end of the BNP's term in 2006 marked the beginning of a new phase of domestic instability. Taking advantage of the fact that it was leading the government, the BNP had been trying over the previous years to create the precon-ditions for a manipulation of the elections scheduled for 22 January 2007 (ICG 2008d: 6). In fact, in 2004 the government had raised the retirement age of judges in order to allow for Justice K.M. Hassan, who had been a member of the BNP, to become head of the CTG (Mukharji 2008a: 63). Moreover, the chief election

---

7 Among them, the operations commander of the JMB, Ataur Rahman, was arrested in December 2005 and the JMB chief, Shaikh Abdur Rahman, as well as its second-in-command, 'Bangla Bhai', were captured within a few days in March 2006 (Gupta 2006: 3). Moreover, five other members of the JMB-JBMB were arrested for the killing of a judge and the August 2005 serial bomb blasts. Six of these terrorist leaders were awarded capital punishment and executed in March 2007 (Behuria 2007).

commissioner was considered to be supportive of the BNP and irregularities had been reported in the composition of the voter list (ibid.: 64).

The possible manipulation of the elections by the ruling party induced the opposition to take to the streets in what had become an almost customary way to deal with political controversies. By October 2006, 19 people had been killed and hundreds injured in increasingly violent protests (*International Herald Tribune* 2006). On a single day in the same month, 12 people were killed and 2,000 injured in clashes between activists of the BNP- and the AL-led coalitions (*The Daily Star* 2006a). Justice Hassan was eventually forced to decline his nomination as chief of the caretaker government. However, ignoring the procedure prescribed by the constitution, on 26 October 2006 the government assigned the post of chief of the CTG to President Iajuddin Ahmed, who had been appointed by the government itself and could therefore not be considered unpartisan (Mukharji 2008a: 64–5). This led to a further intensification of violence and to repeated strikes proclaimed by the opposing AL, which ultimately quit the election race on 3 January 2007 (Habib 2007b).

Given the desperate situation in the country, the armed forces intervened – in line with their almost traditional role as a political force in Bangladesh. Iajuddin was forced to resign as chief of the CTG (while retaining, however, his position as president), to dissolve the CTG itself, to declare the state of emergency on 11 January 2007, and to delay the elections (ICG 2008d: 8).[8] The 'tacit support of the United Nations and not so tacit instigation of [...] Western diplomats' (Ahmed 2009), who had pressurized both parties to find a compromise on elections,[9] reportedly played a significant role in encouraging this 'soft' military coup, which enjoyed a high degree of popular support and was widely perceived as necessary, given the escalation of violence in the country.

2007–8: The Caretaker Government under Fakhruddin Ahmed

After the intervention of the military, on 12 January 2007 a new interim CTG was established under the leadership of Fakhruddin Ahmed, an economist who had been a governor of the Bangladesh National Bank (Mukharji 2008a: 66). Despite this civilian leader, the military played a fundamental role behind the scenes and enjoyed 'immense power and control' over the government (Dutta 2008a: 216).

First of all, the army-backed CTG stabilized the situation on the streets, putting a sudden end to strikes and demonstrations by declaring the state of emergency (ICG 2008d: 9). Going beyond the 'routine functions' prescribed by the consti-tution, the CTG announced a wide-ranging reform agenda as a precondition for

8 Given its brief period in power, the CTG under President Iajuddin Ahmed is not considered as a distinct phase in the present study but rather as an interlude between the BNP term and the subse-quent military-backed CTG.
9 The EU and the UN had also announced that they would suspend their planned support for elections (United Nations – Secretary General 2007).

holding democratic elections. In his first address to the nation on 21 January 2007, Fakhruddin outlined the goals of the CTG: besides the preparation for free and fair elections these were the 'de-politicization of civil administration; separation of judiciary from the executive; stern drive against "listed criminals, terrorists, godfathers, extortionists and anti-social elements;" and measures to curb price hike of essentials and increase power supply' (Jahan 2007). The ultimate aim of the military-backed CTG was 'to change the way Bangladeshi politics work[ed] – attempting to embed military influence in "depoliticised" state institutions and use anti-corruption charges to weaken the parties and marginalise their main leaders' (ICG 2008d: 16).

On the one hand, therefore, the CTG promoted a reform of the electoral machinery and of related institutions in view of the elections: it restructured the Election Commission, it introduced a new electronic voters' list and voters' ID cards, and it redrew the borders of constituencies.[10] Moreover, some institutional reforms were carried out, among them the separation of the judiciary from the executive by ordinance, and the reconstitution of the Public Service Commission, the body responsible for appointments to the civil service (Habib 2007a; Dutta 2008a: 208–9).

On the other hand, the military-backed CTG pursued the goals of fighting corruption and weakening the established political parties. In March 2007, all political activities were prohibited (*The Daily Star* 2007b).[11] This came in the wake of the imposition of emergency regulations and a countrywide curfew imposed by the military. The army raided the homes of AL and BNP politicians arresting over 2,500 people; a further 10,000 were arrested in a time span of three days at the beginning of February 2007; after some months this number had risen to an estimated 100,000 to 200,000, and after a year to 400,000 (ICG 2008d: 17). The arrests were targeted especially at members of the political parties, with a series of high-profile arrests of some BNP and AL leaders on charges of anti-state activities, sabotage, and corruption (*The Daily Star* 2007a). The army and the CTG rather explicitly tried to remove the political leaders Sheikh Hasina and Khaleda Zia from politics in what came to be called a 'minus two' strategy (*The Daily Star* 2007g).[12] The CTG went so far as to pressurize the two leaders to go into exile, banning the former from returning to Bangladesh after a trip to the US and trying to convince the latter to move to Saudi Arabia. However, given the international pressure to allow Shekh Hasina to return to the country and since Khaleda Zia was not willing to go into exile, the CTG resorted to harder measures: in July and

---

10 The latter point is of particular relevance in Bangladesh's first past the post electoral system, where it is not the number of votes, but the number of constituencies that counts.

11 In September 2007, these provisions were eased, allowing 'indoor' political activities again in Dhaka (ICG 2008d: 11).

12 To this end, the formation of a 'third force', the *Nagorik Shakti* (Citizen's Power) under the leadership of Nobel Prize laureate Mohammed Yunus, was encouraged by the CTG (Islam 2007).

September 2007, respectively, the two leaders were arrested on corruption charges (Anam 2007; *The Daily Star* 2007h).

As for the activities of Islamist groups under the CTG, a series of arrests took place in 2007, with over 250 JMB and HuJI activists jailed. The military-backed government also implemented the death sentences of six Islamist leaders arrested in 2006, showing an unprecedented commitment in fighting radical Islamists (Sengupta 2007). At the same time however, under the CTG rule, the Jamaat was not limited in its activities to the same extent as the political parties since it enjoyed the status of a religious organization (ICG 2008a: 10), and Islamist parties were not heavily affected by the CTG's anti-corruption drive (ICG 2008d: 25). Moreover, attacks by Islamist groups continued under the state of emergency: members of the Jamaat student wing ICS attacked other students and journalists, while a new extremist group, the Jadid al-Qaeda Bangladesh (New al-Qaeda Bangladesh) carried out attacks at railway stations in May 2007.

While the anti-corruption measures introduced by the CTG had initially been welcomed by the population, the marginalization of political leaders was a highly unpopular measure (Habib 2007c). Moreover, repeated violations of due process, reported cases of torture in the anti-corruption drive, and the intimidation of journalists, human rights organizations, and social activists provoked increasing criticism (ICG 2008d: 18). In July and August 2007, dissatisfaction about the suspension of democracy and the tight control by the army over university campuses led to strikes and violent agitations among student organizations (*The Daily Star* 2007e, 2007d). The parties, on their part, demanded the lifting of the emergency regulations and the reinstatement of political freedoms to allow for a smooth preparation of elections (Habib 2007c). This induced the CTG to ultimately give in to both the parties' and the demonstrators' demands, and to release Sheikh Hasina and Khaleda Zia on parole in June and September 2008, respectively. As an Indian analyst put it, '[t]he military's attempt to create divisions within political parties […] failed completely […]. The popularity of Khaleda and Hasina remain[ed] intact, frustrating the efforts of the military-backed CTG' (Pattanaik 2008a: 184).

The continuing protests of the parties and the considerable pressure exerted by Western countries critical of human rights violations and abuses by the security forces finally induced the CTG to announce, in September 2008, that elections would take place by the end of the year (*The Associated Press* 2008). Consequently, the state of emergency was lifted in December 2008 (Alamgir 2009: 52) and the elections were carried out on 29 December. The AL-led Grand Alliance won a landslide victory with 262 seats out of 299, while the BNP-led four-party coalition managed to secure only 32 seats, its worst electoral result ever (Habib 2009). The elections also marked a defeat of Islamist forces, with the Jamaat getting only two seats in parliament as opposed to the 17 it previously held. As a consequence, the 2008 elections were interpreted in terms of a rejection of religious extremism and a clear sign of popular support for moderate, secular political forces – a result particularly welcome to India. Given the 'watershed' character of these elections, they are taken as the final point of the analysis in the present study.

India's Foreign Policy Strategies Towards Bangladesh

Having outlined the main domestic events in Bangladesh in the years 2001–8, the strategies pursued by India in dealing with this country will now be analysed by taking into consideration the means employed by India, the reactions and perceptions of Bangladesh, and the goals of both the countries. As we will see, the government of India employed predominantly hard hegemonic tools in its interactions with Dhaka in the first phase analysed (2001–6), while relations became somewhat easier under the CTG (2007–8), leading to the adoption of an intermediate hegemonic foreign policy strategy. Due to the widespread suspicion about India, however, it was impossible for New Delhi to be successful in achieving its goals in dealing with Bangladesh. Specifically, India was unable to solve the security problems emanating from Bangladesh, according to its own preferences.

From Pressure and Threats to Concessions and Soft Persuasion: India's Foreign Policy Means

During the first phase analysed, which corresponded to the second tenure in government of Khaleda Zia and her BNP-led alliance, bilateral relations were 'at a nadir since 1971' (Mehta 2004: 150).[13] This was related to the traditionally antagonistic attitude of the BNP towards India (ibid.) and was particularly true until 2004, when the National Democratic Alliance (NDA) under the leadership of the Hindu nationalist Bharatiya Janata Party (BJP) was in power in India. During this phase of bilateral relations, India extensively resorted to diplomatic pressure, threats, and accusations, as well as to hard persuasion in dealing with Bangladesh. Moreover, some border incidents took place during which India even resorted to displays and threats of force – that is, to means typical of an imperial strategy.

The most controversial security-related topics in bilateral relations in the years 2001–6 were the problem of the persecution of minorities after the 2001 elections in Bangladesh; the issue of 'illegal' migration of Bangladeshis to India and, related to that, the topic of border management; Islamic extremism and the wave of terrorist attacks that took place in Bangladesh in 2005; and the issue of insurgents from the north-eastern states of India operating from the territory of Bangladesh.

In the period following the 2001 elections, repeated episodes of violence against Bangladesh's Hindu minority were reported. Since the BJP-led government of India was particularly sensitive to this topic, it reacted to the reports by putting pressure on Dhaka: the issue was raised by the Indian high commissioner to Bangladesh on 16 October 2001, and the Indian prime minister even sent a special envoy to Dhaka to convey India's concern (Lok Sabha 2001; SAHRDC 2001). However, despite the reassurances on the part of Dhaka, these forms of pressure

---

13   See also Dutta (2009: 86).

had no consequences. After the peak that followed the elections in October 2001, episodes of violence continued in the following years.[14]

New Delhi also tried to exert pressure on Dhaka – with little success – on the problem of the so-called 'illegal' migration of Bangladeshis to India. The number of Bangladeshis who crossed the border to India during the past decades is not known, with estimates varying between a few hundred thousand to 20 or even 35 million (Dutta 2009: 97). 'In reality, the numbers nation-wide are perhaps closer to 2 million than to 20, but these are only guesstimates' (Varadarajan 2005b: 53). These migrants are mainly driven by economic motives,[15] but in India the perception is widespread that the government of Bangladesh is 'sending so many people'[16] or, as Mehta (2004: 149) puts it, '[t]he export of manpower, both legal and illegal, appears to have become part of Bangladesh's foreign policy'. Many of the Bangladeshi immigrants live in India's main urban centres and cannot be distinguished from Indian citizens coming from West Bengal (Ramachandran 2005: 8–9). The main root of the problem is the lack of a procedure to get work or residence permits for migrants in India. As a consequence, Bangladeshi economic migrants have no other options than to cross the border illegally and live and work in India as if they were Indian citizens (Varadarajan 2005b: 54). Given the lack of an ID card system in India, several immigrants have acquired Indian ration cards and used them to obtain voter cards, thereby becoming de facto Indian citizens (Ramachandran 2005: 9–10). This has often happened as a part of 'vote bank politics' in the Indian states bordering Bangladesh (Kaur 2003; Chattopadhyay 2007), where some parties traditionally supported by Muslims have turned a blind eye to 'illegal' migration in order to get new voters.[17] The issue of the undocumented migration from Bangladesh was raised and politicised in the 1980s by the Hindu nationalist BJP, which characterized Muslim migrants from Bangladesh as 'infiltrators' increasing the Muslim population of India, as opposed to Hindu migrants defined as 'refugees' escaping persecution from Islamic Bangladesh (Shamshad 2008: 3; Ramachandran 2005: 14). The topic of migration has been one of the most contentious bilateral issues between India and Bangladesh, especially since it became related to the problem of the spread of Islamist terrorism under both the NDA government led by the BJP and the Congress-led UPA administration (ibid.: 13; GOI 2006).

In the years 2001–6, New Delhi tried to pressurize the government of Bangladesh to take some measures to prevent migration, repeatedly expressing its concern about the issue (e.g., Rajya Sabha 2003c). In January 2003, Indian Deputy Prime Minister L.K. Advani estimated the number of immigrants from Bangladesh at 15 millions and went so far as to define them as a 'serious threat to the

---

14 See, for example, Rajya Sabha (2002).
15 Interview with expert, New Delhi, 7 November 2008.
16 Interview with government official, New Delhi, 20 November 2008.
17 Interview with expert, New Delhi, 7 November 2008. For example, the Left Front government of West Bengal was considered to be responsible for supporting migration from Bangladesh in order to gain votes (Shamshad 2008: 6).

country's internal security' (Dubey 2003; Kaur 2003). At the beginning of 2003, a large number of immigrants from Bangladesh were arrested in Mumbai and Delhi and sent to Kolkata with the aim to forcibly repatriate them to Bangladesh (Chattopadhyay 2003). The tension between the two countries over the problem of migration became evident during a border incident which saw over 200 nomadic 'snake-charmers' from Bangladesh stranded in the no man's land between the two countries. The Bangladesh Rifles (BDR)[18] on the one side and the Indian Border Security Forces (BSF) on the other, both refused to recognize them as the citizens of their respective countries and to allow them to enter their territory. The situation escalated when both the BSF and the BDR called for reinforcements and their posts were put on high alert. According to the Indian press, the BDR were the first to threaten to open fire and the BSF reacted by threatening retaliation (ibid.). However, this claim cannot be confirmed. Even though, at first glance, it seems difficult to categorize this episode as the use of 'imperial' means given the vague and non-specific nature of military action, the fact that the Bangladeshi side also put its posts on alert allows us to consider this episode as one of 'threat of use of force' and 'display of force' according to the COW guidelines (Jones et al. 1996: 169).[19] While the stalemate was solved some days later (Ramachandran 2005: 2), this incident is symptomatic of the degree of tension in bilateral relations between India and Bangladesh as well as of the failure of both countries' border management efforts.

India and Bangladesh share a 4,096.7 km long border, which is not only extremely difficult to control because of the many rivers and the muddy terrain of the Sunderbans, but which has not even been completely settled after the formation of Bangladesh as an independent state. In fact, 6.5 km of the land border still have to be demarcated, and both countries possess several enclaves in each other's territory.[20] Similarly, the Indo–Bangladesh maritime boundary and the corresponding control over Exclusive Economic Zone (EEZ) and continental shelf are contested – especially since huge gas reserves were found in the Bay of Bengal, conferring great economic relevance to the issue of maritime boundary demarcation (Dutta 2009: 95–6). While a Land Boundary Agreement was signed in 1974, it was never implemented, and the activities of two Joint Boundary Working Groups established in 2001 were limited (Das 2008: 381). Moreover, director-general level talks between the BDR and the BSF had taken place since March 2002 to 'promote a better understanding and coordination between the two forces guarding the borders' (Lok Sabha 2002a). But even the adoption of potentially constructive measures like an agreement to 'combat cross-border terrorism, have coordinated

---

18 The BDR was renamed Border Guard Bangladesh (BGB) after a mutiny in 2009 (*The Hindu* 2011).
19 If the initiator of the threat of force was Bangladesh, India's corresponding reaction would equally be imperial. In fact, we can always assume the existence of alternative, 'softer' form of behaviour, even in such situations.
20 Bangladesh possesses 51 enclaves in Indian territory, and India 111 enclaves in Bangladeshi territory, to which it does not have administrative control or access (Rajya Sabha 2006b). An exchange of enclaves was agreed upon in 1974, but never implemented (*The Economist* 2011).

patrolling on the frontiers and work closely on the issues of "Indian insurgent hideouts" in Bangladesh and "anti-Bangladeshis" in India' in September 2004 (Habib 2004) had little repercussion on the ground. Clashes and gunfire exchanges along the Indo–Bangladesh border continued to take place, with the BSF and the BDR repeatedly on the verge of a more serious military confrontation (ibid.).

Besides the issues of minorities, of migration, and of border management, the single main security concern for India, which was raised with a great deal of vehemence on the part of New Delhi during the years 2001–6, was that of alleged anti-India activities by groups operating from Bangladeshi territory. In fact, representatives of the Indian government assumed the existence of linkages between Bangladeshi and international Islamic fundamentalist groups, the Pakistani secret service ISI, and insurgents from the north-eastern states.[21]

The seven north-eastern states of India are almost entirely surrounded by Bangladesh, Bhutan, China, and Myanmar/Burma, while their connection to India is constituted by a narrow strip of land called Siliguri Corridor or Chicken's Neck. Also from an ethnic and cultural point of view, the north-eastern states have little in common with the rest of India and present, instead, larger affinities to the countries bordering them (Kamboj 2005). The low degree of integration with the rest of India and a number of grievances related to the economic backwardness of this area contributed to the formation of several insurgent groups fighting against the Indian state. Some of them have demanded the establishment of a separate state, others have demanded greater administrative autonomy from New Delhi, and still others have been fighting for complete 'independence' of small territorial units. Nearly thirty of these groups were considered to have their bases in Bangladesh during the period analysed. Among them were the National Socialist Council of Nagaland (NSCN), United Liberation Front of Asom (ULFA), National Democratic Front of Bodoland (NDFB), All Tripura Tiger Force (ATTF), National Liberation Front of Tripura (NLFT), and the Muslim United Liberation Tigers of Assam (MULTA) (Mehta 2004: 148; Dutta 2009: 98). According to reports to the Indian government, these groups had their training camps in the Bangladeshi districts of Sylhet Division, Chittagong, and Chittagong Hill Tracts on the border to India (Lok Sabha 2005). To counter militancy, the Indian government declared large parts of the north-eastern states as 'disturbed areas' and resorted to the deployment of the Central Police Forces and the Army to fight the insurgents (MHA 2005: 34–5).

In its interactions with Bangladesh in 2001–6, the Indian government repeatedly raised the issue of north-eastern insurgent groups, including at the highest level with Khaleda Zia in July 2004.[22] The repeated denials by Bangladesh's

---

21 Interview with government official, New Delhi, 20 November 2008.
22 For example, the Indian high commissioner in Dhaka expressed the allegation in October 2003 that Bangladesh was offering protection to a wanted leader of ULFA, which, in turn, led to the issuing of a note verbale, a form of diplomatic protest, by the government of Bangladesh criticizing the high commissioner's statement (Malhotra 2003).

authorities provoked a high degree of discontent in India (e.g., Lok Sabha 2005; Rajya Sabha 2003a). During the BDR-BSF meetings, India handed over lists of insurgent training camps in Bangladesh to the BDR to act upon.[23] However, since little happened, New Delhi was reinforced in its belief that Dhaka was actively supporting the insurgents. In a parliament session in August 2006, the Indian minister of state in the MEA made the Indian accusation explicit:

> Indian insurgent groups continue to misuse Bangladesh territory for sanctuary, training camps, transportation of arms, and transit. These insurgents are being supported by intelligence agencies, both civilian and military, of Bangladesh. A list of 172 Indian insurgent group camps and 307 criminals/insurgents was handed over in the DG level Border Security Force (BSF) – Bangladesh Rifles (BDR) talks held in September-October 2005. However, Bangladesh continues to maintain a policy of complete denial.
>
> (Lok Sabha 2006)

Besides these verbal protests, the Indian government tried to cope with the problem of insurgent group activities, as well as with the issues of migration and smuggling, by building a fence along its border with Bangladesh. The fencing was initiated as early as 1989, and discussions about the construction of a fence had been going on since the 1960s (Shamshad 2008: 1). While the BJP-led government, which tripled the budget for border security in 2003, particularly promoted the construction of the fence, the UPA government temporarily put the fencing on hold and discussed its usefulness before resuming construction work (ibid.: 10). Dhaka, on its part, strongly opposed the fencing, considered to be a violation of the 1975 Border guidelines, which prohibited the construction of any kind of defensive structure within 150 yards of the 'zero line' (Das 2008: 376). As we will see, the fencing of the border was perceived as a hard measure by Bangladesh. Given the slow and irregular progress of the work, however, by the end of January 2006 only 1,275.4 km of the border were fenced (MHA 2006: 160). The difficult conditions on the ground determined by erosion, shifting river routes, and repeated floods made the fence easy to circumvent and, therefore, hardly effective (Shamshad 2008: 9).[24]

In the context of a general sensitization to the issue of Islamist terrorism after the attacks of 9/11 in the US, the apparent impunity of Islamist groups in Bangladesh represented a further, major source of concern for New Delhi. India particularly feared the alleged ties existing between al-Qaeda and terrorist groups in Bangladesh (Dutta 2009: 87).

During the first phase analysed, a series of accusations related to Islamist terrorism made by representatives of the Indian government contributed to a

---

23 In 2002, these training camps were 99 in number (Lok Sabha 2002b). In 2004, the director-general of the BSF handed over a new list of 195 training camps and 126 insurgents to be deported to India (Habib 2004).

24 Interview with expert, New Delhi, 3 November 2008.

decline in bilateral relations with Bangladesh. For example, in November 2002, the Indian deputy prime minister, L.K. Advani, explicitly expressed concern about the activities of the ISI and al-Qaeda in Bangladesh, as well as about the support given to north-eastern insurgent groups under the BNP-led government (PTI 2002).

However, it was not only the BJP-led government in New Delhi that put pressure on Bangladesh. The Congress-led UPA government that came to power after the May 2004 elections also engaged in blame games with Dhaka, but was ultimately unable to substantially improve cooperation on that matter with the neighbouring country. In October 2006, Prime Minister Manmohan Singh explicitly linked the issue of migration with the problem of externally supported terrorism against India – an association which up to that point had been typical of the BJP: 'The economic pull on migrants from Bangladesh of the Indian market offers opportunities to our enemies who seek to incite terrorism in India' (GOI 2006).

A further serious crisis in Indo–Bangladesh relations was unleashed by India's decision not to take part in the SAARC summit scheduled to take place in Dhaka on 6–7 February 2005 given 'recent developments in our neighbourhood, which have caused us grave concern' (MEA 2005m). These 'developments' referred not so much to the coup staged by King Gyanendra in Nepal, as rather to the 'deteriorated' security situation in Dhaka 'following the fatal attack on the former Finance Minister of Bangladesh, Mr. SAMS Kibria', as outlined by Foreign Secretary Shyam Saran (ibid.). New Delhi's decision to boycott the SAARC summit was interpreted by the government of Bangladesh as an attempt to undermine its international reputation and even as a sign of India's support for the opposition led by the Awami League (Habib 2005). This again, is an indicator of the high degree of politicization of relations with India that was prevalent among the political parties in Bangladesh.

Similarly, the terrorist attacks that took place in 2005 unleashed a series of accusations and counter-accusations between Dhaka and New Delhi. For example, when the leader of Jamaat and a minister in the government of Bangladesh, Maulana Matiur Rahman Nizami, blamed the Indian secret service RAW, along with the Israeli Mossad, for an alleged involvement in the bomb blasts of August 2005 (ibid.; *The Daily Star* 2005b), India reacted expressing a vague threat against Bangladesh: 'Statements of this kind undermine efforts to promote the friendly and good neighbourly relations between Bangladesh and India' (MEA 2005c).

The blame game continued after some bomb blasts hit the Indian cities of Varanasi and Hyderabad in March 2006 and August 2007 respectively, and Bangladeshi citizens were found out to have been involved (Gupta/Singh 2007).[25] In October 2006, India's National Security Advisor M. K. Narayanan accused Bangladesh of being a 'sanctuary' of terrorism and a 'launching pad' (*The Hindu* 2006) for terrorists operating in India. Moreover, he complained about the

---

25 In November 2007, moreover, three Islamist terrorist cells were discovered in Indian cities, and evidence was collected of terror networks having links to Bangladesh (Dutta 2009: 87).

cooperation with the government of Bangladesh on this issue, considered 'not as forthcoming as it should be' (ibid.).

Therefore, the problem of terrorism severely affected bilateral relations between India and Bangladesh, inducing New Delhi to take a hard stance in its verbal inter-actions with Dhaka. Even though the UPA government displayed somehow more cooperative attitudes towards Bangladesh,[26] it continued to employ typical hard hegemonic foreign policy means and to engage in a series of mutual accusations with Dhaka.

Besides these huge security-related problems in bilateral relations, tensions between India and Bangladesh also concerned other long-standing disputes in different issue areas, which reveal both Bangladesh's concerns vis-à-vis India, and the difficulties both countries faced in finding a common ground for cooperation. Among these issues were the sharing of water of common rivers, with the lower riparian Bangladesh depending on India for a regular and sufficient flow of water (Dutta 2009: 101–4), or the denial of transit facilities to India by the government of Bangladesh, which forced Indian goods to be transported all the way around Bangladesh through the Siliguri corridor to the north-east (ibid.: 104). Another major issue in bilateral relations has always been Bangladesh's huge trade deficit with India.[27] Over the past decades, Dhaka has demanded greater market access in Indian markets (De/Bhattacharyay 2007: 12), especially in the textile and garment sector, which, however, is heavily protected by India. Even though New Delhi made some concessions in matters of trade to Bangladesh in 2002 and 2003, the textile sector remained protected by 'prohibitively high' (Mukherji 2006: 109) specific duties introduced in 2001.[28]

This uncooperative attitude on the part of India was mirrored by Bangladesh in the area of gas exports. The option of exporting gas to India from the fields of the Bay of Bengal inflamed the political debate in Bangladesh. As Mohan (2002) puts it, '[i]n a typical fashion of the subcontinent, extraordinary emotional baggage was loaded onto what was a simple commercial decision'. In 2006, the BNP and the opposition AL agreed – in a rare moment of political unity – to refuse to export gas to India (Wagner 2008: 26). Dhaka ultimately granted China the exploration rights for its gas fields at Barakpuria, where a Chinese company also set up a coal-fired power plant (Aneja 2006: 7). Similarly, the project of a pipeline, which would have been used to transport gas from Myanmar/Burma to India through Bangladesh, was never implemented despite the high revenues it would have provided to Dhaka (ibid.). A further episode of this kind concerned a US$ 3 billion investment proposal made by the Indian Tata group in 2004. This project too was ultimately

---

26 For example, the frequency of bilateral meetings of government representatives increased and Prime Minister Manmohan Singh adopted a cooperative tone during Khaleda Zia's state visit in 2006 (MEA 2006l).

27 For an analysis of bilateral trade relations, see De/Bhattacharyay (2007).

28 As an Indian scholar put it, 'India has to take care of how it opens up'. Interview with expert, New Delhi, 3 November 2008.

refused by Bangladesh and, again, negative perceptions about India and the fear of selling out the country's national interest led to the failure of a potentially lucrative project for Bangladesh (*The Hindu* 2008b).

After the difficult years of Khaleda Zia, during the brief phase of the caretaker government headed by President Iajuddin Ahmed, under which Bangladesh precipitated into a situation of almost complete anarchy and violence, India followed a low-key approach towards Dhaka. Remarkably, New Delhi did not try to influence the domestic events in Bangladesh and resorted, instead, to soft persuasion tools – for example, expressing the 'hope that the people of Bangladesh [would] be able to elect a government of their own choice in a free, fair, credible and democratic election' (MEA 2007b). As in other cases, New Delhi paid attention not to appear to be interfering with Bangladesh's domestic politics in order to avoid a further outbreak of anti-India resentment. However, despite this restraint on domestic issues, India continued to raise the 'usual' topics of immigration, exchange of enclaves, and border management (e.g., Rajya Sabha 2006a).

In summary, mutual distrust, and historically and geographically determined threat perceptions on the part of Dhaka, contributed to a great extent to making a constructive approach to Bangladesh almost impossible for India during the first phase analysed. The fear of spill-over effects and of actual threats for India's security induced policy-makers from both the BJP and the Congress to adopt an intransigent attitude towards Dhaka and to resort to pressure, accusations, and threats – that is, to typical hard hegemonic tools. Besides these hard hegemonic tools, the problem of border security also led to the (sporadic) adoption of typical 'imperial' measures (see Chapter Two), as in the case of the display and threat of force in the above-mentioned confrontation with the Bangladesh Rifles.[29]

The takeover of the military-backed caretaker government led by Fakhruddin Ahmed marked the beginning of the second phase analysed (2007–8), in which bilateral relations between India and Bangladesh got decisively more relaxed. Despite initial apprehensions, India, along with the international community, supported the military-backed CTG. Decision-makers in New Delhi were well aware of the fact that carrying out elections as scheduled would have destabilized Bangladesh beyond any realistic possibility of control. Moreover, the marginalization of Bangladesh's two main parties from political life allowed Indo–Bangladesh relations to take a more pragmatic turn. Correspondingly, New Delhi shifted to softer foreign policy means, with some important concessions made to Bangladesh in the economic field and the adoption of soft persuasion tools.

An expression of the improved bilateral relations was the 'unmatched' spate of bilateral talks and meetings taking place at different levels during this phase (Dutta 2008b: 193). The government of India took the first step in this regard by sending the minister of external affairs, Pranab Mukherjee, to visit Bangladesh

---

29 However, the border clashes *per se* are not defined as imperial means adopted by India given the uncertainty about the initiator.

just a month after the establishment of the military-backed CTG – an expression of 'unequivocal support' to the government headed by Fakhruddin (Dutta 2009: 88–9). On that occasion, Mukherjee engaged in an open cajoling of Bangladesh: 'India attaches the highest importance to its relations with Bangladesh. I have reiterated India's desire to strengthen and further enhance the friendly cooperative relations between our two countries' (MEA 2007g).[30]

Even more importantly, India displayed an entirely new readiness to make concessions by announcing duty-free access to its market for two million ready-made garments from Bangladesh – an otherwise heavily protected sector in India (ibid.). This was a response to Bangladesh's repeated complaints about India's protectionist policies in sectors vital for Bangladesh and, thereby, a clear effort to ease tensions in bilateral trade relations. At the 14th SAARC summit in April 2007, moreover, India announced its intention to provide duty-free access to its market for products from the Least Developed Countries (LDCs) in SAARC (GOI 2007). The only relevant beneficiary of these concessions was Bangladesh, since India's trade arrangements with the other LDCs in the region already contained more liberal provisions (Nepal and Bhutan have long had duty free access to India's market on the basis of bilateral treaties), and given the limited relevance of trade with the Maledives as well as the difficulties for India to trade with Afghanistan given the physical barrier constituted by Pakistan (World Bank 2006). As a consequence of these trade concessions, 86 per cent of Bangladesh's tariff lines were exempted from import duties to India starting from 1 January 2008 (Dutta 2009: 90). India also made some efforts to reduce its non-tariff barriers towards Bangladesh by accepting Dhaka's long-standing request to establish a testing facility at the Petrapole border checkpoint and not, as originally planned, in Kolkata, thereby allowing for a faster processing of customs controls (ibid.). Similarly, Bangladesh's request to lift the ban on FDI by Bangladeshi companies in India was satisfied in July 2007 (ibid.: 91), and in the field of 'connectivity' relations improved with the decision to start a passenger train service between Dhaka and Kolkata (MEA 2007c).

When a cyclone hit Bangladesh in November 2007, India promptly provided assistance in the form of food aid and relief material worth US$ 1 million and agreed to the request of Bangladesh to lift its ban on rice exports for 50,000 tons of rice (MEA 2007d; 2007i). The Indian minister of external affairs visited the devastated country and announced the symbolic 'adoption' and reconstruction of ten heavily affected coastal villages on the part of India (MEA 2007h). However, some of these overtures were implemented only half-heartedly, thereby provoking a further increase in Bangladesh's negative perceptions about India. In the case of the agreed export of rice, for example, procedural obstacles at customs led to a delay in delivery. This conveyed the impression among the population of

---

30 Similar reiterations of the friendly character of bilateral Indo–Bangladesh relations took place repeatedly during this phase.

Bangladesh that India was intentionally creating procedural obstacles to the consignment (ur Rashid 2008).

It is difficult to say to what extent the government of India planned the concessions outlined above as *incentives* targeted at specific policy changes on the part of Bangladesh. From the official statements analysed, no inferences can be made in this regard since no explicit request or condition was formally attached to the concessions made by New Delhi. The following statement by former Indian ambassador I. P. Khosla suggests that concessions may have been made more in an effort to improve overall bilateral relations and to build confidence than in an effort to obtain concrete and immediate foreign policy changes on the part of Bangladesh:

> 'India's policy in this regard is actually not very clear. Our policy makers tell us that the aim of Indian foreign policy is to ensure that our overall economic targets are achieved. The policy seems to suggest if one tempts the neighbours with economic inducements, political gains will follow. Presumably the idea is to offer economic inducements for political purposes. Possibly it could be a circular thing – economic inducement leading to political gains, which would create an atmosphere of peace leading to further economic gains'.
>
> (Andley/Mahanta 2007)

This much more positive picture of bilateral relations in the years 2007–8 needs, however, to be qualified. Despite the clear improvement in bilateral relations, the main problems remained in place and 'the core Indian concerns *vis-à-vis* Bangladesh, namely security issues, [were] not [...] addressed adequately' in the eyes of New Delhi (Dutta 2008a: 215). The issues of migration, smuggling, human trafficking, and other illegal activities continued to affect the border areas (Rashid 2008). Correspondingly, New Delhi took some measures to increase border security, among others a strengthening of the BSF and an acceleration of border fencing (Lok Sabha 2007a). Similarly, on the issue of Islamist terrorism, India's apprehension about the activities of groups operating in Bangladesh remained in place. After the serial bomb blasts that took place in the Indian city of Hyderabad in August 2007, it was discovered that the culprit had relations to members of HuJI, while a HuJI operative was arrested after the attacks in Jaipur in May 2008. In August 2008, at the home secretary-level meeting between India and Bangladesh, the Indian side requested Bangladesh to arrest three suspects, whose names and contact data were provided by India (Dutta 2009: 107). However, Bangladesh, according to the well-known pattern of interaction with New Delhi, rejected any involvement of its citizens in the Hyderabad attacks and refused to cooperate with India.

To summarize, during the second phase analysed, New Delhi considerably reduced its pressure on Dhaka in comparison to the years under BNP rule. The softening of India's approach was related to a great extent to the more cooperative attitude of the CTG, which adopted some steps to accommodate Indian demands – for example, on the extradition of wanted insurgents, as will be illustrated later. Therefore, the less heated domestic political climate in Bangladesh opened up new space for India to adopt predominantly intermediate hegemonic foreign policy means, mainly in the form of economic concessions. While this did not allow for a radical change in the pattern of strategic interaction between India and Bangladesh, 'certain incremental steps were taken that contributed to creating a conducive atmosphere for future engagement with each other' (Dutta 2009: 86).

Threat Perceptions, Resistance, and Counter-Accusations: Bangladesh's Approach

As mentioned above, mutual negative perceptions contributed to make bilateral relations between India and Bangladesh particularly difficult in the time span analysed, as well as in previous decades. As a diplomat from Bangladesh put it when interviewed, 'our perceptions and their perceptions are clouded. There are many disappointments. Because of history, we have a lot of psychological... you know, memories...'.[31] One of the issues looming large in Bangladesh's image of India (and vice-versa) is the liberation war of 1971 and the problem of 'gratitude'. In fact, while India was disappointed about Bangladesh's short-lived gratitude for the role it played during the war, the Indian expectation of gratitude was resented by Bangladeshis: 'Immediately after independence, when the Bangladeshis wanted to assert their autonomy, the Indians saw that as ingratitude. That really didn't help'.[32] On the contrary, in Bangladesh the view gained a foothold that it was India that should have been grateful to Bangladesh for having weakened its enemy Pakistan (Khosla 2005).[33]

Moreover, since Bangladesh 'cannot ignore powerful India' due to its geographical position, '[t]he anti-India sentiment in Bangladesh appears to be the manifestation of [a] "small country syndrome"' (ur Rashid 2008). This combination of historical and geographical factors has therefore produced 'a stereotyped vision about the Indian threat which hinders beneficial cooperative ventures with India' (Yasmin 2004). All this has been reinforced by 'politically motivated media campaigns and highly nationalistic and sovereignty-sensitive elites that seek their political sustenance through non-cooperation' (Pattanaik 2011: 74).

These negative perceptions did not change much across the time span analysed, even though a slight improvement took place in the second phase. At the same time, it was during this phase that India consciously tried to improve its image by presenting itself as a 'benevolent' neighbour willing to make concessions to smaller states in the region. As External Affairs Minister Mukherjee put it in June 2008, '[i]t is also in this spirit of engagement that India has made several unilateral gestures in the recent past to Bangladesh. These gestures are precisely *to build trust and mutual confidence* in each other [emphasis added]' (MEA 2008e).

31 Interview with Bangladeshi diplomat, New Delhi, 24 November 2008.
32 Interview with Bangladeshi diplomat, New Delhi, 24 November 2008.
33 Interview with expert, New Delhi, 7 November 2008.

However, despite India's concessions on single issues, the BNP's and AL's desire to distance themselves as much as possible from India in order not to appear to be 'selling out the national interest' contributed to frustrate India's efforts.[34] As two of the interviewees put it, 'India–Bangladesh relations are a victim of Bangladeshi politics' and 'there are political parties that have a vested interest in continued tensions and a lack of trust in India'.[35]

Correspondingly, under the BNP-led government between 2001–6, Bangladesh's relations with India were extremely tense. New Delhi's pressures and accusations were met by Dhaka with a pattern of reactions entailing passive resistance and denial, diplomatic protests, and ultimately counter-accusations on a range of issues.

This pattern became evident, for example, on the issue of the persecution of the Hindu minority after the 2001 elections, when the government of Bangladesh initially provided assurances about its intention to protect minorities,[36] but subsequently resorted to an approach of partial denial, highlighting that many of the incidents were not communal in nature and amounted, instead, to private disputes (Rajya Sabha 2003b).

On the issue of migration to India, the denial on the part of the government of Bangladesh was even more open and consistent. As early as in the 1980s, the government of Bangladesh had refused to acknowledge the movement of people to India, as highlighted by one of the experts interviewed, a former Indian diplomat who had been serving in Bangladesh:

> 'And when I talked to Ershad, [...] he said "Bangladesh, have you looked at Bangladesh? Look at it, it's such a beautiful country: it's so fertile, green, fertile, it's rich, it's prosperous. Do you think anybody wants to leave this country? No, only you want to leave it when your term comes to an end!" There is not a single occasion when any official Bangladeshi has ever admitted that there is any migration from Bangladesh to India'.[37]

This kind of reaction remained almost unchanged during the time span analysed. A high diplomatic representative of Bangladesh interviewed in 2008, for example, not only denied the existence of a huge exodus of Bangladeshis to India but also affirmed that '[t]he environment of India is not very conducive to attract people to India. Bangladesh has done much better in terms of inclusive growth than neighbouring Indian states', implying therefore that there are no reasons for Bangladeshis to migrate.[38]

---

34 Interviews with government official, New Delhi, 17 November 2008; with expert, New Delhi, 7 November 2008; with expert, New Delhi, 3 November 2008.
35 Interviews with journalists, New Delhi, 10 December and 26 November 2008.
36 See, for example, Rajya Sabha (2001).
37 Interview with expert, New Delhi, 7 November 2008.
38 Interview with Bangladeshi diplomat, New Delhi, 24 November 2008. The approach of denial on the issue of migration continued all over the two phases analysed.

The discussion on migration also led to some serious confrontations between India and Bangladesh. For example, after Indian Deputy Prime Minister Advani claimed that 15 million Bangladeshis were living illegally in India and constituted a serious security threat, the foreign secretary of Bangladesh summoned the Indian high commissioner to express his country's indignation about the statement, rejecting it as 'an inspired anti-Bangladeshi propaganda ploy done from time to time seeking to project Bangladesh in a negative light internationally' (Kaur 2003). Besides this open denial, the government of Bangladesh ultimately resorted to counter-accusations in the first phase analysed, highlighting the existence of a 'contrary' migration movement from India to Bangladesh enforced by the government of India or by single Indian states. In October 2004, the government of Bangladesh sent an aide-memoire to India expressing concern about the alleged attempts by the BSF to push Bengali-speaking Indian Muslims into Bangladesh (Habib 2004). Dhaka's counter-allegations had already had repercussions on the ground in episodes like the aforementioned refusal on the part of the BDR to allow the stranded nomadic people to enter the country in 2003, which had led to a serious confrontation at the border.

The same pattern of resistance and counter-accusations on the part of Dhaka also applied to India's pressures on the issue of insurgent groups operating from Bangladesh. In fact, after having repeatedly denied the existence of insurgent camps and having reassured India that the list of camps provided by the BSF was verified but that no camps were found,[39] Bangladesh resorted to counter-accusations. In October 2004, the director-general of the BDR reacted to his Indian counterpart handing over to him a new list of camps and insurgents to be deported by submitting himself a list of 95 camps allegedly run by Bangladeshi insurgents on Indian territory (Habib 2004). Shortly before, in September 2004, Bangladeshi Foreign Minister M. Morshed Khan had made the following exasperated statement: 'The list of insurgent camps from their side increases at every meeting between us. But they have not been able to provide us a single phone number or address of these camps' (*Star* 2004). More than this, bilateral relations with India had reached a new low when Morshed Khan, on the same occasion, openly accused New Delhi of turning a blind eye on the activities of anti-Bangladesh insurgent groups and enforced his accusation with a threat: New Delhi should not forget that though Bangladesh is India-locked, the north-east of India is Bangladesh-locked too – and his government possessed the capability to harm India's export industry by issuing a statutory regulatory order on imports from India, which at the time were worth US\$ 3 billion.[40]

Finally, India's last minute announcement that it would not participate in the SAARC summit scheduled to take place in Dhaka in February 2005 provoked

39   See for example ExpressIndia (2005b).
40   See *Star* (2004); Lok Sabha (2004). The statement on the north-east's locked character led, in turn, to a confirmation of the fear in conservative circles in India that Bangladesh wanted to isolate the north-east (see below). Interview with expert, New Delhi, 7 November 2008.

angry reactions and protests on the part of the government of Bangladesh (*The Daily Star* 2005c). As on other occasions, the postponement of the SAARC summit was soon politicised by the main parties in Bangladesh, with the BNP alleging an involvement of the AL in persuading India to boycott the summit in order to damage the government's image (*The Daily Star* 2005a).

The fencing of the border, by which India hoped to dam up the incoming migrants from Bangladesh, was a further object of dispute between the two countries for several years.[41] 'Various officials and non-governmental circles' in Bangladesh were opposed to the fencing, perceived as 'a security structure encircling their country' (Dutta 2009: 99) and as a hard measure on the part of India.[42] On this issue, there were repeated bilateral disputes, as well as protests along the border hampering the construction of the fence (ibid.; *The Daily Star* 2006b). These reactions and perceptions on the part of Bangladesh help define the fencing as a hard hegemonic tool on the part of India.[43]

In summary, the contentious bilateral issues along with the 'small country syndrome' related to the geographic situation of Bangladesh, the 'ingratitude problem' dating back to 1971, and the politicization of issues related to India contributed to worsen pre-existing negative perceptions of the larger neighbour. At the official level, this found expression in statements like that of the planning and finance minister of Bangladesh, who in December 2002 openly defined India as 'an aggressive and difficult country to live with' (Dubey 2003). The gradual worsening of bilateral relations under the BNP-led government reached an all-time low with the previously mentioned allegation by the leader of Jamaat that India had been involved in the 2005 coordinated attacks in Bangladesh (Habib 2005b). Similarly, the director general of the BDR alleged that the suspected perpetrators of the terrorist attacks had links with India – a charge New Delhi immediately denied.[44]

All this led, during the first phase analysed, to a sort of dialogue of the deaf between the two countries, and to a spiral of accusations and increased threat perceptions apparently impossible to overcome.

The CTG takeover under Fakhruddin Ahmed in 2007 marked a remarkable change in Bangladesh's approach to India on a number of issues. As a result, Dhaka

---

41 See, for example, *The Daily Star* (2006c).
42 Informal conversation with scholar from Bangladesh, New Delhi, 6 November 2008.
43 According to the COW project, fortifying the border – that is, the 'explicit attempt to publicly demonstrate control over a border area through the construction of military outposts to defend or claim territory' (Jones et al. 1996: 172) – constitutes a display of force. Although it is difficult to define the fence as a military outpost, its mainly 'practical' goal of stopping migration and smuggling qualifies its nature as an object displaying military power. Given the negative perceptions and reactions about fencing on the part of Bangladesh, the most suitable solution seems to take the fence as an indicator of a hard hegemonic strategy employed by India.
44 See ExpressIndia (2005a). For the Indian reaction, terming the allegation 'baseless and scurrilous', see MEA (2005i).

adopted a much more cooperative attitude towards New Delhi thanks to the less heated domestic political climate. India's concessions and gestures of goodwill in the years 2007–8 were broadly replicated by the military-backed caretaker government of Bangladesh. The increased propensity to dialogue on the part of both countries led to the reopening of fora, such as the talks over the sharing of common rivers, which were resumed in 2007 after having been stalled for over two years (Dutta 2008b: 193); the director general meetings between the BSF and BDR, which resumed from April 2008 (Dutta 2009: 89); and the joint Land Record and Survey team responsible for a survey of the border in disputed areas (ibid.: 94). Moreover, in September 2008, expert talks were held on the issue of maritime boundary demarcation – a topic on which bilateral consultations had been avoided since the 1980s (ibid.: 96–7). As far as high level visits are concerned, besides the two visits of External Affairs Minister Mukherjee to Bangladesh, the army chief of Bangladesh, Moheen U. Ahmed, visited India in February 2008 with the aim of strengthening bilateral defence ties and security cooperation, as well as of gaining political support for the military-backed caretaker regime in Dhaka (*India Defence* 2008).

In addition to that, Dhaka's new approach to New Delhi was marked by a series of goodwill gestures. For example, Indian veterans of the 1971 war of liberation were invited to take part in the Bangladesh Independence Day celebrations in 2008 (Rashid 2008), a gesture 'well received by Indians' (Kapila 2008). Also, the fencing of the border came to be formally accepted by Bangladesh, which recognised India's right to build defensive structures beyond 150 yards from the border as provided for by the Border Guidelines of 1975 (Dutta 2009: 99). Overall, tensions on the border were reduced with a corresponding decline in border clashes between BSF and BDR (ibid.: 100). Substantial progress was even made on the issue of insurgents operating against India from the territory of Bangladesh under the military-backed CTG, since the BDR 'facilitated' the surrender of a wanted militant leader operating from the Chittagong Hill Tracts, and also handed over to India 18 militants suspected of terrorist activities in September 2008 (ibid.: 98).

Despite these overtures to India, however, Bangladesh continued to stick to its intransigent position on other contentious issues. One of them was the problem of transit, on which the CTG agreed to hold discussions with New Delhi – something previous governments of Bangladesh had always straightforwardly rejected (Dutta 2008b: 193) – but refused to make any concessions to India due to 'strong resistance from various quarters' (Rashid 2008) at the domestic level. This was related to the fear that India would use the transit issue to extract further concessions from Bangladesh, and that the benefits from transit would flow exclusively to India to the detriment of Bangladesh (Ahmed 2008).

Similarly, the government of Bangladesh continued to pursue its approach of resistance and denial on the issues of migration (e.g., Sobhan 2007) and terrorism. After a first terrorist attack in Hyderabad in May 2007, Bangladesh's Foreign Affairs Adviser Iftekhar Ahmed Chowdhury reacted by defining India's allegation of an involvement of Bangladeshi citizens as 'purely speculative and unsubstantiated', and by underlining that '[f]inger pointing of this kind without adequate proof is extremely unhelpful to the spirit of good neighbourliness' (*The Daily Star* 2007f). Similarly, India's allegation of an involvement of HuJI members in the serial blasts that hit Hyderabad in August 2007 was also dismissed as 'baseless' by Chowdhury (*The Daily Star* 2007c), and Dhaka refused to cooperate with New Delhi when, at the home minister-level talks, the Indian side handed over to its Bangladeshi counterpart the names of three suspects from Bangladesh (Dutta 2009: 107).

The economic concessions made by India were also still considered insufficient by the CTG of Bangladesh. The existence of non-tariff barriers continued to be interpreted as a 'hard measure' by Dhaka.[45] As a Bangladeshi diplomat put it, 'obviously, economic prosperity gave India a strengthened position to engage with us. But the facts or the unresolved issues – they are the same'.[46] Therefore, despite the substantial improvement in relations during the second phase analysed, the resilience of negative perceptions about India significantly reduced the impact of New Delhi's cooperative overtures. As an Indian expert described Bangladesh's attitude, 'even when the situation on the ground has changed completely, you still stick ... to what you thought five years ago. So that makes [cooperation] very difficult'. [47]

India and Bangladesh: Diverging Goals

Having assessed in detail the foreign policy means employed by India and the reactions and perceptions on the part of Bangladesh, the analysis of both countries' foreign policy goals and of their quite apparent divergence can be carried out very succinctly. As in the previous chapters, the focus will be on 'core' goals and on more specific objectives.

The *limitation of negative security externalities* to neighbouring Indian states and to the country as a whole can be identified as New Delhi's core foreign policy goal in its relations with Bangladesh. The content analysis of the MEA statements, speeches, press briefings, press releases, media interactions, and Q&A sessions in parliament referring to Bangladesh has revealed that 27.3 per cent of the utterances expressing India's goals concerned the limitation of spill-over effects.[48] This goal entails several aspects already widely discussed in the previous sections, particularly the containment of migration and the need to avoid the use of Bangladesh's territory for activities directed against India. In both phases analysed, the latter objective was very explicitly stated by Indian foreign policy makers in their inter-

---

45 Interview with Bangladeshi diplomat, New Delhi, 24 November 2008.
46 Ibid.
47 Interview with expert, New Delhi, 7 November 2008.
48 Further, 15.1 per cent of the utterances were referred to economic issues (connectivity, gas imports, FDI to Bangladesh, transit, promotion of India's economy through tied aid to Bangladesh) and 5.2 per cent to the goals of democracy and secularism. Several other minor goals were equally expressed, among them border demarcation (11 per cent), protection of religious minorities (11 per cent), progress and prosperity (5.2 per cent), and peace and stability (4.6 per cent).

actions with Bangladesh (e.g., MEA 2005a; Lok Sabha 2007c). The limitation of activities inimical to India referred to three main actors: Islamist militants, north-east insurgents, and the Pakistani secret service ISI.

Concerning the last actor, which was assumed to have 'strong ties' (Mehta 2004: 148) with Bangladesh's main intelligence agency, the Directorate General Field Intelligence (DGFI), it was considered to be involved in the support of anti-India activities. Accordingly, the Indian government had repeatedly expressed the allegation of the involvement of the ISI in the activities of Islamic fundamentalists and secessionist insurgents operating in Bangladesh. There was also a widespread view among Indian analysts that Pakistan tried to gain a foothold in Bangladesh in order to destabilize India (e.g., Kamboj 2005). From this perspective, limiting the ISI's presence and its presumed attempts to destabilize India from Bangladesh naturally constituted a key objective for New Delhi.

Other security-related core goals, which were not explicitly stated by the government of India, but can be inferred from India's behaviour and were highlighted by some of the interviewees, were the *limitation of China's influence on Bangladesh* and the *limitation of Bangladesh's influence on India's north-east*.

China's presence in Bangladesh had been rapidly growing over the years analysed, and particularly under the government of Khaleda Zia (Aneja 2006: 3). China became Bangladesh's main provider of military hardware and training, leading to preoccupied assessments by Indian analysts (e.g., Kapila 2003). China's replacement of India as Bangladesh's largest trade partner in 2005 equally irritated Indian experts, who highlighted that Bangladesh unfairly complained only about its trade deficit with India, but never about that with China.[49] In the field of energy, Bangladesh–China relations became equally close. As outlined above, Bangladesh granted China exploration rights for developing some of its gas fields after having denied India the rights to import gas. Even more disturbing from the Indian point of view was the signing of the Cooperation Agreement on the Peaceful Usage of Nuclear Energy between China and Bangladesh (Aneja 2006: 4), with the Indian government stating that it would 'remain vigilant with regard to further developments in the matter' (Rajya Sabha 2005a). Equally, China invested massively in Bangladesh's infrastructure and got naval access to the port of Chittagong – another concession India had long sought but never managed to get from Dhaka (ibid.: 7; *India Defence* 2006). These failures to gain a foothold in Bangladesh contributed to strengthen India's resolve to limit Beijing's influence on Dhaka, which corresponds to India's broader goal of avoiding challenges to its own supremacy in South Asia (ibid.: 9). The 'positive' side of the coin was India's effort to increase its influence on Bangladesh by making economic concessions. The provision of incentives in the second phase analysed can be interpreted as an indicator of New Delhi's desire not to 'lose' Bangladesh to the Chinese as in the cases of Sri Lanka and Nepal.

49   Interviews with experts, New Delhi, 7 November 2008; New Delhi, 20 November 2008.

Among the less obvious of India's unstated goals was the desire to limit relations between India's north-east and Bangladesh. While the UPA government highlighted, at the rhetorical level, the need to provide for deeper integration and connectivity in the sub-region comprising India's east, its north-east, and Bangladesh,[50] sections of the Indian foreign policy making elite feared that Bangladesh might try to gain increasing influence on the north-eastern states of India.[51] As an Indian government official put it with some degree of preoccupation, hinting at the 'Bangladesh-locked' geopolitical situation of the north-eastern states, '[i]n the north-east, Bangladesh is a superpower'.[52] As a consequence of this assessment, if we take a closer look at India's foreign policy approach to Bangladesh, we find out that Indian governments have tried to limit relations between the north-eastern states and Bangladesh. The long-standing desire on the part of India to get transit through Bangladesh to its north-eastern states seems to have been related to the need to strengthen the economies of this region (Dutta 2009: 104) and to provide for a better integration of these states with the rest of India, rather than to the need of improving ties between the north-east and Bangladesh. Accordingly, Bangladesh's refusal to grant India transit rights to the north-east was at times perceived by India as an explicit attempt on the part of Dhaka to isolate India's north-eastern states.[53] The existence and relevance of this unstated goal on the part of New Delhi was further underlined by India's refusal to agree to the establishment of a Bangladeshi trade mission in one of India's north-eastern states in order to improve trade relations with this part of India (Rajya Sabha 2005f). The following reply by Minister of External Affairs Yashwant Sinha to a question on the reasons for New Delhi's hurdles on greater economic integration between the north-east and Bangladesh is telling:

'We welcome your country's close business links with our North-eastern States. Therefore, there is no question of anyone creating hurdles in this regard. However, you will be well advised to look at business links with our North-eastern States in the overall context of your dealings with our country as a whole. A narrow segmentary approach will be counter productive. We are inviting you to increase your business links with the whole of India.'

(MEA 2002d)

On an operational level, India's objectives with respect to the core goal of security were an improvement of border security and, related to it, of border management;

---

50 This was expressed in terms of a vision of a sub-region 'seen not as the periphery of the Indian subcontinent but [as] the core of a thriving, dynamic and integrated economic space with a network of highways, railways, pipelines, transmission lines criss-crossing the region' (MEA 2005f).

51 'Then again [...] they [the Bangladeshis] look at the north-east of India as *Lebensraum*. So the one great hope of the Bangladeshis was – some Bangladeshis, not all obviously – that if India goes to pieces, then this land [will belong to them]'. Interview with expert, New Delhi, 7 November 2008.

52 Interview with government official, New Delhi, 20 November 2008.

53 Ibid.

and a settlement of the pending issues on border demarcation and the exchange of enclaves.[54] Moreover, India had a clear interest in the protection of minorities in Bangladesh after the episodes of harassment in 2001. In addition to that, on a more general note, the Indian MEA repeatedly expressed New Delhi's preference for a 'peaceful, stable, democratic, secular and prosperous Bangladesh', considered to be 'in India's own national interest' (MEA 2007f). As mentioned above, however, New Delhi took an extremely low-key approach in dealing with domestic developments in Bangladesh in order not to appear as interfering.

If we proceed to discuss the goals of Bangladesh, a high degree of divergence from the core objectives of India is almost self-evident. This divergence was related, among other things, to a different prioritization of issues: while security issues were at the centre of India's interests, Bangladesh focused on such topics as its trade deficit with India and the management of rivers. The interviews with two Bangladeshi diplomats carried out in New Delhi in November 2008 help identify Bangladesh's foreign policy goals. According to the interviewees, Dhaka's primary objective was autonomy in decision-making. As one of the diplomats put it, 'there is a tendency in dictating things to you. Many of the things which have gone wrong are due to a role played by outside powers. Even politically, turmoil ... many of these things are due to external influence'.[55] When asked to name these outside powers, the diplomat replied very directly: 'Pakistan and India – both have an interest in how things should go in Bangladesh. Pakistan would like us to be as conservative as they are and India would like us to develop in the totally contrary trajectory, similarly to India'.[56] Therefore, India's repeated assertion of the importance of secularism in Bangladesh was clearly resented by Bangladesh's government representatives: 'People in Bangladesh are not as fundamental as in Pakistan or Afghanistan, they are much more liberal. They [the Indians] are totally misled: they think Bangladesh is supporting the Islamists but it's not like that'.[57]

Bangladesh's growing ties to China were a result of these influence attempts by India and Pakistan, according to the interviewee: 'As all small countries we want to have flexibility in our foreign policy decision-making. [...] We also stitch up alliances with other countries, like China'.[58] This goal and the corresponding policy of cooperation with Beijing pursued by Dhaka in both phases analysed directly oppose India's non-stated goal of keeping China out of Bangladesh.

Further goals outlined by the diplomats were economic security (and particularly the reduction of Bangladesh's trade deficit with India, estimated to be as high

---

54 The goal of border demarcation was also one of the most frequently expressed goals in the MEA official statements and parliament Q&A sessions analysed, making up for 11 per cent of the utterances referring to New Delhi's goals for Bangladesh.

55 Interview with Bangladeshi diplomat, New Delhi, 24 November 2008.

56 Ibid.

57 Ibid.

58 Ibid.

as US\$ 2 billion), the tackling of challenges related to climate change, and 'another issue, *but not as pressing*, is the unbridled growth of extremist groups'.[59]

These statements confirm what has been inferred from the patterns of interaction between India and Bangladesh: India's core goal, the limitation of spill-over effects from Bangladesh, and most notably the fight against migration and against groups carrying out anti-India activities from Bangladesh's territory, did not coincide with Dhaka's main objectives. However, on the issue of insurgent groups having their camps in the areas bordering India, and on militant Islamism, a shift was observed between the first and the second phase analysed. While the BNP government resorted exclusively to denial and counter-accusations, the CTG took some cooperative measures in fighting Indian insurgents in 2008 (Dutta 2009: 98). Similarly, after the bomb blasts of August 2005, Dhaka's readiness to fight Islamists increased and a rapprochement between India's and Bangladesh's goals in this regard took place. This found expression in an – at least rhetorical – recognition that both countries were victims of terrorism and 'need[ed] to join hands in fighting this scourge' (MEA 2006c). However, as emerges from the statement of the Bangladeshi diplomat cited above, there were huge differences in the prioritization of this goal between New Delhi and Dhaka.

With regard to operational and secondary goals, divergences persisted on border demarcation throughout the time span analysed, although a rapprochement took place on border management under the CTG with the acknowledgement of India's right to build defensive structures beyond 150 yards from the border, and a reduction in border clashes. On the issue of border demarcation and exchange of enclaves, Dhaka shared in principle India's goal of settling those pending issues, but divergences emerged on the modalities (*The Economist* 2011). In addition, no convergence in goals could be achieved on New Delhi's unstated objective of avoiding the integration between the north-eastern states and Bangladesh by strengthening the north-eastern states' ties with India. In fact, Dhaka continued to deny transit rights to India throughout the period under scrutiny.

Overview: Failed Hegemonic Strategy

The assessment of a clear divergence on core goals, of the foreign policy means employed by India, and of the perceptions and strategies of resistance employed by Bangladesh leads to the conclusion that India's foreign policy approach towards Bangladesh between 2001–8 should be characterized as hegemonic. During the first phase analysed – that is, during the BNP's term in Bangladesh – India's hegemonic foreign policy clearly took the form of a *hard hegemonic strategy* given the resort to diplomatic pressure and threats, and the clear attitude of resistance on the part of Dhaka. Moreover, elements of an imperial strategy could be observed in the confrontation between BSF and BDR, with the display and threat of force on the part of the BSF. During the second phase, when the military-backed CTG

---

59 Ibid.

ruled in Bangladesh, the more rational and sober attitude of Bangladesh towards India allowed New Delhi to pursue a *predominantly intermediate hegemonic strategy* based on economic concessions. Some elements of a soft hegemonic strategy could equally be observed given India's restraint on the questions of democracy and domestic developments in Bangladesh, mainly addressed through soft persuasion. The persistence of hegemony during this phase was confirmed by Dhaka's continued resistance on issues like transit and migration.

Interestingly, in the case of Bangladesh, there was a relatively high degree of consistency in India's foreign policy goals, with a strong focus on security-related issues. Especially on the core goals related to the limitation of security externalities, this consistency in India's foreign policy took place across different administrations in New Delhi – that is, both under the BJP-led NDA and the Congress-led UPA governments. In fact, given the strained relations with Bangladesh, there was no pro-Bangladesh constituency that could have contributed to promote a more cooperative approach by New Delhi.

Table 6.1   India–Bangladesh: goals, means, and perceptions

		India	*Bangladesh*
GOALS Core goals	*Issue Area* Security	• Limiting negative security externalities: – Fight against 'illegal' migration – Fight against actors engaged in anti-Indian activities (Islamists, North-east insurgents, ISI)	• Non-intervention of India and Pakistan in internal affairs • (2007–8: fighting terrorism)
		• Limiting China's influence -> Increasing India's influence • Limiting Bangladesh's influence on the North-east	• Limiting India's influence. Increasing China's influence • Increasing influence on India's North-east
Secondary goals	General goals	• Peace and stability • (Democracy) • Secularism	• Autonomy in decision-making • Reduction of trade imbalance with India 2007–8: • Peace and stability • Democracy
	Operational/ specific goals	• Border fencing and increased Patrolling • Border demarcation • Protection of minorities (especially 2001–6)	• No border fencing • Border demarcation • (Protection of minorities)

	India	*Bangladesh*
MEANS (actions / reactions)	2001–6 • Diplomatic pressure • Threats • Hard persuasion • Displays and threats of force (border incidents) • Fencing • (Soft persuasion, esp. since 2004 and during Iajuddin Ahmed's CTG)	2001–6 • Resistance (denial, counter-accusations, protests, ignoring India) • Readiness to resist militarily (border incidents) • Rhetorical compliance on protection of minorities
	2007–8: • Soft persuasion • Concessions (on trade and FDI) • Assistance • Soft persuasion on reinstatement of democracy (restraint) • Request for cooperation on terrorism (hard persuasion)	2007–8: • Gestures of goodwill • Compliance on secondary issues (fencing, insurgents) • Resistance on issues vital for Bangladesh: transit, migration
PERCEPTIONS		2001–8: • Bangladesh India-locked • India should be more cooperative • India ungrateful after 1971 • India as a supporter of Bangladesh's insurgents

Source: Author's composition.

Overall, the analysis of India's strategic interactions with Bangladesh, like those with Sri Lanka and Nepal, disproves the hypotheses about the 'leadership' of regional powers, and about the cooperative nature of Indian foreign policy since the 1990s. Despite the significant improvement observed under the caretaker government, Bangladesh remained a 'basket case' for India. Consequently, the dominating feeling among the Indian foreign policy-making elite was that it was impossible to engage in a constructive dialogue with Bangladesh. This led to an often passive attitude on the part of New Delhi in dealing with this neighbouring state.[60] As an Indian analyst poignantly puts it, 'a sense of helplessness has engulfed

---

60 For example, the issue of border demarcation was ignored in India for a long time since it was considered to be 'a minor issue'. Interview with expert, New Delhi, 7 November 2008.

Indian foreign policy makers on relations with Bangladesh' (Singh 2007: 6). Or, in the words of a former diplomat with experience on Bangladesh:

> 'Indians can be blamed for a lot of things: lack of stamina, lack of engagement. But [...] we don't wish to hurt anyone, it doesn't help us. But if you have decided initially that the Indians are not to be trusted, [...] how do I move forward? [...] What is India to do, I mean?'[61]

As a consequence, a sort of resignation spread among the Indian foreign policy elite, disguised in terms of a readiness to make concessions and to wait until Bangladesh would be ready to become more cooperative. As a government official put it in 2008, 'the strategy we are adopting with Bangladesh is we leave it to them. We say: "When you're ready [to make some steps, then we will act accordingly], we wait". We leave it to them, when they're comfortable...'.[62]

To conclude, the analysis of Indo–Bangladesh relations has revealed that India as a regional power had almost no leverage on this neighbouring country despite its overwhelming superiority in terms of material capabilities. The hegemonic strategies pursued by New Delhi were clearly unsuccessful: India was not able to achieve its core goals – to induce Bangladesh to tackle the problems of migration, insurgency, and terrorism. Moreover, there was nothing India could do to limit China's influence on Bangladesh. The strong resistance on the part of Dhaka made India's efforts ineffective. This resistance had its roots in the negative perceptions about India derived from historical animosities, and from a geographically deter-mined fear of being absorbed by India, as well as in the politicization of these threats by Bangladesh's main political parties.

---

61 Interview with expert, New Delhi, 7 November 2008.
62 Interview with government official, New Delhi, 20 November 2008.

7 South Asia

Lessons Learned

The aim of this book was to provide a theoretically informed account of India's foreign policy with regard to its 'Eastern neighbourhood' in South Asia, which has been the subject of divergent interpretations in the literature on international relations in the region. At the same time, the book had the broader objective of discussing the different facets of the exercise of power on the part of dominant states by resorting to a continuum of ideal-typical foreign policy strategies. The theory-led conceptual distinction and clarification of the notions of empire, hegemony, and leadership constitutes a contribution to the debate on power in the discipline of International Relations. While these three contested concepts have been an integral part of the debates on the role of powerful states over the past decades, they have previously neither been accurately distinguished from each other, nor been systematically operationalized. The application of these concepts to the analysis of the foreign policy strategies that can be employed by powerful states in dealing with weaker neighbours allows us to move from a notion of power based on the mere possession of power capabilities, to an assessment of power as 'the production, in and through social relations, of effects that shape the capacities of actors to determine their circumstances and fate' (Barnett/Duvall 2005: 42). The issue of legitimacy, which becomes prominent when we think about foreign policy strategies as based upon a conflict-cooperation or 'coercive'-'benevolent' continuum, is of central importance in this regard.

The detailed assessment of India's foreign policy strategies in its Eastern neighbourhood in South Asia confirms the centrality of the legitimation of power on the part of smaller states. Negative perceptions about the dominant country, and the policies of resistance deriving from those perceptions, can greatly contribute to limiting the actual influence of a 'powerful' state. The South Asian region, with its unequivocal power asymmetry and India's clear predominance as the regional power, is perfectly suited to illustrate the discrepancy between the possession of power capabilities and the ability to exercise power. As Lukes (2005b: 478) puts it, '[…] having the means of power is not the same as being powerful'. At the same time, the South Asian case shows that the mere 'exercise' of power – that is, the 'causing of an observable sequence of events' (ibid.) should not be automatically equated with power itself. According to Lukes (ibid.: 479), 'observing the exercise of power can give evidence of its possession and counting power resources can be a clue to its distribution, but power is a capacity, and neither the exercise nor the vehicle of that capacity'. In this regard, India's difficulties in 'exercising power' in its neighbourhood, in keeping its leverage over much smaller and weaker countries, do not imply that India is not powerful. The widespread threat perceptions and the resistance of India's neighbouring countries are rather a clue of India's immense – sometimes 'inactive' (ibid.: 479) – power.

The fine-grained analysis of India's relations with Sri Lanka, Nepal, and Bangladesh has revealed that India pursued predominantly hegemonic strategies in its interactions with these three countries over the time span analysed. These hegemonic strategies had different nuances specific to the cases and the periods under consideration.

In its relations with Sri Lanka during the years 2003–9 India initially pursued a soft hegemonic strategy mainly based on persuasion efforts. However, starting from 2005, when a deterioration of the security situation in Sri Lanka took place, an increased sense of urgency was conveyed by Indian policy makers, who repeatedly expressed their concern about the developments on the island. This verbal behaviour, paired with the continued provision of economic and development-related incentives, allows us to identify a shift from the soft to an intermediate hegemonic strategy during the first phase. The second phase analysed, covering Eelam War IV, was characterized by the coexistence of two parallel strategies on the part of New Delhi. At the rhetorical level, India adopted a hard hegemonic strategy towards Sri Lanka, exerting a considerable degree of pressure to induce President Rajapaksa to take into consideration the Tamil population during the military offensive. At the same time, at the level of actual, 'non-verbal' behaviour, India pursued an intermediate hegemonic strategy based on a tacit support of the Sri Lankan military effort. That is, starting from 2007, India significantly contributed to the weakening of the LTTE through a crackdown on the LTTE network in Tamil Nadu and the provision of 'defensive' weapons and, more importantly, of military training to the Sri Lankan army.

In its relations with Nepal, India also pursued predominantly hegemonic strategies. During the first phase (2002–5), the provision of incentives to induce the king to reinstate democracy prevailed. The second phase, covering the period of Gyanendra's authoritarian rule between 2005 and 2006, was characterized by India's resort to hard hegemonic means. In fact, New Delhi tried to force the king to re-establish the 'twin-pillar' system of constitutional monarchy and multiparty democracy by imposing an embargo on arms supplies to Nepal. However, the risk of being 'replaced' by China as Nepal's most influential neighbour induced India to continue training Nepalese troops and supporting the monarchy. The most significant trait of India's approach to Nepal during this phase was, however, the coexistence of two different strategies at different levels. At the same time as the above-mentioned course was followed by the government, representatives of the Indian foreign policy establishment also facilitated – at an informal level – talks between the Maoist rebels and the Nepalese political parties, thereby paving the way for the signing of the Comprehensive Peace Agreement. Therefore, besides the 'official' strategy of intermediate hegemony, a parallel – and rather successful

– strategy of informal leadership was pursued by New Delhi. Finally, the third phase analysed, which covered the period of democratic transition between 2006 and 2008, was characterized by the adoption of a soft hegemonic strategy on the part of India, based on diplomatic praise, soft persuasion, and expressions of commitment for the peace process.

The analysis of India's foreign policy strategies towards Bangladesh focused on the issues of Islamist extremism, migration, border security, and anti-India insurgency, which were all closely interrelated from the Indian point of view. Under the BNP-led government (2001–6), New Delhi resorted to a hard hegemonic strategy, which was reciprocated by a high degree of resistance on the part of Dhaka. The two governments indulged in accusations and counter-accusations on issues ranging from migration to the spread of Islamist terrorism and the activities of rebels allegedly operating from the other country's territory. Moreover, the situation came to a head with repeated incidents along the border, which saw India resorting to the display and threat of force. During the second phase analysed, when a military-backed caretaker government was in power and the two main competing parties were excluded from political life in Bangladesh (2007–8), the bilateral relationship could be placed at a more rational and unemotional level. During this phase, India could resort to a predominantly intermediate hegemonic strategy based on economic concessions. However, on issues considered vital by Dhaka, most notably transit and migration, India continued to encounter a high degree of resistance on the part of Bangladesh.

Therefore, in all three cases, and for the region as a whole, India has been unable to develop a 'leadership project' (Schirm 2010: 199) generating followership on the part of neighbouring regional states. At the same time, New Delhi's preference for a stable and peaceful region in which to prosper and focus on its own growth and development underscores India's intrinsic interest in the South Asian region. While India is trying to 'break the confines of [...] merely being a "South Asian" power' (Pant 2008: 11), the 'core issues' in India's international relations, from territorial disputes to energy security, are all related to the region (Mitra 2011: 178), and regional tensions are widely acknowledged to have contributed to hamper India's rise to great power status (Feigenbaum 2010: 84–5; Mitra 2011: 197; Mohan 2006: 22). The centrality of South Asia in Indian foreign policy has been unequivocally outlined by Foreign Secretary Shyam Saran in 2005,

> '[i]t is said that the logic of geography is unrelenting and proximity is the most difficult and testing among diplomatic challenges a country faces. Frontiers with neighbours are where [...] domestic and foreign policies become inextricable and demand sensitive handling. It should come as no surprise therefore, that in defining one's vital national and security interests, a country's neighbourhood enjoys a place of unquestioned primacy'.
>
> (MEA 2005b)

The fact that, during the period analysed in this book, India kept reiterating that it did not want to interfere with the neighbouring countries' internal affairs should not lead us to assume that India is not interested in the region. It indicates, however, the need on the part of New Delhi to take into account the sensitivity of its smaller neighbours. Therefore, instead of assuming an unwillingness on the part of India to act as a leading power in South Asia, we need to acknowledge the basic problem of a lack of common core goals between India and its neighbours, which could have been the basis on which to establish a leader-follower relationship. In the cases under scrutiny, India's own goals clearly stood in the forefront for New Delhi's policy-makers. Besides the objective of stabilizing the neighbourhood, India aimed to avoid spill-over effects from neighbouring countries, and to limit the influence of competing powers in India's traditional sphere of influence. These goals, and particularly the latter, stood in contrast to Sri Lanka's, Nepal's, and Bangladesh's efforts to emancipate themselves from Indian influence by cooperating with competitors of India like China and Pakistan.

Threat perceptions about India were widespread in the countries of India's 'Eastern neighbourhood', making the adoption of cooperative strategies on the part of New Delhi very difficult, if not impossible in the first place. The degree of hostility towards India, however, varied considerably. Bangladesh was the worst case in this regard, since its India-locked geopolitical position and the need to affirm a distinct national identity vis-à-vis India became the topic of heated domestic political debate. Similarly, the geopolitical setting of Nepal and the history of extensive Indian involvement in Nepalese domestic affairs led to a certain – albeit lower – degree of suspicion towards New Delhi. And in the case of Sri Lanka too, public opinion reacted unfavourably to the assertive statement by the Indian foreign secretary, who highlighted India's role as the dominant South Asian power in 2007.

The different degrees of hostility and resistance towards India and its policies contribute to an explanation of the failure of New Delhi's hegemonic approach in the three cases under scrutiny. In dealing with the civil war in Sri Lanka, India was unable to successfully pursue its original preference for a peaceful political settlement of the conflict. Instead, as seen in the chapter on Indo–Sri Lankan relations, it was quietly dragged into the conflict and came to follow the approach preferred by the Sri Lankan government in order to avoid losing its leverage on the island to China and Pakistan. In its relations with Nepal, India's approach was partially successful since New Delhi assisted in stabilizing the situation within the country and its informal contribution to the peace process through the facilitation of talks between the Maoist rebels and the democratic parties was highly constructive. However, in the case of Nepal too, India was unable to limit the influence of external actors on this country, which has traditionally been extremely close to New Delhi. Bangladesh proved to be the case in which India's policies failed most extensively. None of the security-related issues in bilateral relations could be effectively settled according to India's preferences given the high degree of resistance and suspicion towards India prevailing in Bangladesh. Even India's cooperative overtures in the fields of investments and trade were dismissed by Dhaka.

In summary, what does the analysis of India's foreign policy strategies towards the three main countries in its Eastern neighbourhood tell us?

First of all, India's inability to pursue a leadership strategy in all three cases (with the exception of informal leadership in the case of Nepal) clearly refutes the 'leadership hypothesis' developed by a large part of the literature on regional powers: that is, not only does India obviously not act as a leader in its relations with its 'Western' neighbour, Pakistan, but it is also unable to pursue a leadership strategy in dealing with the much smaller and weaker countries in its Eastern neighbourhood. Despite this, India's extraordinary predominance in terms of material power capabilities continues to qualify it as the 'regional power' in South Asia. The results from the South Asian case confirm the usefulness of adopting a broader approach to regional powers, which considers them as dominant states within a given region and assumes that they can pursue a broad range of strategies – cooperative as well as coercive – in their efforts to influence neighbouring countries.

Second, and related to the previous considerations, the empirical analysis refutes the 'cooperative hypothesis' elaborated by a part of the literature on India's foreign policy towards its Eastern neighbourhood. Despite the abandonment of the Indira Doctrine and the rhetorical shift to a much softer foreign policy approach to the region in the 1990s, this study has shown that India has continued to pursue an overall hegemonic strategy towards the major countries in the 'Eastern neighbourhood'. The desire to keep external actors out of India's regional neighbourhood has remained a central element of New Delhi's regional policy, particularly if the external actors are competitors of India, like China and Pakistan. At the same time, however, India has become more tolerant towards the influence of external actors like the UN, the Norwegian mediators in Sri Lanka, or the US in the case of Nepal. The fine-grained diachronic analysis of the three cases of Sri Lanka, Nepal, and Bangladesh has allowed us to identify nuances in India's foreign policy approach, and to unravel some of the dynamics of strategic interaction between India and its smaller neighbours. Importantly, the expected reactions of the smaller neighbours seem to have substantially contributed towards determining the foreign policy strategies adopted by India. The high degree of continuity in India's approach to Bangladesh under the NDA and the UPA governments during the years 2001–6 is telling in this regard – especially if compared to the substantial improvement in bilateral relations determined by the takeover of the caretaker government in Bangladesh in 2007: this change of government in Dhaka seems to have contributed to the shift in bilateral relations much more extensively than the change of government in New Delhi. In other terms, we can assume that the expectation of meeting less resistance to cooperative policies after the takeover by the caretaker government has induced India to act in a more cooperative manner. In the case of Sri Lanka, we have seen that this small neighbour of India has been able to gain New Delhi's support for its military campaign by actively promoting the involvement of external powers. The need to avoid being replaced by China as the dominant country in Sri Lanka has contributed to New Delhi's tacit support of the military efforts of President Rajapaksa from 2007 onwards.

These empirical findings derived from the nuanced assessment of India's policies in its Eastern neighbourhood in South Asia are equally of interest for the broader debate on power and influence in international relations. In fact, what we see in the South Asian case is an impressively predominant regional power that is unable to convert its superior power capabilities into actual leverage over its smaller neighbours. The analysis of the South Asian region would therefore lead us to hypothesize that overwhelmingly superior regional powers may be severely constrained in their foreign policy making and in the success of their policies by their much smaller and weaker neighbouring states if a range of conditions apply. Those conditions would refer to the domestic level in the regional power itself; to the regional level, in particular to the threat perceptions of neighbouring countries; and to the global or inter-regional level of analysis concerning the role of external actors.

At the domestic level, the lack of a coherent foreign policy approach and of a working coordination between different ministries and agencies within the regional power obviously contributes to make successful foreign policy more difficult. The reactive and uncoordinated approach pursued by India in its interactions with Nepal is the most glaring example of these domestic factors undermining the leverage of a regional power. A more detailed assessment of bureaucratic hurdles in foreign policy decision-making would be an interesting field of further research to address the domestic-level impact on the success of the foreign policy strategies of regional powers.

At the regional level, the historically or geopolitically determined threat perceptions on the part of smaller neighbours are the factor most likely to contribute to limit the policy options available to the regional power by making cooperative overtures fruitless. This was the case with the cooperative projects envisioned between India and Bangladesh, which were refused altogether by Bangladesh out of the fear of 'selling out' the national interest to India. Only consistent efforts at improving bilateral ties and a strict refraining from inter-ventionist policies on the part of the regional power may generate the necessary confidence among smaller neighbours in the long term. With increasing levels of confidence comes a growing readiness and willingness to cooperate, which in turn may lead the regional power to adopt more cooperative policies given the increased expectation of success.

At the global level of analysis, the main condition contributing to enable small states to undermine the policies of regional powers is certainly the influence of competitors of the regional power. While this is in line with the expectations of traditional 'balancing' approaches, it also highlights the peculiarities of the regional setting, which can be penetrated and substantially influenced by external actors. As emerges from the three cases examined in this book, the growing influence exercised by China on South Asia over the past years has had a significant impact on India's standing in the region.

In order to draw more general conclusions about the impact of these different factors, and about the actual power and influence of the countries in a region, further studies are needed at the nexus of (Comparative) Area Studies, International

Relations, and Foreign Policy Analysis. The counter-intuitive findings about India's policies in its Eastern neighbourhood have proved to be a first useful step in that direction.

Bibliography

Ahmed, R. (2009) '1/11: An obituary', *Forum* 4 (no. 2). Online. Available at: <http://www.thedailystar.net/forum/2009/february/obituary.htm> (accessed 25 August 2009).

Ahmed, T. (2008) 'Turmoil over transit', *New Age*, 24 July 2008. Online. Available at: <http://www.newagebd.com/2008/jul/24/edit.html#2> (accessed 21 September 2009).

Alam, A. (2005) 'Extremist strategy', *Frontline* 22 (no. 4). Online. Available at: <http://www.frontlineonnet.com/fl2204/stories/20050225005813200.htm> (accessed 15 June 2009).

Alamgir, J. (2009) 'Bangladesh's fresh start', *Journal of Democracy*, 20: 41–55.

Alden, C. and Vieira, M.A. (2005) 'The new diplomacy of the South: South Africa, Brazil, India and trilateralism', *Third World Quarterly*, 26: 1077–95.

Allison, R. (2009) 'The Russian case for military intervention in Georgia: International law, norms and political calculation', *European Security*, 18: 173–200.

Amnesty International (2007) 'Nepal report 2007'. Online. Available at: <http://www.amnesty.org/en/region/nepal/report–2007> (accessed 10 June 2009).

Anam, M. (2005) 'One by one opposition leaders are being killed', *The Daily Star*, 29 January 2005. Online. Available at: <http://www.thedailystar.net/2005/01/29/d5012901033.htm> (accessed 26 August 2009).

— (2007) 'This is no way to strengthen democracy: Just as "Command economy" failed, so will "Command politics"', *The Daily Star*, 11 July 2007. Online. Available at: <http://www.thedailystar.net/2007/07/17/d7071701022.htm> (accessed 25 August 2009).

Andley, P. and Mahanta, U. (2007) 'The 14th SAARC summit: An assessment. Report of the panel discussion held at the IPCS, New Delhi', 13 April 2007. Online. Available at: <http://www.ipcs.org/article_details.php?articleNo=2270> (accessed 19 September 2009).

Aneja, U. (2006) *China-Bangladesh relations: An emerging strategic partnership?*, IPCS Special Report, 33, New Delhi: IPCS.

Ayoob, M. (1999) 'From regional system to regional society: Exploring key variables in the construction of regional order', *Australian Journal of International Affairs*, 53: 247–60.

Azar, E.E. (1993) *The codebook of the conflict and peace data bank (COPDAB): A computer-assisted approach to monitoring and analyzing international and domestic events*, College Park, MD: Center for International Development and Conflict Management.

Bajpai, K. (2003a) 'Crisis and conflict in South Asia after September 11, 2001', *South Asian Survey*, 10: 197–213.

— (2003b) 'Managing conflict in South Asia', in P.F. Diehl and J. Lepgold (eds) *Regional conflict management*, Lanham: Rowman & Littlefield.

Baldwin, D.A. (1985) *Economic statecraft*, Princeton: Princeton University Press.

Bansal, A. (2008) 'Prachanda's visit to India: Beginning of a new dawn', *IDSA Strategic Comment*, 8 October 2008. Online. Available at: <http://www.idsa.in/publications/strat-comments/AlokBansal081008.htm> (accessed 28 July 2009).

Baral, L.R. (2004) 'Democracy and Indo-Nepal relations', in Observer Research Foundation (ed.) *India-Nepal relations: The challenge ahead*, New Delhi: Rupa & Co.

— (2008) 'Nepal: The restructuring of a 'neo-patrimonial' state', in L.R. Baral (ed.) *Nepal: New frontiers of restructuring of state*, New Delhi: Adroit.

Barnett, M. and Duvall, R. (2005) 'Power in international politics', *International Organization*, 59: 39–75.

Basrur, R.M. (2000) *India's external relations: A theoretical analysis*, New Delhi: Commonwealth.

Baxter, C. (1997) *Bangladesh: From a nation to a state*, Boulder, CO: Westview.

Bayles, M. (1972) 'A concept of coercion', in J.R. Pennock and J.W. Chapman (eds) *Coercion*, Chicago: Aldine.

BBC News (2008) 'Renegade sworn in as S Lanka MP', 7 October 2008. Online. Available at: <http://news.bbc.co.uk/2/hi/south_asia/7657668.stm> (accessed 22 May 2009).

— (2009) 'UN supports Sri Lanka aid effort', 27 May 2009. Online. Available at: <http://news.bbc.co.uk/2/hi/south_asia/8070964.stm> (accessed 31 May 2009).

BBC Sinhala (2007) 'British HC summoned by Gotabaya'', 19 April 2007. Online. Available at: <http://www.bbc.co.uk/sinhala/news/story/2007/04/070419_britishghota.shtml> (accessed 14 October 2009).

Behuria, A.K. (2007) 'Uneasy stability: Bangladesh, Sri Lanka, Myanmar', in S. Kumar (ed.) *India's national security annual review 2007*, New Delhi: KW Publishers.

Bemelmans-Videc, M.-L. (1998) 'Introduction: Policy instrument choice and evaluation', in M.-L. Bemelmans-Videc, R.C. Rist and E. Vedung (eds) *Carrots, sticks & sermons: Policy instruments & their evaluation*, New Brunswick: Transaction Publishers.

Bernauer, T. and Ruloff, D. (1999) 'Introduction and analytical framework', in T. Bernauer and D. Ruloff (eds) *The politics of positive incentives in arms control*, Columbia: University of South Carolina Press.

Bidwai, P. (2005) 'India's u-turn on Nepal', *Frontline* 22 (no. 10). Online. Available at: <http://www.frontlineonnet.com/fl2210/stories/20050520004111700.htm> (accessed 27 July 2009).

Biswas, B. (2006) 'The challenges of conflict management: A case study of Sri Lanka', *Civil Wars*, 8: 46–65.

Boggs, C. (2005) *Imperial delusions: American militarism and endless war*, Lanham: Rowman & Littlefield.

Bouffard, S. and Carment, D. (2006) 'The Sri Lanka peace process: A critical review', *Journal of South Asian Development*, 1: 151–77.

Breuning, M. (2007) *Foreign policy analysis: A comparative introduction*, New York: Palgrave Macmillan.

Brighi, E. and Hill, C. (2008) 'Implementation and behaviour', in S. Smith, A. Hadfield and T. Dunne (eds) *Foreign policy: Theories, actors, cases*, Oxford: Oxford University Press.

Bull, H. (1977) *The anarchical society: A study of order in world politics*, London: Macmillan.

Burges, S.W. (2008) 'Consensual hegemony: Theorizing Brazilian foreign policy after the cold war', *International Relations*, 22: 65–84.

Burns, J.M. (1978) *Leadership*, New York: Harper and Row.

Bussmann, M. and Oneal, J.R. (2007) 'Do hegemons distribute private goods? A test of power-transition theory', *Journal of Conflict Resolution*, 51: 88–111.

Buzan, B. (1998) 'The Asia-Pacific region: What sort of region in what sort of world?' in A.G. Mc Grew and C. Brook (eds) *Asia-Pacific in the new world order*, London: Routledge.

— (2002) 'South Asia moving towards transformation: Emergence of India as a great power', *International Studies*, 39: 1–34.

Buzan, B. and Waever, O. (2003) *Regions and powers: The structure of international security*, Cambridge: Cambridge University Press.

Byman, D. and Waxman, M. (2002) *The dynamics of coercion: American foreign policy and the limits of military might*, Cambridge: Cambridge University Press.

Calder, K.E. (2006) 'China and Japan's simmering rivalry', *Foreign Affairs*, 85: 129–39.

CAMEO (2009) 'Cameo code summary: Version 0.9b5'. Online. Available at: <http://cameocodes.wikispaces.com/EventCodes> (accessed 23 June 2009).

Chadda, M. (2000) *Building democracy in South Asia: India, Nepal, Pakistan*, Boulder: Lynne Rienner.

Chandrasekharan, S. (2006) 'Nepal: Municipal elections: No winners but only losers', *South Asia Analysis Group Update* (no. 83). Online. Available at: <http://www.southasiaanalysis.org/%5Cnotes3%5Cnote295.html> (accessed 5 February 2009).

Chattopadhyay, S.S. (2003) 'A border face-off', *Frontline* 20 (no. 4). Online. Available at: <http://www.frontlineonnet.com/fl2004/stories/20030228003210100.htm> (accessed 27 April 2009).

— (2007) 'Constant traffic', *Frontline* 24 (no. 11). Online. Available at: <http://www.frontlineonnet.com/fl2411/stories/20070615003701400.htm> (accessed 27 April 2009).

Cherian, J. (2003) 'A friend in need', *Frontline* 20 (no. 12). Online. Available at: <http://www.frontlineonnet.com/fl2012/stories/20030620005001700.htm> (accessed 30 March 2009).

— (2006a) 'Indian flip-flop', *Frontline* 23 (no. 9). Online. Available at: <http://www.frontlineonnet.com/fl2309/stories/20060519004801000.htm> (accessed 27 July 2009).

— (2006b) 'King size crisis', *Frontline* 23 (no. 8). Online. Available at: <http://www.frontlineonnet.com/fl2308/stories/20060505006312900.htm> (accessed 28 April 2009).

Chomsky, N. (2003) *Hegemony or survival: America's quest for global dominance*, London: Hamilton.

CIA World Factbook (2011) 'Sri Lanka'. Online. Available at: <https://www.cia.gov/library/publications/the-world-factbook/geos/ce.html> (accessed 26 April 2011).

Cohen, S.P. (2002) *India: Emerging power*, Washington, DC: Brookings Insitution Press.

Cohen, W.I. (2005) *America's failing empire: U.S. Foreign relations since the Cold War*, Malden: Blackwell.

Colás, A. and Saull, R. (eds) (2006) *The war on terror and the American 'empire' after the cold war*, London: Routledge.

Cooper, A.F., Higgott, R.A. and Nossal, K.R. (1991) 'Bound to follow? Leadership and followership in the gulf conflict', *Political Science Quarterly*, 106: 391–410.

Cortright, D. (1997) 'Incentives and cooperation in international affairs', in D. Cortright (ed.) *The price of peace: Incentives and international conflict prevention*, Lanham: Rowman & Littlefield.

Cortright, D. and Lopez, G.A. (eds) (2002) *Smart sanctions: Targeting economic statecraft*, Lanham: Rowman & Littlefield.

Cox, R.W. (1983) 'Gramsci, hegemony and international relations: An essay in method', *Millennium: Journal of International Studies*, 12: 162–74.

— (1996) 'Labor and hegemony (1977)', in R.W. Cox and T.J. Sinclair (eds) *Approaches to world order*, Cambridge: Cambridge University Press.

Cronin, B. (2001) 'The paradox of hegemony: America's ambiguous relationship with the United Nations', *European Journal of International Relations*, 7: 103–30.

Das, P. (2008) 'India-Bangladesh border management: A review of government's response', *Strategic Analysis*, 32: 367–88.

Davies, J.L. and Mcdaniel, C.K. (1994) 'A new generation of international event-data', *International Interactions*, 20: 55–78.

Dawisha, K. and Parrott, B. (eds) (1997) *Analyzing the transformation of the Soviet Union in comparative perspective*, Armonk: M.E. Sharpe.

De, P. and Bhattacharyay, B.N. (2007) *Prospects of India-Bangladesh economic cooperation: Implications for South Asian regional cooperation*, ADB Institute Discussion Paper, 78, Tokyo: ADB.

De Silva, K.M. (1986) *Managing ethnic tensions in multi-ethnic societies: Sri Lanka 1880–1985*, Lanham: University Press of America.

— (1991) 'Indo-Sri Lankan relations, 1975–1989', in K.M. De Silva and R.J. May (eds) *Internationalization of ethnic conflict*, London: Pinter Publishers.

— (1995) *Regional powers and small state security: India and Sri Lanka, 1977–90*, Washington, DC: The Woodrow Wilson Center Press.

Denzin, N.K. (1978) *The research act: A theoretical introduction to sociological methods*, New York: McGraw-Hill.

Destradi, S. (2010) 'Regional powers and their strategies: Empire, hegemony, and leadership', *Review of International Studies*, 36: 903–30.

DeVotta, N. (2010) 'When individuals, states, and systems collide', in S. Ganguly (ed.) *India's foreign policy: Retrospect and prospect*, New Delhi: Oxford University Press.

— (2011) 'Sri Lanka: From turmoil to dynasty', *Journal of Democracy*, 22: 130–44.

Dixit, J.N. (1999) *Liberation and beyond: Indo-Bangladesh relations*, Delhi: Konark.

— (2003) 'Sri Lanka', in J.N. Dixit (ed.) *External affairs: Cross-border relations*, New Delhi: Roli Books.

Dorussen, H. (2001) 'Mixing carrots with sticks: Evaluating the effectiveness of positive incentives', *Journal of Peace Research*, 38: 251–62.

Dos Santos, A.N. (2007) *Military intervention and secession in South Asia: The cases of Bangladesh, Sri Lanka, Kashmir, and Punjab*, Westport: Praeger Security International.

Doxey, M.P. (1996) *International sanctions in contemporary perspective*. 2nd edn, Basingstoke: Macmillan.

Doyle, M.W. (1986) *Empires*, Ithaka: Cornell University Press.

Dubey, M. (2000) 'India: Outstanding achievements and dismal failures', *International Politics and Society* 1. Online. Available at: <http://www.fes.de/IPG/ipg1_2000/Artdubey.html> (accessed 22 October 2009).

— (2003) 'Dealing with Bangladesh – I', *The Hindu*, 5 February 2003. Online. Available at: <http://www.thehindu.com/2003/02/05/stories/2003020500041000.htm> (accessed 31 August 2009).

Dutta [Datta], S. (2009) *Caretaking democracy: Political process in Bangladesh, 2006–08*, New Delhi: IDSA.

Dutta, S. (2008a) 'The Bangladesh military: Power without accountability', in S.D. Muni (ed.) *IDSA Asian strategic review 2008*, New Delhi: Academic Foundation.

— (2008b) 'Will Bangladesh address India's security concerns?' in N.S. Sisodia (ed.) *India and its neighbours: Towards a new partnership*, New Delhi: IDSA.

Ekantipur (2007) 'Historical day in course of forming new Nepal', 1 April 2007. Online. Available at: <http://www.kantipuronline.com/kolnews.php?&nid=105318> (accessed 15 June 2009).

— (2008a) 'Federal democratic republic of Nepal', 28 May 2008. Online. Available at: <http://www.kantipuronline.com/kolnews.php?&nid=148495> (accessed 19 January 2009).

— (2008b) 'Maoist chairman Dahal 1st republican PM', 15 August 2008. Online. Available at: <http://www.kantipuronline.com/kolnews.php?&nid=157120> (accessed 15 June 2009).

— (2008c) 'PM Dahal takes charge of office', 18 August 2008. Online. Available at: <http://www.kantipuronline.com/kolnews.php?&nid=157415> (accessed 15 June 2009).

Embassy of India – Kathmandu (2009) 'India-Nepal relations'. Online. Available at: <http://www.south-asia.com/Embassy-India/indneprel.htm> (accessed 5 February 2009).

Embassy of India – Washington D.C. (1997) '"Defence and security in the post-cold war scenario", address by I. K. Gujral, Minister of External Affairs, Government of India at the United Service Institution of India'. Online. Available at: <http://www.indianembassy.org/policy/Foreign_Policy/coldwar(gujral).htm> (accessed 9 October 2009).

Expressindia (2005a) 'B'desh links India to bombing wave, Delhi denies', 1 October 2005. Online. Available at: <http://www.expressindia.com/news/fullstory.php?newsid=55701> (accessed 25 August 2009).

— (2005b) 'We are not training Indian militants: B'desh', 22 June 2005. Online. Available at: <http://www.expressindia.com/fullstory.php?newsid=49283> (accessed 25 August 2009).

Fawn, R. (2009) '"Regions" And their study: Wherefrom, what for and whereto?' *Review of International Studies*, 35: 5–34.

Federal Foreign Office – Germany (2009) 'Länderinformationen, Sri Lanka'. Online. Available at: <http://www.auswaertiges-amt.de/diplo/de/Laenderinformationen/01-Laender/SriLanka.html> (accessed 20 May 2009).

Feigenbaum, E.A. (2010) 'India's rise, America's interest: The fate of the U.S.-Indian partnership', *Foreign Affairs*, 89: 76–91.

Ferguson, N. (2003) 'An empire in denial: The limits of US imperialism', *Harvard International Review*, 25: 64–9.

— (2004) *Colossus: The price of America's empire*, New York: The Penguin Press.

Ferguson, Y.H. (2008) 'Approaches to defining "Empire" and characterizing United States influence in the contemporary world', *International Studies Perspectives*, 9: 272–80.

Fielding, N.G. and Lee, R.M. (1998) *Computer analysis and qualitative research*, London: Sage.

Finnemore, M. and Sikkink, K. (1998) 'International norm dynamics and political change', *International Organization*, 52: 887–917.

Flemes, D. and Wojczewski, T. (2010) *Contested leadership in international relations: Power politics in South America, South Asia and Sub-Saharan Africa*, GIGA Working Paper, 121, Hamburg: GIGA.

Frazier, D.V. and Stewart-Ingersoll, R. (2010) 'Regional powers and security: A framework for understanding order within regional security complexes', *European Journal of International Relations*, 16: 731–53.

Frieden, J.A. (1999) 'Actors and preferences in international relations', in D.A. Lake and R. Powell (eds) *Strategic choice and international relations*, Princeton: Princeton University Press.

Friedrich Ebert Stiftung (FES) (2006) 'News update from Nepal', 1 July 2006. Online. Available at: <http://library.fes.de/pdf-files/iez/50218/nepalnews0706.pdf> (accessed 26 April 2011).

Fuller, G.E. and Arquilla, J. (1996) 'The intractable problem of regional powers', *Orbis*, 40: 609–21.

Fuller, T. (2009) 'Sri Lanka rejects Tamil call for cease-fire', *The New York Times*, 26 April 2009. Online. Available at: <http://www.nytimes.com/2009/04/27/world/asia/27lanka.html?emc=eta1> (accessed 29 May 2009).

Ganguly, S. (2006) *The rise of Islamist militancy in Bangladesh*, United States Institute of Peace Special Report, 171, Washington, DC: USIP.

Ganguly, S. and Hagerty, D. (2005) *Fearful symmetry: India-Pakistan relations in the shadow of nuclear weapons*, Seattle: University of Washington Press.

Ganguly, S. and Pardesi, M.S. 2010. *South Asia and foreign policy*, in R.A. Denemark (ed.) *The International Studies Encyclopedia*: Blackwell Publishing, Blackwell Reference Online. Available at: <http://www.isacompendium.com/subscriber/book?id=g97814443 36597_9781444336597> (accessed 14 April 2011).

Gellner, D.N. (2007) 'Nepal and Bhutan in 2006: A year of revolution', *Asian Survey*, 47: 80–6.

George, A.L., Hall, D.K. and Simons, W.E. (1971) *The limits of coercive diplomacy: Laos, Cuba, Vietnam*, Boston: Litte, Brown and Company.

Ghosh, J. (2003) 'Continuing conflict in Nepal', *Frontline* 20 (no. 15). Online. Available at: <http://www.frontlineonnet.com/fl2015/stories/20030801003311500.htm> (accessed 9 June 2009).

Ghosh, P.S. (2006) 'India in South Asia: Cooperation amidst tensions', in S.K. Mitra and B. Rill (eds) *India's new dynamics in foreign policy*, München: Hanns-Seidel-Stiftung.

Gilpin, R. (1981) *War and change in world politics*, Cambridge: Cambridge University Press.

Godage, K. (2007) 'Om Narayan om Narayan...' *The Island*, 2 June 2007. Online. Available at: <http://www.lankaweb.com/news/items07/030607–3.html> (accessed 23 October 2010).

Goertz, G. (2006) *Social science concepts: A user's guide*, Princeton: Princeton University Press.

Goethals, G.R., Sorenson, G.J. and Burns, M.J. (eds) (2004) *Encyclopedia of leadership*, Thousand Oaks: Sage.

Gokhale, N.A. (2009) *Sri Lanka: From war to peace*, New Delhi: Har-Anand.

Goldstein, K. (2002) 'Getting in the door: Sampling and completing elite interviews', *PS: Political Science & Politics*, 35: 669–72.

Gopal, N. (1995) *India and the small powers in South Asia (a study in Indo-Nepalese relations)*, Jaipur: RBSA.

Government of India (GOI) – Prime Minister's Office (2005) 'PM's speech at the Haksar Memorial Conference', 9 November 2005. Online. Available at: <http://pmindia.nic.in/speech/content.asp?id=216> (accessed 29 April 2011).

— (2006) 'Extracts of PM's address at the combined commander's conference', 18 October 2006. Online. Available at: <http://pmindia.gov.in/speech/content.asp?id=432> (accessed 26 April 2011).

— (2007) 'PM's address to the 14th SAARC summit', 3 April 2007. Online. Available at: <http://pmindia.gov.in/speech/content.asp?id=517> (accessed 21 September 2009).

Government of Sri Lanka (GOSL) (2004) 'Peace talks should begin soon' president tells Yasushi Akashi', 29 October 2004. Online. Available at: <http://www.priu.gov.lk/news_update/Current_Affairs/ca200410/20041029peace_talks_should_begin_soon_president.htm> (accessed 14 October 2009).

— (2005) 'President's new year message', 1 January 2005. Online. Available at: <http://www.priu.gov.lk/news_update/Current_Affairs/ca200501/20050101pre-sidents_new_year_message.htm> (accessed 14 October 2009).

— (2008) 'Permanent mission of Sri Lanka to the United Nations in New York, foreign minister hails entry of Karuna into parliament', 7 October 2008. Online. Available at: <http://www.slmission.com/statements/88-ministry-statements/180-foreign-minister-hails-entry-of-karuna-into-parliament.html> (accessed 14 October 2009).

— (2009a) 'Address by His Excellency President Mahinda Rajapaksa at the ceremonial opening of parliament, Sri Jayawardhanapura – Kotte', 19 May 2009. Online. Available at: <http://www.priu.gov.lk/news_up-date/Current_Affairs/ca200905/20090519terrorism_defeated.htm> (accessed 29 May 2009).

— (2009b) 'Address by His Excellency President Mahinda Rajapaksa, at the 61st independence anniversary celebrations, Galle Face, Colombo, February 4, 2009, cited in: Government of Sri Lanka, from peace to prosperity – 61st anniversary of independence', 4 February 2009. Online. Available at: <http://www.priu.gov.lk/news_up-date/Current_Affairs/ca200902/20090204_61st_anniversary_of_indepen-dence.htm> (accessed 14 October 2009).

— (2009c) 'Address by President Mahinda Rajapaksa at the G–11 summit, Jordan – 16/05/2009', 16 May 2009. Online. Available at: <http://www.priu.gov.lk/news_update/Current_Affairs/ca200905/20090516i_return_to_my_country_freed_of_ltte_barbarism.htm > (accessed 18 July 2009).

— (2009d) 'Mahinda Chintana'. Online. Available at: <http://www.priu.gov.lk/mahin-dachinthana/MahindaChinthanaEnglish.pdf> (accessed 28 May 2009).

Gramsci, A. (1975) *Quaderni del carcere*. 4 vols, Torino: Einaudi.

Gratius, S. (2004) *Die Außenpolitik der Regierung Lula: Brasiliens Aufstieg von einer diskreten Regional- zu einer kooperativen Führungsmacht*, SWP-Studie, S7, Berlin: Stiftung Wissenschaft und Politik.

Grattan, R.F. (2002) *The strategy process: A military-business comparison*, Houndmills: Palgrave Macmillan.

Gupta, R. (2006) *Bangladesh: Recent developments (Aug 2005-Mar 2006)*, IPCS Special Report, 16, New Delhi: IPCS.

Gupta, S. and Singh, S. (2007) 'Bangla terror group's fingerprints were handed over to Dhaka but no word yet', *Indian Express*, 31 August 2007. Online. Available at: <http://www.indianexpress.com/news/bangla-terror-groups-fingerprints-were-handed-over-to-dhaka-but-no-word-yet/213646/> (accessed 21 September 2009).

Guzzini, S. (2009) *On the measure of power and the power of measure in international relations*, DIIS Working Paper, 28, Copenhagen: DIIS.

Habermas, J. (1973) *Legitimationsprobleme im Spätkapitalismus*, Frankfurt/Main: Suhrkamp.

Habib, H. (2004) 'Tension on the border', *Frontline* 21 (no. 24). Online. Available at: <http://www.flonnet.com/fl2124/stories/20041203000606100.htm> (accessed 2 September 2009).

— (2005) 'Rising terror in Bangladesh', *Frontline* 22 (no. 05). Online. Available at: <http://www.frontlineonnet.com/fl2205/stories/20050311000406200.htm> (accessed 2 September 2009).

— (2007a) 'Enter a new player', *Frontline* 24 (no. 05). Online. Available at: <http://www.frontlineonnet.com/fl2405/stories/20070323000505400.htm> (accessed 25 August 2009).

— (2007b) 'From the brink', *Frontline* 24 (no. 02). Online. Available at: <http://www.front-lineonnet.com/fl2402/stories/20070209001005300.htm> (accessed 26 August 2009).

— (2007c) 'Politics behind bars', *Frontline* 24 (no. 19). Online. Available HTTP: <http://www.frontlineonnet.com/fl2419/stories/20071005504505900.htm> (accessed 26 August 2009).

— (2009) 'Landslide win', *Frontline* 26 (no. 2). Online. Available at: <http://www.flonnet. com/fl2602/stories/20090130260205700.htm> (accessed 26 August 2009).

Hachhethu, K. and Gellner, D.N. (2010) 'Nepal: Trajectories of democracy and restruc- turing of the state', in P.R. Brass (ed.) *Routledge handbook of South Asian politics: India, Pakistan, Bangladesh, Sri Lanka, and Nepal*, London: Routledge.

Hagerty, D.T. (1991) 'India's regional security doctrine', *Asian Survey*, 31: 351–63.

Hanif, M. (2009) *Indian involvement in Afghanistan: Stepping stone or stumbling block to regional hegemony?*, GIGA Working Paper, 98, Hamburg: GIGA.

Hariharan, R. (2007) 'Sri Lanka: LTTE ripples in Tamil Nadu', *South Asia Analysis Group Note* (no. 371). Online. Available at: <http://www.southasiaanalysis. org/%5Cnotes4%5Cnote371.html> (accessed 13 October 2009).

Hennayake, S.K. (1989) 'The peace accord and the Tamils in Sri Lanka', *Asian Survey*, 29: 401–15.

Hermann, M.G. (2008) 'Content analysis', in A. Klotz and D. Prakash (eds) *Qualitative methods in international relations: A pluralist guide*, Houndmills: Palgrave Macmillan.

Hill, C. (2003) *The changing politics of foreign policy*, Houndmills: Palgrave Macmillan.

Holsti, O. (1969) *Content analysis for the social sciences and humanities*, Readin: Addison-Wesley.

Human Rights Watch (HRW) (2009) *War on the displaced: Sri Lankan army and LTTE abuses against civilians in the Vanni*, New York: HRW.

Hurrell, A. (1992) 'Brazil as a regional great power: A study in ambivalence', in I.B. Neumann (ed.) *Regional great powers in international politics*, Basingstoke: St. Martin's Press.

— (2004) 'Hegemony and regional governance in the Americas', Global Law Working Paper, 5, New York: NYU School of Law.

— (2005) 'Pax Americana or the empire of insecurity?' *International Relations of the Asia-Pacific*, 5: 153–76.

— (2006) 'Hegemony, liberalism and global order: What space for would-be great powers?' *International Affairs*, 82: 1–19.

— (2007a) 'One world? Many worlds? The place of regions in the study of international society', *International Affairs*, 83: 127–46.

— (2007b) *On global order: Power, values, and the constitution of international society*, Oxford: Oxford University Press.

Husar, J. and Maihold, G. (2009) 'Einführung: Neue Führungsmächte – Forschungsansätze und Handlungsfelder', in J. Husar, G. Maihold and S. Mair (eds) *Neue Führungsmächte: Partner deutscher Außenpolitik?*, Baden-Baden: Nomos.

Hussain, A. (2005) 'Dancing with the devil', *Star: Weekend Magazine* 4 (no. 74). Online. Available at: <http://www.thedailystar.net/magazine/2005/12/02/cover.htm> (accessed 25 August 2009).

Hutt, M. (2006) 'Nepal and Bhutan in 2005: Monarchy and democracy, can they co-exist?' *Asian Survey*, 46: 120–4.

Ikenberry, G.J. (2001) 'American power and the empire of capitalist democracy', *Review of International Studies*, 27 (Special Issue): 191–212.

Ikenberry, J.G. and Kupchan, C.A. (1990a) 'The legitimation of hegemonic power', in D.P. Rapkin (ed.) *World leadership and hegemony*, Boulder: Lynne Rienner.

— (1990b) 'Socialization and hegemonic power', *International Organization*, 44: 283–315.

India Defence (2006) 'China to build Chittagong naval base in Bangladesh', 12 June 2006. Online. Available at: <http://www.india-defence.com/reports/2076> (accessed 22 September 2009).

— (2007) 'Indian navy strengthens surveillance along Sri Lankan border', 7 April 2007. Online. Available at: <http://www.india-defence.com/reports–3001> (accessed 29 May 2009).

— (2008) 'Bangladesh army chief in India to boost bilateral defence ties', 25 February 2008. Online. Available at: <http://www.india-defence.com/reports–3754> (accessed 8 September 2009).

Indian Express (2005) 'Nepal's King Gyanendra seeks S Asian support', 12 November 2005. Online. Available at: <http://www.expressindia.com/news/fullstory.php?newsid=58224> (accessed 5 August 2009).

International Crisis Group (2003) *Nepal: Obstacles to peace*, Asia Report, 57.

— (2005) *Towards a lasting peace in Nepal: The constitutional issues*, Asia Report, 99.

— (2006a) *Bangladesh today*, Asia Report, 121.

— (2006b) *Nepal: From people power to peace?*, Asia Report, 115.

— (2007a) *Nepal's Maoists: Purists or pragmatists?*, Asia Report, 132.

— (2007b) *Sri Lanka: Sinhala nationalism and the elusive southern consensus*, Asia Report, 141.

— (2008a) *Bangladesh: Elections and beyond*, Asia Briefing, 84.

— (2008b) *Nepal's election: A peaceful revolution?*, Asia Report, 155.

— (2008c) *Nepal's new political landscape*, Asia Report, 156.

— (2008d) *Restoring democracy in Bangladesh*, Asia Report, 151.

— (2008e) *Sri Lanka's return to war: Limiting the damage*, Asia Report, 146.

— (2010) *War crimes in Sri Lanka*, Asia Report, 191.

International Herald Tribune (2006) 'Leader intervenes in crisis in Bangladesh', 29 October 2006. Online. Available at: <http://www.nytimes.com/2006/10/29/world/asia/29iht-bangla.3317595.html?_r=1&scp=2&sq=%22ju-stice%20k.m.%20hasan%22&st=cse> (accessed 26 August 2009).

— (2007) 'Former rebels join Nepal's interim government; Elections planned for June 20', 1 April 2007. Online. Available at: <http://www.iht.com/articles/ap/2007/04/02/asia/AS-GEN-Nepal-Rebels.php> (accessed 26 January 2009).

International Institute for Strategic Studies (IISS) (2008) 'The military balance 2008: International comparisons of defence expenditure and military manpower, 2004–2006'. Online. Available at: <http://www.iiss.org/publications/military-balance/the-military-balance–2008/> (accessed 23 September 2009).

International Monetary Fund (IMF) (2009) 'World economic outlook database', October 2009. Online. Available at: <http://www.imf.org/external/pubs/ft/weo/2009/02/weodata/index.aspx> (accessed 16 April 2011).

Islam, N. (2007) 'Growing our way out of trouble', *Forum* 2 (no. 6). Online. Available at: <http://www.thedailystar.net/forum/2007/july/growing.htm> (accessed 25 August 2009).

Jahan, R. (2007) 'The Fakhruddin government: No easy option', *Forum* 2 (no. 2). Online. Available at: <http://www.thedailystar.net/forum/2007/february/fakhruddin.htm> (accessed 24 August 2009).

Jayanth, V. (2007) 'Alarm bells', *Frontline* 24 (no. 9). Online. Available at: <http://www.frontlineonnet.com/fl2409/stories/20070518003601700.htm> (accessed 1 April 2009).

Jeyaraj, D.B.S. (2003a) 'In dread of democracy', *Frontline* 20 (no. 12). Online. Available at: <http://www.frontlineonnet.com/fl2012/stories/20030620006100900.htm> (accessed 26 March 2009).

— (2004) 'The fall of Karuna', *Frontline* 21 (no. 9). Online. Available at: <http://www.frontlineonnet.com/fl2109/stories/20040507006712200.htm> (accessed 31 March 2009).

— (2007) 'French crackdown', *Frontline* 24 (no. 8). Online. Available at: <http://www.frontlineonnet.com/fl2408/stories/20070504001205100.htm> (accessed 1 April 2009).

Jha, P. (2006) 'Tricky tasks', *Frontline* 23 (no. 11). Online. Available at: <http://www.frontlineonnet.com/fl2311/stories/20060616002004800.htm> (accessed 10 June 2009).

— (2007) 'Maoist muddle', *Frontline* 24 (no. 20). Online. Available at: <http://www.frontlineonnet.com/fl2420/stories/20071019503904900.htm> (accessed 5 August 2009).

— (2008) 'Nepal at the crossroads', *Seminar: The Monthly Symposium, web edition* (no. 584). Online. Available at: <http://www.india-seminar.com/2008/584/584_prashant_jha.htm> (accessed 26 April 2011).

Johnson, C. (2000) *Blowback: The costs and consequences of American empire*, New York: Henry Holt.

— (2004) *The sorrows of empire: Militarism, secrecy, and the end of the republic*, New York: Henry Holt.

Jones, D.M., Bremer, S.A. and Singer, J.D. (1996) 'Militarized interstate disputes, 1816–1992: Rationale, coding rules, and empirical patterns', *Conflict Management and Peace Science*, 15: 163–213.

Kagan, R. (1998) 'The benevolent empire', *Foreign Policy*, 111: 24–35.

Kamboj, A. (2005) *Bangladesh factor affecting insurgency in north-east*, IPCS Article, 1733, New Delhi: IPCS.

Kapila, S. (2003) 'Bangladesh-China defence cooperation agreement's strategic implications', *South Asia Analysis Group Paper* (no. 582). Online. Available at: <http://www.southasiaanalysis.org/papers6/paper582.html> (accessed 22 September 2009).

— (2008) 'Bangladesh-India strategic partnership: The imperatives', *South Asia Analysis Group Paper* (no. 2765). Online. Available at: <http://www.southasiaanalysis.org/%5Cpapers28%5Cpaper2765.html> (accessed 21 September 2009).

Kaur, N. (2003) 'Right-wing politics at play', *Frontline* 20 (no. 4). Online. Available at: <http://www.frontlineonnet.com/fl2004/stories/20030228003510300.htm> (accessed 27 April 2009).

Kaushik, S. (2006) 'The crisis in Nepal', in V.D. Chopra (ed.) *India's foreign policy in the 21st century*, Delhi: Kalpaz.

Kelegama, S. and Mukherji, I.N. (2007) *India-Sri Lanka bilateral free trade agreement: Six years performance and beyond*, Research and Information System for Developing Countries Discussion Paper, 119, New Delhi: RIS.

Kelle, U. (1995) 'Introduction: An overview of computer-aided methods in qualitative research', in U. Kelle (ed.) *Computer-aided qualitative data analysis*, London: Sage.

Kennedy, P. (1991) 'Grand strategy in war and peace: Toward a broader definition', in P. Kennedy (ed.) *Grand strategies in war and peace*, New Haven: Yale University Press.

Khadka, N. (1997) 'Foreign aid to Nepal: Donor motivations in the post-cold war period', *Asian Survey*, 37: 1044–61.

Khosla, I.P. (2005) 'Bangladesh-India relations', *South Asian Journal* 7. Online. Available at: <http://www.southasianmedia.net/Magazine/Journal/7_bangladesh-india_relations.htm> (accessed 26 April 2011).

— (2008) 'Introduction', in I.P. Khosla (ed.) *Spotlights on neighbours: Talks at the IIC*, New Delhi: Konark.

Kindleberger, C.P. (1973) *The world in depression, 1929–1939*, Berkeley: University of California Press.

— (1981) 'Dominance and leadership in the international economy: Exploitation, public goods, and free ride', *International Studies Quarterly*, 25: 242–54.

Knorr, K. (1975) *The power of nations: The political economy of international relations*, New York: Basic Books.

Kogler Hill, S.E. (1997) 'Team leadership theory', in P.G. Northouse (ed.) *Leadership: Theory and practice*, Thousand Oaks: Sage.

Krämer, K.-H. (2006) *Aktuelle politische Lage in Nepal: Schwierige Bemühungen um einen Neubeginn.* Online. Available at: <http://www.nepalresearch.com/publications/lage_0609.pdf> (accessed 26 April 2011).

Krasner, S.D. (2001) 'Rethinking the sovereign state model', *Review of International Studies*, 27: 17–42.

Lake, D.A. (1993) 'Leadership, hegemony, and the international economy: Naked emperor or tattered monarch with potential?' *International Studies Quarterly*, 37: 459–89.

— (1997) 'The rise, fall and future of the Russian empire: A theoretical interpretation', in K. Dawisha and B. Parrott (eds) *The end of empire? The transformation of the USSR in comparative perspective*, Armonk: M.E. Sharpe.

Lake, D.A. and Morgan, P.M. (1997) 'The new regionalism in security affairs', in D.A. Lake and P.M. Morgan (eds) *Regional orders: Building security in a new world*, University Park: Pennsylvania State University Press.

Lake, D.A. and Powell, R. (1999) 'International relations: A strategic-choice approach', in D.A. Lake and R. Powell (eds) *Strategic choice and international relations*, Princeton: Princeton University Press.

Lakshman, K. (2002) *Maoist insurgency and Indo-Nepal border relations*, IPCS Article, 678, New Delhi: IPCS.

Lankanewspapers (2005) 'Sri Lanka tsunami aid becomes geopolitical game', 4 January 2005. Online. Available at: <http://www.lankanewspapers.com/news/2005/1/135.html> (accessed 30 May 2009).

Layne, C. and Thayer, B.A. (2007) *American empire: A debate*, New York: Routledge.

Lemke, D. (2002) *Regions of war and peace*, Cambridge: Cambridge University Press.

Liberation Tigers of Tamil Eelam (LTTE) (2003) 'The proposal by the Liberation Tigers of Tamil Eelam on behalf of the Tamil people for an agreement to establish an interim self-governing authority for the North-east of the island of Sri Lanka', 1 November 2003. Online. Available at: <http://www.tamilnet.com/img/publish/2003/11/proposal.pdf > (accessed 25 May 2009).

Liddell Hart, B.H. (1991) *Strategy*. 2nd rev. edn, New York: Meridian.

Lintner, B. (2003) 'Bangladesh extremist Islamist consolidation', *Faultlines* 14. Online. Available at: <http://www.satp.org/satporgtp/publication/faultlines/volume14/Article1.htm> (accessed 21 August 2009).

Lok Sabha (2001) 'Unstarred question no. 531 to be answered on 22/11/2001', 22 November 2001. Online. Available at: <http://meaindia.nic.in> (accessed 27 April 2009).

— (2002a) 'Unstarred question no. 424 to be answered on 20/11/2002', 20 November 2002. Online. Available at: <http://meaindia.nic.in/> (accessed 27 April 2009).

— (2002b) 'Unstarred question no. 1701 to be answered on 05/12/2002', 5 December 2002. Online. Available at: <http://meaindia.nic.in/> (accessed 27 April 2009).

— (2003) 'Unstarred question no. 2636', 14 August 2003. Online. Available at: <http://meaindia.nic.in/> (accessed 23 February 2009).

— (2004) 'Unstarred question no. 117 to be answered on 01/12/2004', 1 December 2004. Online. Available at: <http://meaindia.nic.in/> (accessed 27 April 2009).

— (2005) 'Unstarred question no. 2005 to be answered on 16/03/2005', 16 March 2005. Online. Available —: <http://meaindia.nic.in/> (accessed 27 April 2009).

— (2006) 'Unstarred question no. 1192 to be answered on 02/08/2006', 2 August 2006. Online. Available at: <http://meaindia.nic.in/> (accessed 27 April 2009).

— (2007a) 'Starred question no. *486 to be answered on 09/05/2007', 9 May 2007. Online. Available at: <http://meaindia.nic.in/> (accessed 27 April 2009).

— (2007b) 'Unstarred question no. 2240', 14 March 2007. Online. Available at: <http://meaindia.nic.in/> (accessed 23 February 2009).

— (2007c) 'Unstarred question no. 4709 to be answered on 09/05/2007', 9 May 2007. Online. Available at: <http://meaindia.nic.in/> (accessed 27 April 2009).

Lukes, S. (2005) *Power: A radical view*. 2nd, revised edn, Houndmills: Palgrave Macmillan.

Lundestad, G. (2003) *The United States and Western Europe since 1945: From "Empire" by invitation to transatlantic drift*, Oxford: Oxford University Press.

Malhotra, J. (2003) 'Dhaka warmth on ULFA leads to chill with New Delhi', *Indian Express*, 16 November 2003. Online. Available at: <http://www.indianexpress.com/oldStory/35457/> (accessed 2 September 2009).

Manchanda, R. (2003a) 'King's gambit', *Frontline* 20 (no. 18). Online. Available at: <http://www.frontlineonnet.com/fl2018/stories/20030912000706300.htm> (accessed 27 July 2009).

— (2003b) 'New guns in an old battle', *Frontline* 20 (no. 3). Online. Available at: <http://www.frontlineonnet.com/fl2003/stories/20030214001105300.htm> (accessed 27 April 2009).

— (2004a) 'Challenging the monarchy', *Frontline* 21 (no. 3). Online. Available at: <http://www.frontlineonnet.com/fl2103/stories/20040213001305400.htm> (accessed 5 August 2009).

— (2004b) 'Nepal at a crossroads', *Frontline* 21 (no. 19). Online. Available at: <http://www.frontlineonnet.com/fl2119/stories/20040924000605800.htm> (accessed 28 April 2009).

— (2004c) 'Towards a showdown in Kathmandu', *Frontline* 21 (no. 9). Online. Available at: <http://www.frontlineonnet.com/fl2109/stories/20040507001105600.htm> (accessed 5 August 2009).

Manik, J.A. (2008) 'Grenade attack accused given BNP nomination', *The Daily Star*, 30 November 2008. Online. Available at: <http://www.thedailystar.net/pf_story.php?nid=65546> (accessed 26 August 2009).

Mann, M. (2003) *Incoherent empire*, London: Verso.

Mastanduno, M. (2002) 'Incomplete hegemony and security order in the Asia-Pacific', in G.J. Ikenberry (ed.) *America unrivaled: The future of the balance of power*, Ithaca: Cornell University Press.

— (2008) 'Economic statecraft', in S. Smith, A. Hadfield and T. Dunne (eds) *Foreign policy: Theories, actors, cases*, Oxford: Oxford University Press.

Mayilvaganan, M. (2009) 'Will the fall of Killinochchi end ethnic crisis in Sri Lanka?' *IDSA Strategic Comment*, 12 January 2009. Online. Available at: <http://www.idsa.in/publications/stratcomments/Mayilvaganan120109.htm> (accessed 25 May 2009).

Mayring, P. (2003) *Qualitative Inhaltsanalyse. Grundlagen und Techniken*. 8th edn, Weinheim: Beltz.

Mehta, A.K. (2001) 'Problems of terrorism and other illegal activities on Indo-Nepal border: Issues in effective border management', in Ramakant and B.C. Upreti (eds) *India and Nepal: Aspects of interdependent relations*, Delhi: Kalinga.

— (2004) 'Strategic neighbourhood: Nepal, Sri Lanka, Bangladesh, Bhutan', in S. Kumar (ed.) *India's national security annual review 2004*, Delhi: KW.

— (2008) 'People's revolution in Nepal', in V. Gupta, S. Kumar and V. Chandra (eds) *India's neighbourhood: Challenges ahead*, New Delhi: Rubicon.

— (2010) 'Political dynamics in Nepal and security implications', in S. Kumar (ed.) *India's national security annual review 2009*, New Delhi: Routledge.

Menon, R. (2001) 'Monarchy is passing through a crisis of survival: Interview with S.D. Muni', *Rediff on the Net*, 12 June 2001. Online. Available at: <http://www.rediff.com/news/2001/jun/12inter.htm> (accessed 18 October 2009).

Ministry of External Affairs – India (MEA) (2002a) 'Challenges ahead – India's views on regional development, Foreign Secretary's presentation at IFRI (French Institute for International Relations), Paris', 17 December 2002. Online. Available at: <http://meaindia.nic.in/> (accessed 23 February 2009).

— (2002b) 'India-Sri Lanka joint statement', 11 June 2002. Online. Available at: <http://meaindia.nic.in/> (accessed 23 February 2009).

— (2002c) 'Response to a question by the official spokesperson', 5 October 2002. Online. Available at: <http://meaindia.nic.in/> (accessed 9 March 2009).

— (2002d) 'Transcript: United News of Bangladesh interview with External Affairs Minister Shri Yashwant Sinha', 24 August 2002. Online. Available at: <http://meaindia.nic.in/> (accessed 27 April 2009).

— (2003a) 'India – Sri Lanka foreign office consultations', 25 July 2003. Online. Available at: <http://meaindia.nic.in/> (accessed 23 February 2009).

— (2003b) 'India – Sri Lanka, joint statement', 10 October 2003. Online. Available at: <http://meaindia.nic.in/> (accessed 23 February 2009).

— (2003c) 'India-Sri Lanka joint statement', 21 October 2003. Online. Available at: <http://meaindia.nic.in/> (accessed 23 February 2009).

— (2003d) 'Interview of External Affairs Minister Shri Yashwant Sinha by Mr. Vijay Kumar Pandey for the Disha Nirdesh Programme of Nepal Tv', 12 December 2003. Online. Available at: <http://meaindia.nic.in/> (accessed 9 March 2009).

— (2003e) 'Press statement on visit of H.E. Mr. Surya Bahadur Thapa, Prime Minister of Nepal', 25 November 2003. Online. Available at: <http://meaindia.nic.in/> (accessed 9 March 2009).

— (2004a) 'External Affairs Minister Natwar Singh in joint press conference with Lakshman Kadirgamar, Foreign Minister of Sri Lanka', 31 May 2004. Online. Available at: <http://meaindia.nic.in/> (accessed 23 February 2009).

— (2004b) 'Joint press conference by Mr. Natwar Singh, External Affairs Minister and Mr. Lakshman Kadirgamar, Foreign Minister of Sri Lanka, South block, New Delhi', 31 May 2004. Online. Available at: <http://meaindia.nic.in/> (accessed 23 February 2009).

— (2004c) 'Joint press release, visit to India of President of Sri Lanka H.E. Mrs. Chandrika Bandaranaike Kumaratunga', 7 November 2004. Online. Available at: <http://meaindia.nic.in/> (accessed 23 February 2009).

— (2004d) 'Media briefing by Foreign Secretary on the visit of His Excellency Mr. Sher Bahadur Deuba, Prime Minister of Nepal', 10 September 2004. Online. Available at: <http://meaindia.nic.in/> (accessed 9 March 2009).

— (2004e) 'On bilateral talks during the visit of the Foreign Minister of Sri Lanka', 29 April 2004. Online. Available at: <http://meaindia.nic.in/> (accessed 23 February 2009).

— (2004f) 'Statement by official spokesperson on the bomb attacks on an Indian joint venture industrial unit in Nepal', 28 August 2004. Online. Available at: <http://meaindia.nic.in/> (accessed 9 March 2009).

— (2004g) 'Working visit of H.E. Mrs Chandrika Bandaranaike Kumaratunga, President of Sri Lanka from November 3rd to 7th, 2004', 2 November 2004. Online. Available at: <http://meaindia.nic.in/> (accessed 23 February 2009).

— (2005a) 'Address by External Affairs Minister Shri Natwar Singh at India-Bangladesh dialogue organised by Centre for Policy Dialogue and India International Centre', 7 August 2005. Online. Available at: <http://meaindia.nic.in/> (accessed 27 April 2009).

— (2005b) 'Foreign Secretary Mr. Shyam Saran's speech on "India and its neighbours" at the India International Centre (IIC)', 14 February 2005. Online. Available at: <http://meaindia.nic.in/> (accessed 23 February 2009).

— (2005c) 'GOI rejects allegations contained in statements by Bangladesh minister of industries reported in the Bangladesh media', 21 August 2005. Online. Available at: <http://meaindia.nic.in/> (accessed 27 April 2009).

— (2005d) 'In response to a question on resumption of military supplies to Nepal', 10 May 2005. Online. Available at: <http://meaindia.nic.in/> (accessed 9 March 2009).

— (2005e) 'In response to a question on the 12-point understanding between political parties and Maoists in Nepal, press briefing', 23 November 2005. Online. Available at: <http://meaindia.nic.in/> (accessed 9 March 2009).

— (2005f) 'India's relations with its eastern neighbours', address by Shri Rajiv Sikri, Secretary, Ministry of External Affairs, at the Bangladesh Enterprise Institute, Dhaka', 31 May 2005. Online. Available at: <http://meaindia.nic.in/> (accessed 27 April 2009).

— (2005g) 'Joint press conference by External Affairs Minister Shri Natwar Singh and Foreign Minister of Sri Lanka Mr. Lakshman Kadirgamar', 10 June 2005. Online. Available at: <http://meaindia.nic.in/> (accessed 23 February 2009).

— (2005h) 'Joint press statement, state visit of Mr. Mahinda Rajapaksa, President of Sri Lanka to India, December 27–30, 2005', 30 December 2005. Online. Available at: <http://meaindia.nic.in/> (accessed 23 February 2009).

— (2005i) 'On the remarks of the visiting Director General of Bangladesh Rifles', 30 September 2005. Online. Available at: <http://meaindia.nic.in/> (accessed 27 April 2009).

— (2005j) 'On the visit of External Affairs Minister Shri Natwar Singh to South Africa and working visit of Foreign Minister of Nepal to India', 7 March 2005. Online. Available at: <http://meaindia.nic.in/> (accessed 9 March 2009).

— (2005k) 'On the visit of President of Sri Lanka and reaction to reports about imposition of sanctions on two Indian firms under the US-Iran proliferation act', 28 December 2005. Online. Available at: <http://meaindia.nic.in/> (accessed 23 February 2009).

— (2005l) 'Press statement on the visit of Sri Lankan leader of the opposition to India from August 16–18, 2005', 22 August 2005. Online. Available at: <http://meaindia.nic.in/> (accessed 23 February 2009).

— (2005m) 'Media Briefing by Foreign Secretary Shyam Saran on the postponement of the 13th Summit conference of the South Asian Association for Regional Cooperation', 2 February 2005. Online. Available at: <http://meaindia.nic.in/> (accessed 9 March 2009).

— (2005n) 'Statement by official spokesperson on the call on External Affairs Minister by Ambassador of Nepal to India', 14 February 2005. Online. Available at: <http://meaindia.nic.in/> (accessed 9 March 2009).

— (2005o) 'Statement by Prime Minister Dr. Manmohan Singh at the 13th SAARC Summit, Dhaka', 12 November 2005. Online. Available at: <http://meaindia.nic.in/> (accessed 23 February 2009).

— (2005p) 'Statement on developments in Nepal', 1 February 2005. Online. Available at: <http://meaindia.nic.in/> (accessed 9 March 2009).

— (2005q) 'Suo moto statement by External Affairs Minister Shri Natwar Singh on developments in Nepal and his visit to Afghanistan and Pakistan in Rajya Sabha', 4 March 2005. Online. Available at: <http://meaindia.nic.in/> (accessed 9 March 2009).

— (2005r) 'Visit of external affairs minister to Sri Lanka, June 9–11, 2005', 9 June 2005. Online. Available at: <http://meaindia.nic.in/> (accessed 23 February 2009).

— (2006a) 'Ambassador of India to Nepal meets the prime minister and other ministers of Nepal', 4 May 2006. Online. Available at: <http://meaindia.nic.in/> (accessed 9 March 2009).

— (2006b) 'Announcement of the candidature of Mr. Shashi Tharoor for UN Secretary General, visit of Amir of Kuwait, Indo-Pak talks and response to questions on India-US talks on civil nuclear cooperation, and Sri Lanka', 15 June 2006. Online. Available at: <http://meaindia.nic.in/> (accessed 23 February 2009).

— (2006c) 'Briefing points by official spokesperson on the talks between India and Bangladesh', 21 March 2006. Online. Available at: <http://meaindia.nic.in/> (accessed 27 April 2009).

— (2006d) '"Does India have a neighbourhood policy?" – talk by Foreign Secretary at ICWA', 9 September 2006. Online. Available at: <http://meaindia.nic.in/> (accessed 23 February 2009).

— (2006e) 'In response to questions on developments in Nepal, press briefing', 6 April 2006. Online. Available at: <http://meaindia.nic.in/> (accessed 9 March 2009).

— (2006f) 'In response to questions on Nepal, press briefing', 12 April 2006. Online. Available at: <http://meaindia.nic.in/> (accessed 9 March 2009).

— (2006g) 'Joint press statement, official visit of Rt. Hon'ble Girija Prasad Koirala, Prime Minister of Nepal, to India from 6–9 June 2006', 9 June 2006. Online. Available at: <http://meaindia.nic.in/> (accessed 9 March 2009).

— (2006h) 'MEA, India, media briefing by Foreign Secretary on 31 July 2006, after conclusion of the first day of the SAARC Standing Committee meeting in Dhaka, Bangladesh', 31 July 2006. Online. Available at: <http://meaindia.nic.in/> (accessed 23 February 2009).

— (2006i) 'On the visit of Prime Minister of Nepal Mr. Girija Prasad Koirala, statement on Sri Lanka and response to questions on media reports on a statement of Foreign Minister of Pakistan and that Pakistan was harassing Kashmiri leaders', 9 June 2006. Online. Available at: <http://meaindia.nic.in/> (accessed 23 February 2009).

— (2006j) 'On the visit to India of President of the government of Spain and Foreign Minister of Argentina, visit of Foreign Secretary to Sri Lanka and response to questions on Indian fishermen in Pakistan and sale of F–16s by US to Pakistan', 3 July 2006. Online. Available at: <http://meaindia.nic.in/> (accessed 23 February 2009).

— (2006k) 'Press briefing by Foreign Secretary Shri Shyam Saran on Nepal', 22 April 2006. Online. Available at: <http://meaindia.nic.in/> (accessed 9 March 2009).

— (2006l) 'Speech by Prime Minister Dr. Manmohan Singh at the banquet in honour of Bangladesh Prime Minister Begum Khaleda Zia', 21 March 2006. Online. Available at: <http://meaindia.nic.in/> (accessed 27 April 2009).

— (2006m) 'Statement by official spokesperson on the municipal elections in Nepal on February 8', 9 February 2006. Online. Available at: <http://meaindia.nic.in/> (accessed 9 March 2009).

— (2006n) 'Statement on Nepal, press release', 21 April 2006. Online. Available at: <http://meaindia.nic.in/> (accessed 9 March 2009).

— (2006o) 'Visit of Minister of State Mr. Anand Sharma to Namibia and response to questions on Sri Lanka and Nepal', 21 April 2006. Online. Available at: <http://meaindia.nic.in/> (accessed 9 March 2009).

— (2007a) '"The challenges ahead for India's foreign policy" – speech by Foreign Secretary, Shri Shivshankar Menon at the Observer Research Foundation, New Delhi', 10 April 2007. Online. Available at: <http://meaindia.nic.in/> (accessed 23 February 2009).

— (2007b) 'In response to a question relating to political developments in Bangladesh today', 3 January 2007. Online. Available at: <http://meaindia.nic.in/> (accessed 27 April 2009).

— (2007c) 'Joint press statement on the occasion of Foreign Office consultations between India and Bangladesh (25–26 June 2007)', 26 June 2007. Online. Available at: <http://meaindia.nic.in/> (accessed 27 April 2009).

— (2007d) 'On India's relief package for cyclone victims in Bangladesh', 19 November 2007. Online. Available at: <http://meaindia.nic.in/> (accessed 27 April 2009).

— (2007e) 'Opening remarks by Foreign Secretary at press conference in Nepal during his visit', 16 September 2007. Online. Available at: <http://meaindia.nic.in/> (accessed 9 March 2009).

— (2007f) 'Speech by Shri Shivshankar Menon, Foreign Secretary at the Bangladesh Enterprise Institute', 27 June 2007. Online. Available at: <http://meaindia.nic.in/> (accessed 27 April 2009).

— (2007g) 'Statement by external affairs minister on departure from Dhaka', 19 February 2007. Online. Available at: <http://meaindia.nic.in/> (accessed 27 April 2009).

— (2007h) 'Statement by External Affairs Minister, Shri Pranab Mukherjee to the Bangladeshi media followed by question and answer session prior to departure from Dhaka', 1 December 2007. Online. Available at: <http://meaindia.nic.in/> (accessed 27 April 2009).

— (2007i) 'Statement by official spokesperson on Bangladesh', 28 November 2007. Online. Available at: <http://meaindia.nic.in/> (accessed 27 April 2009).

— (2007j) 'Statement by official spokesperson on Prime Minister of Nepal's address to the nation', 9 February 2007. Online. Available at: <http://meaindia.nic.in/> (accessed 9 March 2009).

— (2007k) 'Visit of Shri Shyam Saran, special envoy of the Prime Minister to Nepal, press release', 10 December 2007. Online. Available at: <http://meaindia.nic.in/> (accessed 9 March 2009).

— (2008a) 'Briefing by Foreign Secretary Shri Shivshankar Menon on the official visit of Prime Minister of Nepal to India', 16 September 2008. Online. Available at: <http://meaindia.nic.in/> (accessed 9 March 2009).

— (2008b) 'Briefing points by official spokesperson on letters issued by President and Vice President to President and Vice President of Nepal, press briefing', 23 July 2008. Online. Available at: <http://meaindia.nic.in/> (accessed 9 March 2009).

— (2008c) 'In response to a question on the recommendations of the All Party Representatives Conference in Sri Lanka', 24 January 2008. Online. Available at: <http://meaindia.nic.in/> (accessed 23 February 2009).

— (2008d) 'In response to questions about Sri Lankan government's abrogation of ceasefire agreement of 2002', 4 January 2008. Online. Available at: <http://meaindia.nic.in/> (accessed 23 February 2009).

— (2008e) 'Inaugural address by Shri Pranab Mukherjee, Hon'ble Minister for External Affairs at South Asian Free Media Association (SAFMA) conference of journalists from Bangladesh and West Bengal', 30 June 2008. Online. Available at: <http://meaindia.nic.in/> (accessed 27 April 2009).

— (2008f) 'India-Sri Lanka joint press release', 26 October 2008. Online. Available at: <http://meaindia.nic.in/> (accessed 23 February 2009).

—— (2008g) 'Keynote address by Shri Shyam Saran, SEPM on Nepal's political transformation and future of India-Nepal relations', 26 April 2008. Online. Available at: <http://meaindia.nic.in/> (accessed 9 March 2009).

—— (2008h) 'On the summoning of the Sri Lankan Deputy High Commissioner by the National Security Adviser', 6 October 2008. Online. Available at: <http://meaindia.nic.in/> (accessed 23 February 2009).

—— (2008i) 'On the telephone conversation between President of Sri Lanka and Prime Minister', 18 October 2008. Online. Available at: <http://meaindia.nic.in/> (accessed 23 February 2009).

—— (2008j) 'Statement by EAM on situation in Sri Lanka', 16 October 2008. Online. Available at: <http://meaindia.nic.in/> (accessed 23 February 2009).

—— (2008k) 'Suo-motu statement by Shri Pranab Mukherjee, Minister for External Affairs on "Sri Lanka" in parliament', 22 October 2008. Online. Available at: <http://meaindia.nic.in/> (accessed 23 February 2009).

—— (2009a) 'Sri Lanka – Factsheet'. Online. Available at: <http://meaindia.nic.in/foreignrelation/srilanka.pdf> (accessed 30 May 2009).

—— (2009b) 'Statement by EAM in Sri Lanka', 28 January 2009. Online. Available at: <http://meaindia.nic.in/> (accessed 23 February 2009).

—— (2009c) 'Statement by EAM to the media on his visit to Sri Lanka', 28 January 2009. Online. Available at: <http://meaindia.nic.in/> (accessed 23 February 2009).

—— (2009d) 'Statement by External Affairs Minister on the situation in Sri Lanka', 22 April 2009. Online. Available at: <http://meaindia.nic.in/> (accessed 1 June 2009).

—— (2009e) 'Statement by the External Affairs Minister Shri Pranab Mukherjee in Sri Lanka', 28 January 2009. Online. Available at: <http://meaindia.nic.in/> (accessed 23 February 2009).

—— (2009f) 'Statement by the official spokesperson on Sri Lanka', 18 May 2009. Online. Available at: <http://meaindia.nic.in/> (accessed 1 June 2009).

—— (2009g) 'Statement of External Affairs Minister Mr. Pranab Mukherjee on appeal to government of Sri Lanka to work out safe passage for trapped civilians', 28 February 2009. Online. Available at: <http://meaindia.nic.in/> (accessed 1 June 2009).

—— (2009h) 'Visit of Foreign Secretary to Sri Lanka', 18 January 2009. Online. Available —at: <http://meaindia.nic.in/> (accessed 23 February 2009).

Ministry of Foreign Affairs – Sri Lanka (2009) 'Governments refutes false assertions of Arundhati Roy', 2 April 2009. Online. Available at: <http://www.slmfa.gov.lk/index.php?option=com_content&task=view&id=1683&Itemid=1 > (accessed 14 October 2009).

Ministry of Home Affairs (MHA) – India (2005) 'Annual report 2004–05'. Online. Available at: <http://www.mha.nic.in/pdfs/ar0405-Eng.pdf> (accessed 4 September 2009).

—— (2006) 'Annual report 2005–06'. Online. Available at: <http://www.mha.nic.in/pdfs/ar0506-Eng.pdf> (accessed 4 September 2009).

Mishra, R. (2004) 'India's role in Nepal's Maoist insurgency', *Asian Survey*, 44: 627–46.

Mitra, S.K. (2006) 'Engaging the world: The ambiguity of India's power', in S.K. Mitra and B. Rill (eds) *India's new dynamics in foreign policy*, München: Hanns-Seidel-Stiftung.

Mitra, S.K. (2011) *Politics in India: Structure, process and policy*, New York: Routledge.

Mohaiemen, N. (2009) 'Our politics of dispossession', *Forum* 4 (no. 2). Online. Available at: <http://www.thedailystar.net/forum/2009/february/our.htm> (accessed 16 September 2009).

Mohan, C.R. (2002) 'India loses interest in Bangladesh gas?' *The Hindu*, 12 November 2002. Online. Available at: <http://www.hinduonnet.com/2002/11/12/stories/2002111204391200.htm> (accessed 19 September 2009).

— (2005) 'India may have to deal with Gyanendra's China card option', *Indian Express*, 7 February 2005. Online. Available at: <http://www.indianexpress.com/oldStory/64225/> (accessed 4 August 2009).

— (2006) 'India and the Balance of Power', *Foreign Affairs*, 85:17–32.

— (2007) 'Peaceful periphery: India's new regional quest', 24 May 2007. Online. Available at: <http://casi.ssc.upenn.edu/india/iit_Mohan.html> (accessed 25 April 2008).

Motyl, A.J. (2001) *Imperial ends: The decay, collapse, and revival of empires*, New York: Columbia University Press.

Mukharji, D. (2008a) 'Current developments in Bangladesh', in I.P. Khosla (ed.) *Spotlights on neighbours: Talks at the IIC*, New Delhi: Konark.

— (2008b) 'A return to democracy', *Seminar: The Monthly Symposium, web edition* (no. 584). Online. Available at: <http://www.india-seminar.com/2008/584/584_deb_mukharji. htm > (accessed 26 April 2011).

Mukherji, I.N. (2006) 'India's economic diplomacy towards its neighbours', in I.P. Khosla (ed.) *Economic diplomacy*, New Delhi: Konark.

Muni, S.D. (2003) *Maoist insurgency in Nepal: The challenge and the response*, New Delhi: Rupa & Co.

— (2008a) 'Introduction', in S.D. Muni (ed.) *IDSA Asian strategic review 2008*, New Delhi: Academic Foundation.

— (2008b) 'Restructuring of the state in Nepal: The external dimension', in L.R. Baral (ed.) *Nepal: New frontiers of restructuring of state*, New Delhi: Adroit.

Münkler, H. (2005a) *Imperien. Die Logik der Weltherrschaft – vom alten Rom bis zu den Vereinigten Staaten*, Berlin: Rowohlt.

— (2005b) 'Staatengemeinschaft oder Imperium – alternative Ordnungsmodelle bei der Gestaltung von „Weltinnenpolitik"', in S. Jaberg and P. Schlotter (eds) *Imperiale Weltordung – Trend des 21. Jahrhunderts?*, Baden-Baden: Nomos.

Murari, S. (2009) 'Karunanidhi renews resignation threat over Sri Lanka', *Reuters*, 23 January 2009. Online. Available at: <http://in.reuters.com/article/idINIndia–37625720090123> (accessed 22 July 2010).

Nabers, D. (2008) *China, Japan and the quest for leadership in East Asia*, GIGA Working Paper, 67, Hamburg: GIGA.

— (2010) 'Power, leadership, and hegemony in international politics: The case of East Asia', *Review of International Studies*, 36: 931–49.

Nayar, B.R. and Paul, T.V. (2004) *India in the world order: Searching for major power status*. South Asia edn, New Delhi: Cambridge University Press/Foundation Books.

Nepalbiznews (2008) 'Govt., UDMF strike the deal, strike called off', 29 February 2008. Online. Available at: <http://www.nepalbiznews.com/newsdata/Biz-News/signedgovern-mentudmf.html> (accessed 5 February 2009).

Nepalnews (2003a) 'Terrorist label withdrawn', 30 January 2003. Online. Available at: <http://www.nepalnews.com.np/archive/2003/january/arc588.htm#9> (accessed 15 June 2009).

— (2003b) 'Thapa succeeds Chand', 4 June 2003. Online. Available at: <http://www. nepalnews.com.np/archive/2003/june/arc699.htm#1> (accessed 15 June 2009).

Nessman, R. (2009) 'Analysis: Sri Lanka war persists despite criticism', *The Associated Press*, 15 May 2009. Online. Available at: <http://www.google.com/hostednews/ap/article/ALeqM5jWpfDqAvmT1–0u7khJ-oVmnXyBMQD9874RQG0> (accessed 30 May 2009).

Neumann, I. (2008) 'Discourse analysis', in A. Klotz and D. Prakash (eds) *Qualitative methods in international relations: A pluralist guide*, Basingstoke: Palgrave Macmillan.

Neumann, I.B. (ed.) (1992) *Regional great powers in international politics*, Basingstoke: St. Martin's Press.

— (2003) 'A region-building approach', in F. Söderbaum and T.M. Shaw (eds) *Theories of new regionalism*, Houndmills: Palgrave Macmillan.

Nolte, D. (2006) *Macht und Machthierarchien in den Internationalen Beziehungen: Ein Analysekonzept für die Forschung über Regionale Führungsmächte*, GIGA Working Paper, 29, Hamburg: GIGA.

— (2010) 'How to compare regional powers: Analytical concepts and research topics', *Review of International Studies*, 36: 889–93.

Northouse, P.G. (1997) *Leadership: Theory and practice*, Thousand Oaks: Sage.

Nye, J.S. (2004) *Soft power: The means to success in world politics*, New York: Public Affairs.

NZZonline (2007) 'Einigung auf ein Wahldatum in Nepal', 20 December 2007. Online. Available at: <http://www.nzz.ch/nachrichten/startseite/einigung_auf_ein_wahldatum_in_nepal_1.601447.html> (accessed 14 January 2009).

Østerud, Ø. (1992) 'Regional great powers', in I.B. Neumann (ed.) *Regional great powers in international politics*, Basingstoke: St. Martin's Press.

Paige, G.D. (1977) *The scientific study of political leadership*, New York: The Free Press.

Pant, H.V. (2008) *Contemporary debates in Indian foreign and security policy: India negotiates its rise in the international system*, New York: Palgrave Macmillan.

Parajulee, R.P. (2000) *The democratic transition in Nepal*, Lanham: Rowman & Littlefield.

Parchami, A. (2009) *Hegemonic peace and empire: The Pax Romana, Britannica, and Americana*, London: Routledge.

Parthasarathy, G. (2007) 'Sri Lanka's defence needs: Is India behaving like a bully?' *The Tribune*, 14 June 2007. Online. Available at: <http://www.tribuneindia.com/2007/20070614/edit.htm> (accessed 23 October 2010).

Patchen, M. (1988) *Resolving disputes between nations: Coercion or conciliation?*, Durham: Duke University Press.

Pattanaik, S.S. (2008a) 'Bangladesh: Fixing the democratic future', in A.K. Behuria (ed.) *India and its neighbours: Towards a new partnership*, New Delhi: IDSA.

— (2008b) 'Building a new Nepal: Pains of state restructuring', in S.D. Muni (ed.) *IDSA Asian strategic review 2008*, New Delhi: Academic Foundation.

— (2011) 'India's neighbourhood policy: Perceptions from Bangladesh', *Strategic Analysis*, 35: 71–87.

Pedersen, T. (1998) *Germany, France and the integration of Europe: A realist interpretation*, London: Pinter.

— (1999) 'State strategies and informal leadership in European integration: Implications for Denmark', in B. Heurlin and H. Mouritzen (eds) *Danish foreign policy yearbook 1999*, Copenhagen: Danish Institute of International Affairs.

— (2002) 'Cooperative hegemony: Power, ideas and institutions in regional integration', *Review of International Studies*, 28: 677–96.

Pennock, J.R. and Chapman, J.W. (eds) (1972) *Coercion*, Chicago: Aldine.

Perry, A. (2005) 'Reining in the radicals', *Time*, 28 February 2005. Online. Available at: <http://www.time.com/time/magazine/article/0,9171,1032429,00.html> (accessed 21 August 2009).

— (2006) 'Rebuilding Bangladesh', *Time*, 3 April 2006. Online. Available at: <http://www.time.com/time/asia/covers/501060410/story.html> (accessed 21 August 2009).

Press Trust of India (PTI) (2002) 'Dhaka's support to ISI, al-Qaeda will cost it dear: Advani', 7 November 2002. Online. Available at: <http://www.expressindia.com/news/fullstory.php?newsid=16595 > (accessed 2 September 2009).

Price, G. (2004) *India's aid dynamics: From recipient to donor?*, Asia Programme Working Paper, London: Chatham House.

— (2005) *India's official humanitarian aid programme*, HPG Background Paper, London: Humanitarian Policy Group.

Prys, M. (2010) 'Hegemony, domination, detachment: Differences in regional powerhood', *International Studies Review*, 12: 479–504.

Raeper, W. and Hoftun, M. (1992) *Spring awakening: An account of the 1990 revolution in Nepal*, New Delhi: Viking.

Rajagopalan, R. (2008) *Fighting like a guerrilla: The Indian army and counterinsurgency*, London: Routledge.

Rajya Sabha (2001) 'Unstarred question no. 529 to be answered on 22/11/2001', 22 November 2001. Online. Available at: <http://meaindia.nic.in/> (accessed 27 April 2009).

— (2002) 'Unstarred question no. 265 to be answered on 21/11/2002', 21 November 2002. Online. Available at: <http://meaindia.nic.in/> (accessed 27 April 2009).

— (2003a) 'Starred question no. *71 to be answered on 24/07/2003', 24 July 2003. Online. Available at: <http://meaindia.nic.in/> (accessed 27 April 2009).

— (2003b) 'Starred question no. *225 to be answered on 17/12/2003', 17 December 2003. Online. Available at: <http://meaindia.nic.in/> (accessed 27 April 2009).

— (2003c) 'Unstarred question no. 256 to be answered on 20/02/2003', 20 February 2003. Online. Available at: <http://meaindia.nic.in/> (accessed 27 April 2009).

— (2003d) 'Unstarred question no. 2650 to be answered on 14/08/2003', 14 August 2003. Online. Available at: <http://meaindia.nic.in/> (accessed 9 March 2009).

— (2005a) 'Starred question no. *599 to be answered on 05/05/2005', 5 May 2005. Online. Available at: <http://meaindia.nic.in/> (accessed 27 April 2009).

— (2005b) 'Unstarred question no. 365 to be answered on 03/03/2005', 3 March 2005. Online. Available at: <http://meaindia.nic.in/> (accessed 9 March 2009).

— (2005c) 'Unstarred question no. 978 to be answered on 10/03/2005', 10 March 2005. Online. Available at: <http://meaindia.nic.in/> (accessed 9 March 2009).

— (2005d) 'Unstarred question no. 3132 to be answered on 21/04/2005', 21 April 2005. Online. Available at: <http://meaindia.nic.in/> (accessed 9 March 2009).

— (2005e) 'Unstarred question no. 3772 to be answered on 28/04/2005', 28 April 2005. Online. Available at: <http://meaindia.nic.in/> (accessed 9 March 2009).

— (2005f) 'Unstarred question no. 4539 to be answered on 05/05/2005', 5 May 2005. Online. Available at: <http://meaindia.nic.in/> (accessed 27 April 2009).

— (2006a) 'Unstarred question no. 142 to be answered on 23/11/2006', 23 November 2006. Online. Available at: <http://meaindia.nic.in/> (accessed 27 April 2009).

— (2006b) 'Unstarred question no. 1691 to be answered on 07/12/2006', 7 December 2006. Online. Available at: <http://meaindia.nic.in/> (accessed 27 April 2009).

— (2006c) 'Unstarred question no. 2921 to be answered on 24/08/2006', 24 August 2006. Online. Available at: <http://meaindia.nic.in/> (accessed 9 March 2009).

— (2006d) 'Unstarred question no. 2935', 24 August 2006. Online. Available at: <http://meaindia.nic.in/> (accessed 23 February 2009).

— (2008) 'Unstarred question no. 2238 to be answered on 20/03/2008, answer the Minister of External Affairs (Shri Pranab Mukherjee)', 20 March 2008. Online. Available at: <http://meaindia.nic.in/> (accessed 23 February 2009).

Ramachandran, S. (2005) *Indifference, impotence, and intolerance: Transnational Bangladeshis in India*, Global Migration Perspectives, 42, Geneva: Global Commission on International Migration.

Ramana, P.V. (2002) *Cross-country left-wing extremist network is real*, IPCS Article, 833, New Delhi: IPCS.

— (ed.) (2008) *The Naxal challenge: Causes, linkages, and policy options*, New Delhi: Pearson Education.

Rao, P.V. (1988) 'Ethnic conflict in Sri Lanka: India's role and perception', *Asian Survey*, 28: 419–36.

Rapkin, D.P. (1990a) 'The contested concept of hegemonic leadership', in D.P. Rapkin (ed.) *World leadership and hegemony*, Boulder: Lynne Rienner.

— (1990b) 'Japan and world leadership?' in D.P. Rapkin (ed.) *World leadership and hegemony*, Boulder: Lynne Rienner.

— (2005) 'Empire and its discontents', *New Political Economy*, 10: 389–411.

Rashid, A.K. (2008) 'Indo-Bangla relations: A new perspective', *The Daily Star*, 25 August 2008. Online. Available at: <http://www.thedailystar.net/pf_story.php?nid=51703> (accessed 8 September 2009).

Reddy, B.M. (2006a) 'Conflicting signals', *Frontline* 23 (no. 20). Online. Available at: <http://www.frontlineonnet.com/fl2320/stories/20061020003204000.htm> (accessed 1 April 2009).

— (2006b) 'Inviting India', *Frontline* 23 (no. 13). Online. Available at: <http://www.flonnet.com/fl2313/stories/20060714007400800.htm> (accessed 23 October 2010).

— (2006c) 'Merger of North and East provinces null and void', *The Hindu*, 17 October 2006. Online. Available at: <http://www.hindu.com/2006/10/17/stories/2006101712170100.htm> (accessed 25 May 2009).

— (2007a) 'Angry response', *Frontline* 24 (no. 12). Online. Available at: <http://www.frontlineonnet.com/fl2412/stories/20070629002803200.htm> (accessed 30 March 2009)

— (2007b) 'Fall of Vaharai', *Frontline* 24 (no. 2). Online. Available at: <http://www.frontlineonnet.com/fl2402/stories/20070209003102600.htm> (accessed 31 March 2009).

— (2007c) 'India should not return to bad neighbour policy: JVP', *The Hindu*, 6 June 2007. Online. Available at: <http://www.hindu.com/2007/06/06/stories/2007060600821400.htm> (accessed 23 October 2010).

— (2008a) 'Eastern vote', *Frontline* 25 (no. 11). Online. Available at: <http://www.frontlineonnet.com/fl2511/stories/20080606251104200.htm> (accessed 1 April 2009).

— (2008b) 'Indian concerns', *Frontline* 25 (no. 22). Online. Available at: <http://www.flonnet.com/fl2522/stories/20081107252204100.htm> (accessed 23 February 2010).

— (2008c) 'Neighbourly gesture', *Frontline* 25 (no. 26). Online. Available at: <http://www.hinduonnet.com/fline/fl2526/stories/20090102252603800.htm > (accessed 27 April 2011).

— (2008d) 'Political battles', *Frontline* 25 (no. 2). Online. Available at: <http://www.frontlineonnet.com/fl2502/stories/20080201501501000.htm> (accessed 1 April 2009).

Risse, T. and Sikkink, K. (1999) 'The socialization of human rights norms into domestic practices: Introduction', in T. Risse, S.C. Ropp and K. Sikkink (eds) *The power of human rights: International norms and domestic change*, Cambridge: Cambridge University Press.

Roller, E., Mathes, R. and Eckert, T. (1995) 'Hermeneutic-classificatory content analysis: A technique combining principles of quantitative and qualitative research', in U. Kelle (ed.) *Computer-aided qualitative data analysis*, London: Sage.

Rose, L.E. (1971) *Nepal: Strategy for survival*, Berkeley: University of California Press.

Rosecrance, R. and Stein, A.A. (1993) 'Beyond realism: The study of grand strategy', in R. Rosecrance and A.A. Stein (eds) *The domestic bases of grand strategy*, Ithaca: Cornell University Press.

Sambandan, V.S. (2003) 'The India factor', *Frontline* 20 (no. 23). Online. Available at: <http://www.hinduonnet.com/fline/fl2023/stories/20031121006001600.htm> (accessed 23 October 2010).

— (2004a) 'A rebellion in the East', *Frontline* 21 (no. 6). Online. Available at: <http://www.frontlineonnet.com/fl2106/stories/20040326004411400.htm> (accessed 30 March 2009).

— (2004b) 'A tiring battle', *Frontline* 21 (no. 6). Online. Available at: <http://www.frontlineonnet.com/fl2106/stories/20040326004211600.htm> (accessed 30 March 2009).

— (2005a) 'The LTTE's silent vote', *Frontline* 22 (no. 25). Online. Available at: <http://www.flonnet.com/fl2225/stories/20051216000506100.htm> (accessed 31 March 2009).

— (2005b) 'A parting of ways', *Frontline* 22 (no. 14). Online. Available at: <http://www.frontlineonnet.com/fl2214/stories/20050715002503300.htm> (accessed 31 March 2009).

— (2005c) 'War by other means', *Frontline* 22 (no. 13). Online. Available at: <http://www.frontlineonnet.com/fl2213/stories/20050701002304200.htm> (accessed 31 March 2009).

— (2006) 'An air of apprehension', *Frontline* 23 (no. 1). Online. Available at: <http://www.flonnet.com/fl2301/stories/20060127001505200.htm> (accessed 31 March 2009).

Sanchez Nieto, W.A. (2008) 'A war of attrition: Sri Lanka and the Tamil Tigers', *Small Wars & Insurgencies*, 19: 573–87.

Sandschneider, E. (ed.) (2007) *Empire*, Baden-Baden: Nomos.

Schelling, T.C. (1966) *Arms and influence*, New Haven: Yale University Press.

Schimmelfennig, F., Engert, S. and Knobel, H. (2006) *International socialization in Europe: European organizations, political conditionality and democratic change*, Houndmills: Palgrave Macmillan.

Schirm, S.A. (2005) 'Führungsindikatoren und Erklärungsvariablen für die neue internationale Politik Brasiliens', *Lateinamerika Analysen*, 11: 107–30.

— (2010) 'Leaders in need of followers: Emerging powers in global governance', *European Journal of International Relations*, 16: 197–221.

Schoeman, M. (2003) 'South Africa as an emerging middle power: 1994–2003', in J. Daniel, A. Habib and R. Southall (eds) *State of the nation: South Africa 2003–2004*, Cape Town: HSRC Press.

Schrader, L. (2005) 'Diskurse zum "Empire"-Konzept in den Vereinigten Staaten – eine ideologiekritische Dekonstruktion', in S. Jaberg and P. Schlotter (eds) *Imperiale Weltordnung – Trend des 21. Jahrhunderts?*, Baden-Baden: Nomos.

Sengupta, S. (2007) 'Bangladesh hangs 6 Islamist militants in the killings of 2 judges', *The New York Times*, 31 March 2007. Online. Available at: <http://www.nytimes.com/2007/03/31/world/asia/31bangla.html?_r=1&scp=1&sq=jmb%20bangladesh&st=cse> (accessed 25 August 2009).

Shah, S. (2004) 'A Himalayan red herring? Maoist revolution in the shadow of the Legacy Raj', in M. Hutt (ed.) *Himalayan 'People's War': Nepal's Maoist rebellion*, London: Hurst & Co.

Shamshad, R. (2008) 'Politics and origin of the India-Bangladesh border fence', paper presented at 17th Biennial Conference of the Asian Studies Association of Australia, Melbourne, 1–3 July 2008.

Shim, D. (2009) *A shrimp amongst whales? Assessing South Korea's regional-power status*, GIGA Working Paper, 107, Hamburg: GIGA.

Shrestha, G.R. (2003) *Nepal-India bilateral trade relations: Problems and prospects*, Research and Information System for the Non-Aligned and Other Developing Countries (RIS) Discussion Paper 54, New Delhi: RIS.

Shukla, S. (2007) *Foreign policy of India*, New Delhi: Anamika.

Sibal, K. (2009) 'India's relations with its neighbours', *India Quarterly*, 65: 351–9.

Singh, K. (1988) *Small neighbours of big powers: India's attitude towards Nepal (September 1946 – March 1963)*, Delhi: Capital.

Singh, P. (2006) *The Naxalite movement in India*. Revised edn, New Delhi: Rupa & Co.

Singh, S. (2001) *Framing "South Asia": Whose imagined region?*, RSIA Working Paper, Singapore: Institute of Defence and Strategic Studies.

—— (2007) *Bangladesh in 2006: Teetering political edifice and democracy*, IPCS Special Report 35, New Delhi: IPCS.

Sisson, R. and Rose, L.E. (1990) *War and secession: Pakistan, India, and the creation of Bangladesh*, Berkeley: University of California Press.

Smith, C. (2008) 'Sri Lanka returns to war', *Asian Affairs*, 39: 83–94.

Snidal, D. (1985) 'The limits of hegemonic stability theory', *International Organization*, 39: 579–614.

Snyder, G.H. and Diesing, P. (1977) *Conflict among nations: Bargaining, decision making, and system structure in international crises*, Princeton: Princeton University Press.

Soares De Lima, M.R. and Hirst, M. (2006) 'Brazil as an intermediate state and regional power: Action, choice and responsibilities', *International Affairs*, 82: 21–40.

Sobhan, F. (2007) '"The role of Bangladesh in South Asian cooperation", speech at the Carnegie Endowment for the International Peace, Washington, DC', 8 May 2007. Online. Available at: <http://carnegieendowment.org/files/0509carnegie-bangladesh.pdf> (accessed 26 April 2011).

Soko, M. (2008) 'Building regional integration in Southern Africa: South African customs union as a driving force?' *South African Journal of International Affairs*, 15: 55–69.

South Asia Human Rights Documentation Centre (SAHRDC) (2001) *Attacks on Hindu minorities in Bangladesh: The insurgency fallout in north east India*, Human Rights Features, 48/01, New Delhi: SAHRDC.

South Asian Association for Regional Cooperation (SAARC) (2011) 'SAARC Charter, art. X (2)'. Online. Available at: <http://www.saarc-sec.org/SAARC-Charter/5/> (accessed 15 April 2011).

Stachoske, B. (2005) 'Die bilateralen Beziehungen zwischen Indien und Nepal nach dem "Königlichen Staatsstreich"', in G. Schucher and C. Wagner (eds) *Indien 2005. Politik, Wirtschaft, Gesellschaft*, Hamburg: Institut für Asienkunde.

Stamm, A. (2004) *Schwellen- und Ankerländer als Akteure einer globalen Partnerschaft*, DIE Discussion Paper, 1/2004, Bonn: DIE.

Star (2004) 'Morshed blasts India', 17 September 2004. Online. Available at: <http://www.thedailystar.net/magazine/2004/09/03/news.htm> (accessed 16 September 2009).

Sterling-Folker, J. (2008) 'The emperor wore cowboy boots', *International Studies Perspectives*, 9: 319–30.

Stockholm International Peace Research Institute (SIPRI) (2011a) 'Arms transfers database'. Online. Available at: <http://armstrade.sipri.org/> (accessed 16 March 2011).

—— (2011b) 'Military expenditure database'. Online. Available at: <http://milexdata.sipri.org/> (accessed 16 April 2011).

Stogdill, R.M. (1974) *Handbook of leadership: A survey of theory and research*, New York: The Free Press.

Strange, S. (1987) 'The persistent myth of lost hegemony', *International Organization*, 41: 551–74.

Subedi, S.P. (1997) 'Indo-Nepal relations: The causes of conflict and their resolution', in S.K. Mitra and D. Rothermund (eds) *Legitimacy and conflict in South Asia*, New Delhi: Manohar.

Sudarshan, V. (2002) 'Next door boor', *Outlook*, 02 September 2002. Online. Available at: <http://www.outlookindia.com/article.aspx?217049> (accessed 22 October 2009).

Sunday Observer (2008) 'All three communities must put heads together: Conflict essentially a problem of ours', 29 June 2008. Online. Available at: <http://www.sunday-observer.lk/2008/06/29/pol06.asp > (accessed 28 May 2009).

Supreme Court of Bangladesh (2011) 'Constitution of the People's Republic of Bangladesh, Part IV, Chapter IIA, Art. 58C'. Online. Available at: <http://www.supremecourt.gov.bd/constitution/367_IV_II_.pdf> (accessed 28 April 2011).

Suryanarayana, P.S. (2005) 'Building bridges', *Frontline* 22 (no. 10). Online. Available at: <http://www.hinduonnet.com/fline/fl2210/stories/20050520001005300.htm> (accessed 4 August 2009).

Suryanarayan, V. (2010) 'Decline and fall of the Liberation Tigers of Tamil Eelam', in S. Kumar (ed.) *India's national security annual review 2009*, New Delhi: Routledge.

Take, I. (2005) '(Schon) "Empire" Oder (noch) "Hegemon"? Was uns die Hegemonietheorie über die gegenwärtige US-Politik zu sagen hat', in S. Jaberg and P. Schlotter (eds) *Imperiale Weltordnung – Trend des 21. Jahrhunderts?*, Baden-Baden: Nomos.

Tamilnet (2003) 'LTTE suspends negotiations with Sri Lanka pending implementation of agreements reached', 21 April 2003. Online. Available at: <http://www.tamilnet.com/art.html?catid=13&artid=8824> (accessed 25 May 2009).

The Associated Press (2008) 'Officials in Bangladesh set December elections', 20 September 2008. Online. Available at: <http://www.nytimes.com/2008/09/21/world/asia/21bangladesh.html?scp=33&sq=bangladesh&st=cse> (accessed 25 August 2009).

The Daily Star (2005a) 'Alliance to face AL in streets', 4 February 2005. Online. Available at: <http://www.thedailystar.net/2005/02/04/d5020401011.htm> (accessed 19 September 2009).

— (2005b) 'Jamaat blames RAW, Mosad', 21 August 2005. Online. Available at: <http://www.thedailystar.net/2005/08/21/d50821011512.htm> (accessed 3 September 2009).

— (2005c) 'SAARC summit postponed as India pulls out', 3 February 2005. Online. Available at: <http://www.thedailystar.net/2005/02/03/d5020301011.htm> (accessed 19 September 2009).

— (2006a) '12 killed, 2,000 hurt as violence hits country', 29 October 2006. Online. Available at: <http://www.thedailystar.net/2006/10/29/d6102901033.htm> (accessed 26 August 2009).

— (2006b) 'Fresh BSF move to raise fence in Ramagarh border', 23 November 2006. Online. Available at: <http://www.thedailystar.net/2006/11/23/d611230706105.htm > (accessed 19 September 2009).

— (2006c) 'Home Secys meet in Dhaka tomorrow', 23 August 2006. Online. Available at: <http://www.thedailystar.net/2006/08/23/d60823012618.htm> (accessed 2 September 2009).

— (2006d) 'Writ petition filed in HC against govt', 17 April 2006. Online. Available at: <http://www.thedailystar.net/2006/04/17/d60417011812.htm> (accessed 16 September 2009).

— (2007a) 'Caught political bigwigs detained, sent to jail', 6 February 2007. Online. Available at: <http://www.thedailystar.net/2007/02/06/d7020601011.htm> (accessed 25 August 2009).

— (2007b) 'Complete ban on all sorts of political activities', 9 March 2007. Online. Available at: <http://www.thedailystar.net/2007/03/09/d7030901085.htm> (accessed 24 August 2009).

— (2007c) 'Dhaka rejects Delhi's claim of Bangladesh link', 27 August 2007. Online. Available at: <http://www.thedailystar.net/pf_story.php?nid=1650 > (accessed 21 September 2009).

— (2007d) 'DU erupts in violence as army men beat students', 21 August 2007. Online. Available at: <http://www.thedailystar.net/story.php?nid=895> (accessed 25 August 2009).

— (2007e) 'DU teachers skip classes', 23 July 2007. Online. Available at: <http://www.thedailystar.net/2007/07/23/d7072301096.htm> (accessed 25 August 2009).

—(2007f) 'Foreign adviser trashes Indian media reports', 23 May 2007. Online. Available at: <http://www.thedailystar.net/2007/05/23/d70523012414.htm> (accessed 21 September 2009).

— (2007g) 'Hasina arrested, sent to sub-jail', 17 July 2007. Online. Available at: <http://www.thedailystar.net/2007/07/17/d7071701011.htm > (accessed 25 August 2009).

— (2007h) 'Khaleda lands in sub-jail', 4 September 2007. Online. Available at: <http://www.thedailystar.net/story.php?nid=2584> (accessed 25 August 2009).

The Economist (2011) 'Enclaves between India and Bangladesh: The land that maps forgot', 15 February 2011. Online. Available at: <http://www.economist.com/blogs/asiaview/2011/02/enclaves_between_india_and_bangladesh> (accessed 25 March 2011).

The Hindu (2006) 'Bangladesh, a launching pad for terrorists: M.K. Narayanan', 20 October 2006. Online. Available at: <http://www.hindu.com/2006/10/20/stories/2006102010550100.htm> (accessed 8 September 2009).

— (2007) 'Centre considering unified command for armed forces', 1 June 2007. Online. Available at: <http://www.hindu.com/2007/06/01/stories/2007060108050100.htm> (accessed 8 April 2009).

— (2008a) 'Karunanidhi opposes joint patrolling of Palk Strait', 5 October 2008. Online. Available at: <http://www.thehindu.com/2008/10/05/stories/2008100555320800.htm> (accessed 13 October 2009).

— (2008b) 'Tatas drop plans to invest in Bangladesh', 1 August 2008. Online. Available at: <http://www.hinduonnet.com/businessline/2008/08/01/stories/2008080152090200.htm> (accessed 19 September 2009).

— (2011) 'India-Bangaldesh border talks from tomorrow', 8 March 2011. Online. Available at: <http://www.thehindu.com/news/national/article1520140.ece (accessed 30 March 2011).

The Hindustan Times (2009) 'UN Rights Council divided over Sri Lanka', 26 May 2009. Online. Available at: <http://www.hindustantimes.com/StoryPage/StoryPage.aspx?section-Name=RSSFeed-SriLanka&id=c55979e6-cf14–4abe-bafc–91951e0337d9&Headline=UN+rights+council+divided+over+Sri+Lanka> (accessed 31 May 2009).

The Island (2007) 'Problems of being bully's buddy – ii', 2 June 2007. Online. Available —at: <http://www.lankanewspapers.com/news/2007/6/15493.html> (accessed 17 April 2009).

The Kathmandu Post (2006) 'House of Representatives proclamation', 19 May 2006. Online. Available at: <http://www.kantipuronline.com/kolnews.php?&nid=74104> (accessed 14 January 2009).

The New York Times (2001) 'Nepal rebels abandon cease-fire accord', 22 November 2001. Online. Available at: <http://www.nytimes.com/2001/11/22/world/nepal-rebels-abandon-cease-fire-accord.html> (accessed 18 October 2009).

— (2005) 'Series of small bomb blasts rattle Bangladesh', 17 August 2005. Online. Available at: <http://www.nytimes.com/2005/08/17/world/asia/17iht-web.0817bangla.html?_r=1&scp=1&sq=ban-gladesh%20blasts%20august%202005&st=cse> (accessed 10 October 2009).

Thomas, R.G.C. (2002) 'The shifting landscape of Indian foreign policy', in S.W. Hook (ed.) *Comparative foreign policy: Adaptation strategies of the great and emerging powers*, Upper Saddle River: Pearson Education.

Treverton, G. and Jones, S.G. (2005) *Measuring national power*, Santa Monica: RAND Corporation.

Triepel, H. (1938) *Die Hegemonie. Ein buch von führenden Staaten*, Stuttgart: Kohlhammer.

Tucker, R.C. (1981) *Politics as leadership*, Columbia: University of Missouri Press.

U.S. Department of State (2005) 'World military expenditures and arms transfers 2005'. Online. Available at: <http://www.state.gov/documents/organization/121776.pdf> (accessed 16 April 2011).

United Nations (2008a) 'Secretary-General deeply concerned over increased hostilities in northern Sri Lanka', 9 September 2008. Online. Available at: <http://www.un.org/News/Press/docs/2008/sgsm11779.doc.htm> (accessed 26 April 2011).

— (2008b) 'World macro regions and components'. Online. Available at: <http://www.un.org/depts/dhl/maplib/worldregions.htm> (accessed 30 June 2008).

— (2011) 'Report of the Secretary General's panel of experts on accountability in Sri Lanka', Online. Available at: <http://www.un.org/News/dh/infocus/Sri_Lanka/POE_Report_Full.pdf > (accessed 30 May 2011).

United Nations – Secretary General (2007) 'United Nations says Bangladesh political crisis jeopardizes electoral legitimacy, urges all parties to refrain from violence, seek compromise', 10 January 2007. Online. Available at: <http://www.un.org/News/Press/docs//2007/sgsm10838.doc.htm> (accessed 26 April 2011).

United Nations Mission in Nepal (UNMIN) (2005) '12-point understanding reached between the seven political parties and Nepal Communist Party (Maoist)'. Online. Available at: <http://www.unmin.org.np/downloads/keydocs/12-point%20understanding–22%20Nov%202005.pdf> (accessed 26 January 2009).

— (2006a) 'Proclamation to the nation from His Majesty King Gyanendra on 24 April 2006'. Online. Available at: <http://www.unmin.org.np/downloads/keydocs/2006–04–24-Proclaimation_of_HM_King.pdf > (accessed 14 January 2009).

— (2006b) 'Unofficial translation of the comprehensive peace agreement concluded between the government of Nepal and the Communist Party of Nepal (Maoist) (21 November 2006)'. Online. Available at: <http://www.unmin.org.np/downloads/keydocs/2006–11–29-peace_accord-MOFA.pdf> (accessed 14 January 2009).

— (2007) '23-point agreement by the Seven-Party Alliance. Unofficial translation from the original Nepali, by United Nations Mission in Nepal (UNMIN), 23 December 2007'. Online. Available at: <http://www.unmin.org.np/downloads/keydocs/2007–12–24–23.Point.Agreement.SPA.ENG.pdf > (accessed 14 January 2009).

United Nations Security Council (2007) 'Resolution 1740'. Online. Available at: <http://www.unmin.org.np/downloads/keydocs/2007–01–23-UN.political.mission.to.Nepal.ENG.pdf> (accessed 26 January 2009).

Upreti, B.C. (2008) *Maoists in Nepal: From insurgency to political mainstream*, New Delhi: Kalpaz.

Upreti, B.R. (2004) 'External involvement in mediation of Nepalese conflict: Problems and prospects', paper presented at Conference on "Role of political parties, civil society and international communities in conflict management", organized by CDSG/FES, Kathmandu, 25 July 2004.

Ur Rashid, H. (2008) *Saga of Indian rice to Bangladesh*, IPCS Article, 2566, New Delhi: IPCS.

Uyangoda, J. (2009) 'New configurations and constraints', *Frontline* 26 (no. 4). Online. Available at: <http://www.frontlineonnet.com/fl2604/stories/20090227260402200.htm> (accessed 24 September 2009).

Varadarajan, S. (2005a) 'India does a u-turn on arms supplies to Nepal, delivery soon', *The Hindu*, 24 April 2004. Online. Available at: <http://www.hindu.com/2005/04/24/stories/2005042404660100.htm> (accessed 21 March 2011).

— (2005b) 'An overview of Indo-Bangladesh relations: Perceptions of each other's foreign policies', in F. Sobhan (ed.) *Dynamics of Bangladesh-India relations*, Dhaka: Bangladesh Enterprise Institute/The University Press Limited.

— (2006) 'The king is down but not out', *Frontline* 23 (no. 9). Online. Available at: <http://www.frontlineonnet.com/fl2309/stories/20060519004700900.htm> (accessed 27 July 2009).

— (2010) 'The dangers in India's Nepal policy', *The Hindu*, 16 August 2010. Online. Available at: <http://www.thehindu.com/opinion/columns/siddharth-varadarajan/article572789.ece?homepage=true&css=print> (accessed 21 March 2011).

Wagner, C. (2004) *Sri Lanka – a new chance for peace*, European Institute for Asian Studies Briefing Paper, 01–2004, Brussels: EIAS.

— (2005a) *From hard power to soft power? Ideas, interaction, institutions, and images in India's South Asia policy*, South Asia Institute, University of Heidelberg, Working Paper, 26, Heidelberg: SAI.

— (2005b) *Die „verhinderte" Großmacht? Die Außenpolitik der Indischen Union, 1947–1998*, Baden-Baden: Nomos.

— (2006) *Das politische System Indiens. Eine Einführung*, Wiesbaden: VS Verlag für Sozialwissenschaften.

— (2008) *Der Einfluss Indiens auf Regierungsstrukturen in Pakistan und Bangladesch*, DIE Discussion Paper, 12, Bonn: DIE.

Wallerstein, I. (1984) *The politics of the world-economy: The states, the movements, and the civilizations*, Cambridge: Cambridge University Press.

Webb, E.J. (1970) 'Unconventionality, triangulation, and inference', in N.K. Denzin (ed.) *Sociological methods: A sourcebook*, Chicago: Aldine Publishing.

Wendt, A. and Friedheim, D. (1995) 'Hierarchy under anarchy: Informal empire and the East German state', *International Organization*, 49: 689–721.

Whelpton, J. (2005) *A history of Nepal*, Cambridge: Cambridge University Press.

— (2008) 'Nepal and Bhutan in 2007: Seeking an elusive consensus', *Asian Survey*, 48: 184–90.

— (2009) 'Nepal and Bhutan in 2008: A new beginning?' *Asian Survey*, 49: 53–8.

Wiener, J. (1995a) 'Hegemonic leadership: Naked emperor or the worship of false gods?' *European Journal of International Relations*, 1: 219–43.

— (1995b) *Making rules in the Uruguay Round of the GATT: A study of international leadership*, Aldershot: Dartmouth.

Woods, N. (2008) 'Whose aid? Whose influence? China, emerging donors and the silent revolution in development assistance', *International Affairs*, 84: 1205–21.

World Bank (2006) *India-Bangladesh bilateral trade and potential free trade agreement*, Bangladesh Developement Series Paper, 13, Dhaka: The World Bank Office.

— (2011a) 'Data & statistics'. Online. Available at: <www.worldbank.org> (accessed 16 April 2011).

— (2011b) 'South Asia'. Online. Available at: <http://web.worldbank.org/WBSITE/ EXTERNAL/COUNTRIES/SOUTHASIAEXT/0,,pagePK:158889~piPK:146815~theS itePK:223547,00.html> (accessed 26 April 2011).

Yasmin, L. (2004) 'Bangladesh-India tussles', *South Asia Journal* 5. Online. Available at: <http://www.southasianmedia.net/Magazine/Journal/bangladeshindia_tussels.htm> (accessed 18 April 2008).

Young, O.R. (1991) 'Political leadership and regime formation: On the development of institutions in international society', *International Organization*, 45: 281–308.

Index

For Product Safety Concerns and Information please contact our EU
representative GPSR@taylorandfrancis.com
Taylor & Francis Verlag GmbH, Kaufingerstraße 24, 80331 München, Germany

9 780415 721240